More Conversations with Eudora Welty

Literary Conversations Series

Peggy Whitman Prenshaw
General Editor

More Conversations with Eudora Welty

Edited by
Peggy Whitman Prenshaw

University Press of Mississippi
Jackson

Copyright © 1996 by the University Press of Mississippi
All rights reserved
Manufactured in the United States of America

99 98 97 96   4 3 2 1

The paper in this book meets the guidelines for permanence and durability of the Committee
on Production Guidelines for Book Longevity of the Council on Library Resources.

Library of Congress Cataloging-in-Publication Data

More conversations with Eudora Welty / edited by Peggy Whitman
   Prenshaw.
       p.   cm. — (Literary conversations series)
   Includes index.
   ISBN 0-87805-864-8 (cloth : alk. paper). — ISBN 0-87805-865-6
(pbk. : alk. paper)
       1. Welty, Eudora, 1909–   —Interviews. 2. Women authors,
American—20th century—Interviews. 3. Southern States—
Intellectual life. I. Prenshaw, Peggy Whitman. II. Series.
PS3545.E6Z775   1996
813'.52—dc20   95-25720
                                                            CIP

British Library Cataloging-in-Publication data available

Books by Eudora Welty

A Curtain of Green. Garden City: Doubleday, Doran, 1941.
The Robber Bridegroom. Garden City: Doubleday, Doran, 1942.
The Wide Net and Other Stories. New York: Harcourt, Brace, 1943.
Delta Wedding. New York: Harcourt, Brace, 1946.
The Golden Apples. New York: Harcourt, Brace, 1949.
The Ponder Heart. New York: Harcourt, Brace, 1954.
The Bride of the Innisfallen and Other Stories. New York: Harcourt, Brace, 1955.
The Shoe Bird. New York: Harcourt, Brace and World, 1964. (Children's Book)
Losing Battles. New York: Random House, 1970.
One Time, One Place: Mississippi in the Depression: A Snapshot Album. New York: Random House, 1971.
The Optimist's Daughter. New York: Random House, 1972.
The Eye of the Story: Selected Essays and Reviews. New York: Random House, 1978.
The Collected Stories of Eudora Welty. New York: Harcourt Brace Jovanovich, 1980.
One Writer's Beginnings. Cambridge: Harvard University Press, 1984.
Photographs. Jackson: University Press of Mississippi, 1989.
The Norton Book of Friendship, co-editor, Ronald A. Sharp. New York: W. W. Norton, 1991.
A Writer's Eye: Collected Book Reviews, ed. Pearl Amelia McHaney. Jackson: University Press of Mississippi, 1994.
One Time, One Place: Mississippi in the Depression: A Snapshot Album, foreword by William Maxwell. Rev. ed. Jackson: University Press of Mississippi, 1996.

Contents

Introduction

In 1984, the University Press of Mississippi published *Conversations with Eudora Welty,* a volume that initiated a series of collected interviews with twentieth-century writers—*Literary Conversations.* The collection comprised twenty-six interviews covering Welty's literary career from 1942 to 1983, focusing mainly upon such subjects as Welty's views of writers and the craft of writing, the play of the imagination, the southern literary tradition, and her southern upbringing. Those early interviews also revealed a woman who brought a strong sense of privacy and reserve to such conversations, but who nonetheless acquiesced to them, expressing a generous measure of courtesy as well as professional obligation to her reading public.

The twenty-six interviews collected here supplement and extend the earlier volume. They cover the years principally since 1983, although I include a few earlier interviews that were omitted from the first volume and that warrant a rereading for the portrait they offer of Welty. These include a lengthy profile by Jonathan Yardley, a discerning critic of Welty's writing, that is based upon an interview following the award of the 1973 Pulitzer Prize; a conversation between literary scholar Jeanne Rolfe Nostrandt and Welty that largely concerns the author's growing up in Mississippi and her early efforts to establish a literary career; and a long discussion about the South and literature, an exchange sponsored by the USIA's Voice of America Forum that brought together Welty, fellow southerner Shelby Foote, and literary scholar, Louis D. Rubin, Jr.

Also in this early group are several short pieces, memorable for their pictorial and auditory vividness in describing Welty in conversation at her home on Pinehurst Street in Jackson, Mississippi. Henry Mitchell, for example, brings a sharp eye for detail as well as a gardener's sensitivities to a visit with Welty following the awarding of the Presidential Medal of Freedom to her by President Carter in 1980. And Anne Tyler offers her impressions as a younger southern woman writer calling upon an admired predecessor in a conversation in 1980 following the publication of *The Collected Stories of Eudora Welty*.

In 1984 Welty published *One Writer's Beginnings,* autobiographical reflections based upon the William E. Massey, Sr., lectures she had delivered at Harvard in 1983. A new release by Welty always predictably elicited interviews from book editors, but the heavy sales of *One Writer's Beginnings,* surprising to both author and publisher, placed it on national best-seller lists, giving rise to widespread requests for interviews. Many of these focus upon Welty's childhood, the subject of the lectures. Among the most informative of the articles based on interviews following *One Writer's Beginnings* are those by Barbara Lazear Ascher, Thomas Fox, and Leslie Myers.[1] One finds also among the interviews of the mid and late 1980s continuing questions put to Welty about her views of southern culture and literature, her assessment of other writers and their literary influences upon her career, her thoughts concerning creativity and the craft of writing, and her reflections upon the relation of her personal experience to specific characters and works of fiction.

The 1989 University Press of Mississippi publication of Welty's *Photographs* was the occasion for a lengthy interview by Hunter Cole and Seetha Srinivasan that appeared as the introduction to the book. The conversation, which covers technical details about Welty's cameras, the processing of film, her work with the WPA in the 1930s, her photographic subjects, and her comments about the relation of photography to the writing of fiction, substantially extends Welty's introductory comments to the 1971 *One Time, One Place*.

The awarding of the National Book Foundation Medal for Distinguished Contribution to American Letters in 1991 set off another round of newspaper interviews, the most notable of which is that by Elizabeth Bennett in the *Houston Post*. Similarly, the Pen/Malamud Award several years later led to an interview by David Streitfeld, excerpts of which appear in his detailed profile in the *Washington Post*. Articles by Joseph Dumas for *Mississippi Magazine* and Danny Heitman for the Baton Rouge *Advocate* are also included among the 1990s interviews collected here, both notable for the wealth and precision of detail they offer about their conversations with Welty at her home in Jackson. Among newspaper interviews over the past fifteen years, those conducted by Leslie Myers as background for

articles published in the Jackson *Clarion-Ledger* during the period
1984–94 have been most numerous and in many ways most fully
reflective of Welty's recent years. These focus upon new publications,
awards, homecomings at the elementary school in Jackson that Welty
attended, and even include comments by the author on the trial of
Byron De La Beckwith, the man convicted in 1994 for the 1963
murder of the civil rights leader, Medgar Evers. Collected here are
the unpublished transcriptions of Myers's interviews, most of which
were conducted at Welty's home.

I have also sought to locate and include in the collection all detailed
interviews in question-answer format published between 1984 and
1985. Usually conducted by scholars in the humanities, and frequently
by Welty scholars who typically pursue literary matters in greater
depth than is possible in newspaper and magazine articles, these
include interviews by Charles Ruas, Gayle Graham Yates, Albert
Devlin and Peggy Prenshaw, Hermione Lee, *Humanities* magazine,
Sally Wolff, Dannye Romine Powell, Wayne Pond, and Jan Nordby
Gretlund.

Two unpublished transcriptions of videotaped interviews appear in
the volume. In spring 1986 Patricia Wheatley of the British Broadcasting Corporation interviewed Welty in a lengthy videotaping for a
documentary program in the BBC's Omnibus series. The program
was subsequently telecast in Great Britain and the United States. The
interviews were conducted at Welty's home in Jackson and at other
Mississippi sites, including the Natchez Trace south of Jackson and
the Mississippi River town of Rodney. The interview is notable for
the range of topics Welty discusses and for her forthrightness in
responding to a number of direct questions about her life and work.
The transcriptions and other archival material related to the BBC
documentary are housed in the Mississippi Department of Archives
and History.

In May 1992, Clyde S. White of Cabisco Teleproductions, affiliate
of Carolina Biological Supply Company, conducted a two-hour interview in Eudora Welty's house on Pinehurst Street. Filming in prepara-
tion for a documentary aimed at high school and college students,
White put questions to Welty that cover many of the biographical and
literary issues that she has written and talked about over the past fifty
years. At this date, the documentary has not been completed.

Other taped interviews, especially those designed for network dis-
tribution, such as that by Nancy Nichols for the *MacNeil/Lehrer
News Hour* on April 13, 1984—Welty's seventy-fifth birthday—tend
to be brief and general and to elicit responses from Welty that overlap
the author's texts, especially *One Writer's Beginnings,* as well as
repeat responses that appear in published interviews. For that reason,
and lack of space, I have not included transcriptions of these.

Many other interviews, especially interview-based newspaper articles, I have omitted for the same reasons of space and repetitions,
although often there occurs in these a memorable comment by Welty
that demands to be included—her response to Gayle White in 1977 in
the *Atlanta Journal and Constitution Magazine,* for example. Asked
why she had not married, Welty replied, "Various things caused me
to stay single. I don't mean that it was a determination like Joan of
Arc. I'm sure I would have been very happy had I married and had
children. I'm a natural person in that way. But on the other hand, I've
had many compensations. Your personal life is something you work
out as you can."[2] Ten years later when Josyanne Savigneau of the
Manchester Guardian Weekly asked a similar question, she reported
that "Welty would say nothing about her private life, other than
confessing that she 'did not choose' to live alone." Rather, she
considered one's private life "of no use for understanding a writer."[3]

In the most recent interview to date, by Nicholas Dawidoff in *The
New York Times* in August 1995, she gives a similar succinct response
to questions about marriage and career. Acknowledging that going to
a college far from home, taking employment in public relations, and
pursuing an interest in photography were not the usual choices of
young women of her time, she observes: "Days when I was coming
along, girls didn't do that kind of thing much. . . . They stayed home
and went out to dances and things, got married and raised a family."
Dawidoff notes her terse conclusion: "Marriage for her, she said,
'never came up.'"[4]

Many of the interviews not included because of space considera-
tions and repetitions may, of course, amplify the autobiographical
record we have of Welty. In addition to the preceding examples, a few
other such excerpts warrant attention here for the insights they offer
into Welty's early adult years, her relations with other writers, her
love of travel, her pleasure in her hometown connections, and her

humor. One of these occurs in a brief interview by William Ferris that accompanies an article by Patti Carr Black giving details of Welty's "first paying job at WJDX in 1931 as editor of the radio newspaper." Welty explains her father's interest in establishing a radio station: "He was very progressive, and he was also not happy with the newspaper situation in Jackson—or Mississippi. He wanted something that could be reliable and quick with dispensing the real news. . . . Since Mr. [Fred] Sullens [editor of the *Jackson Daily News*] refused to carry the schedule of the radio broadcasts in the paper, we got out a little weekly paper, which we sent out to anyone who wanted it, with the schedule, with the programs that came on, the timing. It was a little leaflet kind of thing, four pages long, and I was the editor of it. I had to make up whatever was in it. It was fun because I could have things about the people who appeared on the programs. . . . It was exciting because everything was new."[5]

Welty's responses to interviewers who have asked her about other writers are usually either warm and generous, such as her several comments about her friend Reynolds Price, or noncommittal. But in talking to George Plimpton in October 1994 about a remembered visit by Henry Miller to Jackson, she pointedly elaborates upon what she found to be a rather disappointing meeting, one she has recounted in earlier interviews and, more recently, in the Dawidoff interview. Asked, "Did you like Mr. Miller?" she replies: "Not much, he was so dull. He never looked at anything. I guess he was bored by being in Mississippi." She recalls that she and friends took him to dinner on successive nights to the best restaurant in town, one that had several entrances. "How is it that a hole like Jackson, Mississippi, has three good restaurants?" she recalls his asking. "We didn't ever tell him it was just one," Welty confesses to Plimpton.[6]

By contrast, her praise of Tennessee Williams in a 1994 interview by Patricia Grierson, a poet and professor of English at Jackson State University, is warm and enthusiastic. Welty speaks of her admiration of Williams's plays, mentioning that she was in New York during the opening run of *Cat on a Hot Tin Roof* and took friends to see it. "It played on Broadway to packed houses." She also singles out *The Glass Menagerie,* which she says she found "more tender and adventuresome than many of the others." Speaking of her two college years in Columbus, Mississippi, Tennessee Williams's birthplace, she remembers that the family tales she heard from classmates were "all so dramatic. Columbus was also a place of intellectual stimulation. There was always so much going on there," but she recalls that for two years teachers at the Mississippi State College for Women taught without pay, "unsupported by Governor Bilbo." Nonetheless, "they just went on teaching anyway, even after he had withdrawn the money to pay them." A little later Welty speaks of the connection between Williams's dramatic sense and his being from Mississippi, though when Grierson asked Welty whether she regarded Williams as a "regional writer," she replies, "I distrust that word. People always use it if you come from Mississippi. I guess I feel regional this morning."[7]

Much more common than defensiveness about Mississippi, however, is Welty's obvious delight in the friendships and spirited use of language that she associates with her home state. In the Dawidoff interview in *The New York Times,* for example, she talks of her friend Bill Matheos, owner of Bill's Greek Tavern, a favorite restaurant and site of birthday parties for Welty hosted by Matheos. One year he hired a belly dancer—"she was a pretty belly dancer," Welty remembers. "On her navel it said, 'Eudora Welty I Love You.' "[8] In 1985, she related to Pamela Blotner a story that, despite a quite different context, similarly depicts her attraction to joyous displays of language and gesture. "There's a legal term in Mississippi called 'A Frolic of His Own,' " she begins. I've just got to use that some time. There's a real case of a man who went to an ice house where he worked by day. He went around at night and just had a wonderful time there by himself. He wasn't doing too much damage, just kind of trespassing. He was arrested for trying to do something to the Morris Ice Company, but the judge said, no, he was on a 'frolic of his own.' I just *love* that!" Welty concludes, in fact, that "some of those people in *Losing Battles* were on 'frolics of their own.' "[9]

Two final excerpts of special interest reflect Welty's love of travel, particularly by train and ship. Speaking to Francoise Sciaky in a 1972 interview for *Women's Wear Daily,* Welty commented: "I just love to take crack trains. I went to Kansas City from Jackson only recently, just so I could take the Super chief to Santa Fe. Of course it costs more and it takes longer than flying, but I like to travel slow. I sit in my roomette, I look at the scenery, I read and move around. There's no telephone. I hate to rush and, after all, I can write anywhere—as long as it's in the morning."[10] Repeating her preference for unhurried, deliberate travel, she describes her notion of a perfect vacation in a *Clarion-Ledger* feature story based on interviews with Mississippians to whom Rebecca Hood-Adams put the question, "If time and space and money were no object, how would you spend your perfect day?" Welty replied: "I'd like to be sitting in a deck chair on board an ocean liner. There'd be a stack of books at my side. I could read when I wanted, watch the waves. I'd look out and see a whale rise from the waters, then dive back into the sea. There's something fabulous about watching the sea—the infinity of water and sky! I just love being on ships. There's a sense of destination. It doesn't matter if it takes a long time getting there; the point is to have a destination. I had a chance several years ago to travel to England on the QE2. A week without pressure—it was so wonderful that just thinking about it makes me want to go right now."[11]

As these excerpts reveal, as indeed the entire collection of interviews here demonstrates, Welty is generous in granting interviews both in person and by telephone. She is unfailingly courteous to her questioners, but she clearly knows how to protect her privacy, as she shows in instances when interviewers press her too sharply about her private life. She is in no way a recluse, however, and her many exchanges with reporters, students, scholars, and visiting dignitaries—literary and otherwise—give evidence of the pleasure she takes in conversation and, especially, of her professional sense of obligation to her readers to reciprocate their interest in and support of her work by granting interviews that focus upon this work.

As with all books in the Literary Conversations Series, the interviews are reprinted as they originally appeared. Obvious errors have been silently corrected. A chief frustration in editing a collection such as this, which is directed both to a general and a scholarly audience, is that in the effort to provide uncut texts of interviews that are essential to a scholar's work, inevitably one must acknowledge and acquiesce to repetitions in the interviews that the general reader may question. Noting that repetitions may provide significant insights into a writer's turn of mind and use of language, and thereby to a more insightful analysis of the fiction and understanding of the literary career, I would ask the general readers to indulge the scholars on this point. I might add that in the case of a subject whose candor, wit, and sensitivity to the nuances of language are those of a Eudora Welty, one may understandably even savor familiar questions for the revised tellings they evoke from this master storyteller.

In dating the interviews for this volume, I have cited the date on which an interview takes place, following interviewers' explicit statements and internal evidence. For example, in the Charles Ruas interview, which is not dated in the original text, Welty mentions that Katherine Anne Porter had died the week before the interview took place, and thus it is possible to date the interview as September 1980. In cases in which it is impossible to determine the actual date of the conversation, I have used the publication date.

The present volume would have been impossible but for the generous assistance of the interviewers and publishers who have permitted these conversations to be collected here. Sarah Griffin, graduate assistant at Louisiana State University, has also provided significant help. Above all, it is to Eudora Welty herself that the deepest expression of gratitude must be tendered. Not only has she given readers the immeasurable pleasure of her fiction for over half a century; she has shared with us as well her living presence—her conversation.

PWP
August 1995

Notes

1. The unpublished transcription of the Myers interview is collected in this volume. The published article appears as "New Welty Work Taps Talented Mind's Eye," *The Clarion-Ledger,* 17 January 1984, F 1, 3.

2. Gayle White, "Eudora Welty: The Central Thing Is a Sense of Belonging," *Atlanta Journal and Constitution Magazine,* 15 May 1977, 6, 42–44.

3. Josyanne Savigneau, "French About to Discover the Little Old Lady from Jackson," *Manchester Guardian Weekly,* 13 December 1987, 16.

4. Nicholas Dawidoff, "Eudora Welty's Typewriter May Be Silent, But She's Still Telling Stories," *The New York Times,* 11 August 1995, B 12.

5. William Ferris, "One Writer's First Job," *Reckon: The Magazine of Southern Culture,* I (Premiere 1995), 141. See also Patti Carr Black, "Eudora Welty's Radio Days," 140–41.

6. George Plimpton, "Two Encounters," *The Paris Review*, 37 (Spring 1995), 260.

7. Patricia Grierson, "Eudora Welty Speaks of Tennessee Williams," *Mississippi Quarterly*, 48 (Fall 1995).

8. Dawidoff, B 12.

9. Pamela Blotner, "Eudora Welty: Making Things," *In Art* [Houston, TX], 2 (Spring 1985), 23.

10. Francoise Sciaky, "Healthy, Welty and Wise," *Women's Wear Daily*, 19 June 1972, 8.

11. Rebecca Hood-Adams, "Fantasies, Anyone? Mississippians Tell All," *The Clarion-Ledger*, 2 July 1989, E 1.

Chronology

1909   13 April, Eudora Alice Welty born in Jackson, Mississippi, to Mary Chestina Andrews Welty and Christian Webb Welty

1925   Graduates from Central High School, Jackson

1925–27   Attends Mississippi State College for Women, Columbus

1927–29   Attends University of Wisconsin, Madison; B.A. degree with a major in English.

1930–31   Studies advertising at Columbia Graduate School of Business, New York

1931   Death of father; returns to Jackson to live. Begins to work part-time for local radio station and to take free-lance jobs as newspaper correspondent, publicist.

1933–36   Works as publicity agent for the WPA in Mississippi

1936   Publishes "Death of a Traveling Salesman" in *Manuscript;* exhibits photographs in one-woman show in New York City.

1937   Publishes "A Piece of News" and "A Memory" in *Southern Review*

1940   Begins association with Diarmuid Russell as literary agent

1941   *A Curtain of Green,* with introduction by Katherine Anne Porter; O. Henry Award, second prize for "A Worn Path."

1942   *The Robber Bridegroom;* O. Henry first prize for "The Wide Net"; awarded Guggenheim Fellowship.

1943   *The Wide Net and Other Stories;* O. Henry Award, first prize for "Livvie Is Back."

1944   American Academy of Arts and Letters award of $1000; works for six months on staff of *New York Times Book Review;* uses pseudonym of Michael Ravenna when reviewing war books.

1946   *Delta Wedding;* in November, begins five-month stay in San Francisco.

1947   Gives lecture, "The Reading and Writing of Short Stories," at writers' conference, University of Washington, Seattle; August–November, in San Francisco.

1949   *The Golden Apples;* Guggenheim Fellowship; travels to Europe.

1951   March to July in England; visits Elizabeth Bowen in Ireland.

1952   Election to National Institute of Arts and Letters

1954   *The Ponder Heart* and *Selected Stories* (Modern Library edition); July–October, Europe; gives lecture, "Place in Fiction," at Cambridge University.

1955   *The Bride of the Innisfallen;* mother's eye surgery in March; receives William Dean Howells Medal.

1956   Attends Broadway opening of Chodorov-Fields production of *The Ponder Heart* in February; show runs until late June.

1958–61 Honorary Consultant, Library of Congress; illnesses of mother and brother, Walter, who dies January 1959.

1964   *The Shoe Bird,* a book for children

1966   Death of mother in January; unexpected death of brother Edward a few days later; O. Henry first prize for "The Demonstrators."

1969   "The Optimist's Daughter," 15 March, in *The New Yorker*

1970   *Losing Battles;* awarded the Edward McDowell Medal.

1971   *One Time, One Place: Mississippi in the Depression, A Snapshot Album,* introduction by Welty; named to American Academy of Arts and Letters.

1972   *The Optimist's Daughter;* Gold Medal for the Novel, National Institute of Arts and Letters; appointed to the National Council of the Arts.

1973   Pulitzer Prize for *The Optimist's Daughter;* Diarmuid Russell dies.

1978   *The Eye of the Story: Selected Essays and Reviews*

1980   *The Collected Stories of Eudora Welty*

1981   National Medal of Literature and Medal of Freedom awards

1984   *One Writer's Beginnings;* Modern Language Association
        Commonwealth Award.

1986   Jackson Public Library named in honor of Eudora Welty;
        National Medal of Arts.

1987   Named Chevalier de L'ordre d'Arts et Lettres (France)

1989   *Photographs;* portrait of Welty added to National Portrait
        Gallery of the Smithsonian Institution.

1991   *The Norton Book of Friendship,* ed. Eudora Welty and
        Ronald A. Sharp; National Book Foundation Medal; Helm-
        erich Distinguished Author Award; Cleanth Brooks Medal
        (Southern Letters); Eudora Welty Society organized.

1992   Awarded the Frankel Prize by the National Endowment for
        the Humanities

1993   Receives PEN/Malamud Award (excellence in the short
        story); honorary doctorate, University of Dijon (France).

1994   *A Writer's Eye: Collected Book Reviews,* ed. Pearl Amelia
        McHaney

1995   Eudora Welty Writers' Center established by Mississippi
        legislature on site of Welty's childhood home, 741 N. Con-
        gress St. in Jackson.

1996   Inducted into France's Legion of Honor

More Conversations with Eudora Welty

A Quiet Lady in the Limelight

Jonathan Yardley / 1973

The Miami Herald, 17 February 1974. The interview was conducted in May 1973 in Jackson, Mississippi. Reprinted by permission of *The Miami Herald.*

Midafternoon on a Monday of last May, the telephone rang at Eudora Welty's house on Pinehurst Street in Jackson, Mississippi. The caller was Frank Hains, arts editor of the *Jackson Daily News,* who jokingly told her that he was thinking of printing up cards reading, "Congratulations, Eudora, on _____," the blank to be filled in with whatever her latest honor might be. She laughed, and began thanking him once again for his role in the staging, five days earlier, of Jackson's "Eudora Welty Day." Finally Hains interrupted: "Do you mean, Eudora, that you don't know about the Pulitzer?"

Thus did Eudora Welty learn that she had been awarded the 1973 Pulitzer Prize in fiction. That the news was delivered in lighthearted and informal fashion, and that the messenger was a good home-town friend, may not have been in true Pulitzer tradition—somehow one thinks of the awards issuing forth to drum rolls and trumpet flourishes—but it was entirely appropriate for Miss Welty. Utterly without pomp or pretense, treasuring her friends and her home, she would have been uncomfortable with fanfare and ceremony.

It must be said, however, that last May she had her full share of both. In rapid succession, she was given her special "Day," by her fellow Mississippians; the Pulitzer, for her novel *The Optimist's Daughter;* the "Order of the South," by the newly-established Southern Academy of Arts, Letters and Science; and an honorary Doctor of Humanities, by Queens College in Charlotte, N.C. For a writer who values her insulation from the hurly-burly—who has said that "fiction has, and must keep, a private address"—it was a rare venture into the limelight. But if the pace and the excitement wearied her, she did not betray it. With each new honor she was genuinely surprised, genuinely pleased, genuinely grateful.

Above all, she was grateful for "Eudora Welty Day," and for the

3

Distinguished Mississippian Award given her then by Governor William Waller. Though critics and fellow writers have applauded her for three decades, she has remained resolutely home-folks, and this swell of affection from her native state has touched her deeply, far more so than the Pulitzer. No Mississippi writer—and there have been plenty of good ones—has been saluted by the state in a remotely comparable manner. Why Miss Welty was singled out is suggested by her close friend Charlotte Capers, former director of the state's department of Archives and History:

"I think she's almost beatified in Jackson. Jackson is so proud of Eudora and she is such a nice and friendly person. Jacksonians, along with Mississippians, have a terrible inferiority complex—they feel that everything in the world people say about them is bad and they have the feeling somehow that everything she's saying about Mississippi is good and funny and true. Where Faulkner didn't give a damn, and his writings were difficult, her personal popularity and the feeling of gratitude that she has represented us so well—we need this, and we're grateful for it."

The object of this adulation is a deceptively soft-spoken 64-year-old lady who has published five novels, four collections of short stories, a photographic portrait of Mississippi in the Depression, and innumerable essays and book reviews. Her critical reputation is secure: she is widely regarded, though she and many perceptive readers dispute it, as the "last" of the great Southern writers. If Mississippians love her for her personal kindness and generosity, and for the warmth and humor with which she writes about them, critics admire her for her lyrical prose, her mastery of a wide variety of fictive forms, her comprehension of life's complexity and ambiguity, her refusal to pass moral judgment on her characters, her sense of place.

"Place" is central to her fiction, as it has been to her private life. Jackson now is a metropolitan sprawl with a population nearing 300,000; it suffers from all the familiar problems of pollution, highways and unplanned growth. But when she was born there in 1909, it was a close-knit community of 25,000 which, she says, "we thought was a very great town." Then, as now, it was Mississippi's largest city, but a child growing up in those days had nearby the pristine Pearl River and the historic Natchez Trace, and the hours Miss Welty spent at those lovely, magical places are still vivid in her mind.

Though she might now be regarded as such, Miss Welty was not "old Jackson" at birth. Her father, an insurance executive, was from Ohio and her mother was a West Virginian: "I had a northerner and a southerner for parents, and I was always aware that there were two sides to most questions." They were a loving and attentive couple, and Eudora's childhood was happy, carefree, rather sheltered. No one in Jackson was rich then—not many Jacksonians are now—but the Weltys evidently had everything they needed and "I never gave a thought to money."

There were always books in the house, and as soon as Eudora learned to read she threw herself into the realm of books; she once wrote that "the pleasures of reading itself—who doesn't remember?— were like those of a Christmas cake, a sweet devouring." She read voraciously and with childish indiscrimination, but she was unerringly drawn to "the fairy tales and the myths and the legends," books that "rely on the imagination." Children today, she thinks, are deprived of that pleasure: "The disquieting thing now about children's books is that they don't dare use the imagination. Things have to be based on a certain very small set of facts and realities, without anything that would excite a child's imagination." This affinity for fable and fantasy has never left her—it is a dominant strain in her own fiction, the early stories especially—and "imagine" is a key word in an understanding of her work. "I try," she says, "to imagine myself into other people's lives."

After high school she went to Mississippi State College for Women, "with the understanding that if I went there for two years I could transfer for the other two." That she did, enrolling upon her father's urging at the University of Wisconsin, which "at that time was supposed to be very much in the forefront of progressive education." Many courses influenced her there, but none more than one in 18th-century English literature, taught by the noted Ricardo Quintana: "I had never heard a teacher use the word 'passion' before, and it really taught me what was meant by that word, and the whole meaning of the poetic imagination." Socially she was happy and had many friends, but she enrolled too late to join a sorority and largely missed out on Jazz Age campus excitement, being "too naive and inexperienced and shy" to "experience any wild life."

Wisconsin heightened her interest in writing fiction, though anything she wrote at the time was pure apprentice-work and she regards it as eminently forgettable. Her father was not ecstatic about her writing plans, but he helped; he gave her "the best advice there was—if you were going to be a writer you needed to have another way of earning your living," and he sent her to Columbia to study advertising. She stayed there for the 1930–31 academic year, living at Johnson Hall on 116th Street, but any hopes she had of a New York career were ended by the Depression and the death of her father in the fall of 1931; he was 52 years old, victim of "the first case of leukemia that I'd ever heard of." Her mother put no pressure on her to stay in Jackson, but with jobs unavailable in New York and with two younger brothers still in school, she decided to remain at home.

For a time she worked for WJDX, Jackson's first radio station, which her father had founded; the staff was small, and she "did all sorts of things." She wrote occasionally on her own, but "it couldn't have been any good; I never showed it to anyone." In 1933, however, she went to work as a "junior publicity agent" for the W.P.A., and in her growth as a writer "that was it." She describes her W.P.A. experience and her response to it:

"It was a matter of getting to see something of the state. I'd never seen any of it before, except on family car trips. I hadn't realized anything about the life here. It was a wonderful year. I was independent and on my own, traveling. I went to every county seat in the state. It was a—I almost said "heart-opener"—a real eye-opener. My feelings were engaged by the outside world, I think for the first time. Of course I'd had romantic feelings of all kinds, but I never had really understood what was going on in the world until I saw it by myself. I'd always been sheltered, traveling with my father. I was shown the Grand Canyon, but that's not the same as seeing one family, living by the side of the road. That was when I really started writing stories."

Suddenly this shy young woman discovered that a real world beckoned to her, engaged her imagination, and provided breathing room for her vivid fantasies. In what she recalls as a "compulsive and spontaneous" rush, she began to write stories about the ordinary Mississippians she had met during her travels. Looking back on those early days, she realizes that she was possessed by a heady exhilaration: "I may be more cautious now. I think I try things that are really harder than that now. I like to do the hardest thing I can do. I don't mind things being hard. But I don't even know that was hard—it was just pure pleasure."

It took a while for editors to appreciate the merit of her stories, but those early tales—"The Wide Net," "Why I Live at the P.O.," "A Worn Path," "Lily Daw and the Three Ladies"—are the work of a fully mature writer. The themes that have consistently marked her work emerged at once: the senses of place and community (the latter, as in "Lily Daw," often embodied in a Greek chorus of chattering ladies); the living presence of memory and the past; love and grief; magic and mystery; the comedy of human error. "The excursion is the same," a character in "The Wide Net" says, "when you go looking for your sorrow as when you go looking for your joy." These stories, taken as a whole, are themselves an excursion, exploring the emotions and sensations of life with extraordinary scope and variety.

The editor who "found" Miss Welty was John Rood of *Manuscript,* who published "Death of a Traveling Salesman" in 1936. Other stories followed, in other small magazines, and they attracted the attention of two men who would become her most influential champions: Diarmuid Russell, the literary agent, and John Woodburn, the Double-day & Doran editor. Russell steered her stories into magazines of national circulation; Woodburn cajoled his Doubleday colleagues into violating publishing convention by issuing a collection of short stories as her first book.

That was *A Curtain of Green,* published in 1941. It contained a glowing introduction by Katherine Anne Porter (another early cham-pion, as was Robert Penn Warren), and it was received with enthusias-tic reviews. Eudora Welty was on her way: *The Robber Bridegroom,* an incandescent novella about the Natchez Trace, appeared in 1942; *The Wide Net,* a second story collection, in 1943; *Delta Wedding,* a full-length novel and her first notable popular success, in 1946; *The Golden Apples,* a collection of interrelated stories of which she says, "It takes the form of a novel without any of the responsibilities," in 1949.

During all this time many Mississippians were aware of Miss Welty, but it is likely that few read her until the publication, in 1953, of the short novel *The Ponder Heart.* The story of Edna Earle Ponder and her charmingly irresponsible Uncle Daniel, it made her for the first time a local celebrity. People thought they saw themselves, or their relatives or friends, in it, and they still do. Last May Miss Welty and I made a sightseeing trip to Vicksburg, and when we entered a popular restaurant there she was greeted with a great flutter of excitement from a table jammed with elderly ladies. One rose and greeted her: "Eudora, I'm Edna Earle!" She was an acquaintance of many years past, and she had one question: "Did you name Edna Earle Ponder after me?" The answer, alas, was no: Edna Earle was the name of the heroine of a syrupy 19th-century novel called *St. Elmo,* and countless turn-of-the-century Mississippi daughters were thus christened.

The Ponder Heart (which had a successful Broadway run in an adaptation by Jerome Chodorov and Joseph Fields) was followed in 1955 by another book of stories, *The Bride of the Innisfallen*—and then by a long period of silence. With the exception of a handful of stories and magazines pieces, Miss Welty did not publish for 15 years. In part it was because, in order to earn a more regular living than fiction provides, she undertook a rigorous schedule of readings and lectures. In part it was because she had begun work on what was to become *Losing Battles,* an epic folk novel that was a decade in the making. But in great measure it was because she had, as she says with great reticence, "troubles in the house."

Those troubles were illness and death. The younger of her brothers, Walter, died in 1959, and her mother's health was failing. Miss Welty lived with her mother in the Pinehurst Street house, and her nursing obligations mounted over the years. It is a period she clearly prefers not to talk about, but as one friend says, "It was rough." At last her mother became too ill to stay at home, and Miss Welty put her in a nursing home in Yazoo City, 45 miles away; she drove between Jackson and Yazoo almost every day, sometimes making notes for *Losing Battles* with her right hand while she held the steering wheel with her left. On January 22, 1966, her mother died; five days later her brother Edward, who had been ill for some time, also died.

For one so steeped in family as Miss Welty, it was a hard and inexpressibly painful time. But she is, in the words of her friend James Wooldridge, a person of "character and integrity," and she was not long in getting back to *Losing Battles.* "I felt I needed to put my life back in order," she says. "It had been haunting me all this time that here was all this work but without proper shape. I had so many friends who had been patient and helpful and encouraging, and nobody ever

said, 'Why don't you finish it?' " So, she went back to work: "What
I had to do was get the whole thing out and put it on the floor or the
bed or something and start at the beginning and assemble and dis-
card." Snipping away with scissors, putting pages together with pins,
she produced a 436-page comic masterpiece told almost exclusively in
dialogue, and the manuscript she delivered to Random House was
published without change—not once, in all these years, has an editor
laid a finger on her copy.

The schoolteacher in *Losing Battles* is loosely based on Miss
Welty's mother, one of the few figures in her work who derives from
her private life. A similar character appears in *The Optimist's Daughter,* which she describes as her "most personal book." In this case it
is the mother of Laurel Hand, who has returned to Mississippi
because of her father's illness. His death stirs up loving memories of
her mother, and though Miss Welty has said she did not write the
novel as "therapy," it obviously draws from sources deep within her:

"I had been through these personal experiences, and I had to write
about loss and understanding and so on, because that was what my
experience was. I identify with Laurel only in sensibilities and understanding; that's true of a lot of my work. You can't make up emotions,
but you can invent people who can act them out or embody them.
Certainly I have felt all the things that Laurel felt—but her life is
not mine."

That is true not merely in biographical detail but in spirit, for
Eudora Welty and Laurel Hand actually have very little in common.
Peter Taylor, the short-story writer and a good friend of Miss Welty's,
has said of her, "I don't see her anywhere in her work"—and
certainly one will not find her in Laurel Hand, whom Miss Welty
concedes to be "something of a prig." Miss Welty herself is shy, and
she is single, but she is anything except a prig. Her soft voice,
modesty and low-key demeanor are all genuine, but they are decep-
tive. She has a kinky and irreverent sense of humor which she is quick
to turn on herself; she loves her friends, has scores of them all over,
and sees them as often as possible; she is anything but a recluse,
venturing regularly into the daily life of Jackson and making an annual
trip (by train—she hates flying) to New York; she follows political and
social matters with an active and highly opinionated interest; she is
an outspoken book reviewer, with some enthusiasms—S.J. Perelman

and Ross MacDonald, for example—that hardly conform to the image of a sheltered Southern lady.

She is a person of routine, but she is not fussy about it. An inveterate early riser, she is usually up by six. She fixes coffee, and if she is writing—as usually she is—she is at the typewriter quickly. "When I'm working on something in particular," she says, "I work as long and hard as I can on it every day. I don't work at all unless I have something to work on." Her typewriter is in her upstairs bed-room, and she may stay at it until late afternoon. If she isn't writing, she may do gardening or housework; the house, which her father built a half-century ago, is red-brick Tudor, with high ceilings and spacious rooms—a cleaning woman comes in once a week to help keep it up, but otherwise she is on her own.

No matter what she has done during the day, Miss Welty will stop in the evening for a drink, usually bourbon and often at someone else's house: "I like to see a friend at the end of the day," she says, and almost always she does. After dinner, if she isn't going to a concert or a play, she will read; there are books all over the house, and she has arranged them "so that no matter what room you're in, there will be a book you're in the mood to read." Her taste is Catholic: among her favorite authors are E.M. Forster, Jane Austen, Faulkner, Chekhov, Turgenev, Henry Green, "nearly all the Irish writers."

She has the greatest admiration for the work of such friends as Peter Taylor, Jean Stafford, Walker Percy and Ellen Douglas, and the younger writers she likes include Thomas Rogers, Reynolds Price, Anne Tyler and Elizabeth Spencer. She has read too little Norman Mailer to pass judgment, though she says she plans to have a go at his work.

If there is anything in her routine that is virtually inviolable, it is the NBC Evening News, which comes on in Jackson at 5:30 p.m. As we were walking late one afternoon, I suggested that we might be about ready to turn off the tape recorder and call it a day. She glanced at her watch and said, "Oh, let's do. We've got to go and hear the Watergate." Her absorption in the TV news is absolute. One evening in 1970 she was signing copies of *Losing Battles* for a limited edition, scribbling away while she watched the news. She happened to glance down and discovered that she had just signed several copies "David Brinkley."

She also listens to the radio news before going to bed, and she enjoys talking politics "among friends." "I'm a Democrat," she says, "and I suppose I'm fairly liberal, but that doesn't mean I go along with the party every time." She takes wicked delight in Mr. Nixon's Watergate misfortunes—"Nothing could make me vote for Nixon; I've never voted for him"—but her disdain for the President is almost matched by her irritation over her own party's performance in 1972. "That was the most abysmal presidential campaign we've ever had," she says. "It was the one time I've never voted. It was so dispiriting."

As a Southerner and a woman, she is constantly pressed for her opinions on race and Women's Liberation. Her feelings on the racial situation have always been firm: in the late '50s and early '60s, when that sort of thing could be dangerous, she occasionally visited the Social Science Forum at the nearby black college, Tougaloo, and she has never left any doubt about her sympathy for the civil-rights cause. Of the racial situation in Mississippi today she says: "I think it's pretty healthy. I don't think there are any bad sores festering. There may be some, but I don't know about them. The general tenor of things here is easing, instead of tense or ugly. All I can say is that I haven't seen anything that isn't pretty hopeful."

She gets a lot of Women's Lib mail, asking her to take a stand or sign a petition—" 'I have had an abortion,' or something like that!"— and though she always replies politely she does not get exercised about the subject. "I don't think anything is against women writers," she says. "I've always been my own boss, I've never had any prejudice shown to me, so I have no bone to pick. I do think women should be paid as much as men, which I don't suppose anyone would disagree with. I don't see why, just because I write stories, that should give me any authority about, say, what should happen about abortion. Maybe I'm shirking responsibility, but I don't think so. Everything I feel is in my stories."

The question of the writer's political role pressed in on her with force during the height of the civil-rights battle, when she was getting late-night phone calls from out-of-staters demanding to know what she was doing for the cause. The calls irritated and troubled her, and finally in response she wrote an essay called "Must the Novelist Crusade?" In it she explained why she would not use the art of fiction to advocate a cause:

"Indifference would indeed be corrupting to the fiction writer, indifference to any part of man's plight. Passion is the chief ingredient of good fiction. It flames right out of sympathy for the human condition and goes into all good writing. . . . But to distort a work of passion for the sake of a cause is to cheat, and the end, far from justifying the means, is fairly sure to be lost with it."

Eudora Welty's fiction draws not from what is manufactured, but from what is seen and felt and, out of that, imagined. "Her stories emerge," she finds, "when I touch the match to something that's been smoldering for a good long while—in most cases something you could put a general word on, such as grief or love. All of a sudden something in the outside world will suggest a form it can take. Then you can write the story, but you've got this whole build-up of feeling behind it. You have everything inside you waiting for a clue, for an entry to the form of a story." Often a story will be set off by a mere glimpse—an observed face, an object, a small place. When the story starts in the typewriter, Miss Welty may not know where it will take her: "I learn in the doing. I'm not very smart ahead of time about my stories. I guess I depend on them to teach me."

As that suggests, Miss Welty is a natural writer. She works with the utmost craftsmanship and discipline, and can handle almost any fictive device or method, but her stories flow naturally from within her and from what she observes. The latter, of course, is Jackson and the surrounding Southern landscape, and she agrees that she has been influenced by this seeing—"just this kind of day," she said happily one afternoon, pointing out the window to balmy sunlight and rich green foliage. But unlike a Faulkner, a Robert Penn Warren, an Allen Tate, she does not feel especially burdened by the weight of the Southern past: "If I had been born in Manitoba or anywhere else I could have used what sensibilities I'm blessed with, and I feel that I would have been a writer." When I suggested to her that "place" is more important than where "place" is, she responded with enthusiasm:

"Oh, that's exactly what I mean. I think it can be a springboard. I think you have got to have some place on which to stand, then you can jump anywhere. You can't start swimming without something to push against, you can't dive off without a diving board, you can't really see anything until you have the frame."

By happy coincidence of birth Eudora Welty's "frame" is the Mississippi world in which she and her fiction are so firmly rooted—as firmly rooted as the great tree under which the family gathers in *Losing Battles*. But though her place may seem a small one, she is far less a "Southern" writer than a universalist, and the central concerns of her fiction know no iron boundaries. "I'm so much a person interested in the individual, the one person. I'm just aware of that person as singular and remarkable." More than anything else, it is this respect for individual human dignity, this abiding tolerance, this refusal to pass judgment on the actors in the human comedy, that pervade Miss Welty's work, that give it compassion, humor, integrity and beauty.

"My wish," she wrote not long ago, "indeed my continuing passion, would be not to point the finger in judgment but to part a curtain, that invisible shadow that falls between people; the veil of indifference to each other's presence, each other's wonder, each other's human plight." It is a wish that has been richly fulfilled, in her fiction and in her life.

Fiction as Event: An Interview with Eudora Welty

Jeanne Rolfe Nostrandt / 1978

From *New Orleans Review*, 7 (1979), 226–34. Reprinted by permission of the Loyola University of New Orleans Press.

Eudora Welty was born and has lived most of her life in Jackson, Mississippi. Her last novel, *The Optimist's Daughter*, won the Pulitzer Prize for fiction in 1973, and her latest book, *The Eye of the Story*, is a collection of her criticism. Her work includes four collections of short stories, two novellas, three novels, a children's book, a book of photographs taken during the 1930's Depression, and one collection of criticism.

This interview took place during our visit to Williamsburg, Virginia, in my room at the Williamsburg Inn on May 13, 1978. We had driven with a friend across the state from the western part to the eastern. It was Miss Welty's first visit to Williamsburg, and we had just returned from sight-seeing, somewhat tired and ready to relax. The tone of the interview, therefore, took on more of a relaxed conversation than question/answer format. Perhaps this is inevitable when two Southerners get together to talk about a common love, in this case—writing.

Eudora Welty is a tall, greying woman whose charm and warmth become apparent with her first words—softly spoken with the musical drawl that characterizes her as Southern. She is eager to talk about her work and more than tolerant of hasty questions put to her by students and interviewers. She is confident in her art and in her presence, but never patronizing or cold. Her knowledge of the human being and his condition, so prevalent in her fiction, becomes equally as obvious as her speaking or reading aloud. Her sense of humor is ever at hand, as the following interview will show.

NOR: As a child, did you hear stories from older people, especially black people?

Welty: Not from black people, mostly because I never saw black people then except in a white household as a servant or something, and though I would hear bits of superstition or remarks that I later remembered, I never heard black people talking among themselves. I heard many white people. I used to hear family stories and also in my neighborhood there were a lot of grand talkers that I used to sit at the feet of and listen to, telling not only family stories but just what went on in their own lives and interpreted in a dramatic way.

NOR: Like people who talk about their operations or some event?

Welty: Yes, exactly, and dramatizing things too, which gave me several ideas in writing. Then I heard my family stories, stories I used to hear when I would go up to West Virginia with my mother into her family. She had five brothers and they had families and they would sort of have a steady reunion while we were up there. I was still a very little girl when I began hearing these stories and it went on as long as they lived, most of them, and I heard many stories as stories well-told by good story tellers, things that were in the good sense of, of what you and I mean. That is, everybody knew these stories, but they just loved telling them and laughing at them and the more because it wasn't 365 days a year, but just in the summers, and I would look forward to it. They could also play all musical instruments—just by ear. They were all musical except for my mother, and they played the banjo and horns and things like that. They lived way up on a mountain. I could just listen enchanted to the old songs and ballads they were singing to the banjos and things—things they would pick up out in the country. These were not family songs handed down, but things they had heard in the mountains that they had learned and could sing, ballads and all kinds of things.

NOR: Where in West Virginia was that?

Welty: It was in Clay County, which is near Charleston, up the Elk River, quite wild and lonely up there in the high mountains.

NOR: That experience is like Laurel's in *The Optimist's Daughter*.

Welty: That's true. I used my own memories of about the age of three. I was there many other times, but I used those sharp memories you have when you first begin to notice things and gave them to Laurel. And also memories of my grandmother and of my mother at that age too. I used some of that personal memory in that book, about the first time I ever did do that without translating them entirely into fictional characters.

NOR: My grandmother used to tell stories more in the fashion of Miss Katie Rainey when she's talking to this obvious stranger in the opening of *The Golden Apples*. My grandmother used to do that for the children—sit on the front porch and snap beans or something like that, and entertain us; really to keep us out of trouble, I think, she would tell us stories.

Welty: Well now, those were the kind of things that I would hear in my neighborhood at home under the same circumstances. My mother would tell us things that she remembered, but they would be too important to throw out like that, to her, you know. She would tell them to us, but maybe after we were in bed at night wanting a story. She'd tell us something, but that's very serious to her—it's about her family. I don't mean pompous; it meant a lot to her.

NOR: Did she make up stories for you?

Welty: No.

NOR: She just told you real experiences. My grandmother tended to make up stories for us (I think they were made up), and she would put riddles in them to keep us quiet for a while. How did you first become interested in telling stories? Did you take courses in high school where you wrote short stories or poetry?

Welty: No. As I remember in high school we had composition, which would be grammar and themes. They were severely corrected and criticized for grammatical mistakes, for which I'm thankful. I remember the Latin grammar, which teaches you English. I liked to write simple narratives—"How I spent my vacation" or book reports. It's all beginning to come back to me. We had to do many book reports, and I used to write the book reports of a good many others besides me, because they didn't want to read the book. That was fun. I used to enjoy that, this early book reviewing. And we had oral themes and written themes. So, I think we were given a sense of being able to express ourselves on a piece of paper, and we had a pretty good literature course, too.

NOR: Did you write in reaction to this literature?

Welty: I guess we did give reports on things, but whether we were asked such personal things as our opinion, I rather doubt. I think it was all too formal. Of course, I contributed to the St. Nicholas League in *St. Nicholas Magazine* and to the children's page of the *Commercial Appeal*. I liked to write at home.

NOR: You've said before that you wanted to write, as far back as you can remember. All this time in school, even elementary school, were you, on your own writing stories?

Welty: I think so; my mother kept some. They are so-called

comicals and poems, you know, funny poems that take off on something. We used to write plays and give them in the garage for the
neighbors. Oh sure, I was always doing that. I won a prize at an early
age. It was a patent something called "Jackie Mackie Pine Oil," and
they gave me a prize for the best poem about it, and I won twenty-five
dollars. Wasn't that great?

NOR: That was; that's a lot of money for a child to win.

Welty: I'll say. That's the reason I remember it; luckily I don't
remember the poem.

NOR: As a student in the Jackson, Mississippi, public schools, did
you feel that any course or teacher was especially important to you
as a writer?

Welty: The level of excellence in the schools was really outstanding.
I'm not speaking only from my memory, but from that of all the kids
I know that have grown up and are my contemporaries. We remember
with much admiration how well we were taught. We had somebody
sort of like Miss Julia Mortimer *(Losing Battles)* who was principal of
my particular elementary school—Miss Lorena Duling, who was
marvelous. And there were a number like her—wonderful teachers. I
think they were missionaries in a sense; I think they felt they were. It
was marvelous; we had good schools. The year I entered Jackson
High School, or somewhere along there, there were only eleven
grades. They added on to make a twelfth grade and they picked a
class to make a graduating class. There were about sixty altogether,
and we were the entire twelfth grade class. I think I know what
happened to just about everybody in that class. We had a reunion (I
hate to tell you the number) last year, and just about everybody came
that was still in the land of the living. The summer I worked on the
New York Times Book Review, one of my jobs was to recruit new
reviewers for the summer. Robert Van Gelder, who was the editor,
wanted to bring fresh reviewers from time to time, in contrast to the
New York Herald Tribune, which used the same stable of reviewers
week after week after week. He wanted all new. One week, as it
happened, there were seven or nine members of my high school class
all reviewing books from different parts of the country. One would be
a professor at Duke, one would be a clergyman on the Gulf coast, and
one would be a teacher at Sewanee, but we were all members of that
same high school class. I think it was rather extraordinary; it shows

the way we were taught. I mean, it proves what I said, that we were well grounded in getting an education later in college.

NOR: How did Robert Van Gelder know of all these people?

Welty: He didn't. He interviewed me about a book I'd written, and then offered me a job. I was amazed, naturally, but I was quite young and I thought, "Why not try it?" He knew exactly my limitations; it was just a summer job. So, I stayed in New York and did it, and I was the one who suggested these other people, that was part of my job.

NOR: That was after the first collection of your stories. A friend has a letter from you just before that first collection came out, in which you ask him and others you knew in Raleigh, North Carolina, to help you find a title. How did you decide on *A Curtain of Green,* also the title of one of the stories, though not a central one?

Welty: The way it was decided was funny; no one could agree. And so the editors decided. That was the only story that there wasn't a strong feeling about from everybody. Nobody really cared about that title, but they wanted a title of one of the stories. The editor said no one objects to "A Curtain of Green," and then he laughs (this is John Woodburn, who's so wonderful) and says that settles it for the future; you can call your next book "A Curtain of Red," and "A Curtain of Blue," and a curtain of so on. And then he laughed and said, the last book can just be "Curtains."

NOR: "June Recital" from *The Golden Apples* was once entitled "The Golden Apples." Did the editors change this?

Welty: Yes, and they thought, and quite rightly, that this book, being connected stories, should have a title that none of the single stories had. I think that was proper. All my life I've been plagued by the inability to find a title for anything.

NOR: Can you remember any other special teachers?

Welty: I think, without question, the teacher who influenced me because he showed me something about the profundity or the scope of great literature was at the University of Wisconsin—Mr. Ricardo Quintana, who taught me Swift and Milton.

NOR: He's got a wonderful name.

Welty: And he was a wonderful person, and he's still there. I asked the other day when I met somebody. I think he's retired, but he's around. This was not a class where we did much reciting. It was a lecture course and, really, he began with the seventeenth century which he said Swift was the child of. So we had almost a course in John Donne and all of those other people, and then on through Swift. It gave us a whole (concept). I know he used words I never heard a teacher use—like "passion"; he really made us realize the strength and truth of poetic feeling and depth of feeling and emotional drive. I saw what a vast force literature was and the seriousness of the whole thing. It was exhilarating. It really opened the door to me.

NOR: The vast force; the connection in all of life. That's what a good teacher does, I think.

Welty: Yes, exactly, exactly. It really does come as a revelation. I always loved the things he was talking about, but I had never realized that it was all right to be so wholly enraptured by things. That it was part of it, you know, those were the feelings it reached. And there was also another teacher, I can't think of his name right now, I'm sorry. I had a course in logic under him that was a great help to me to show me how to organize my thoughts, which I'd never learned, to make an outline of things and to set things in order. How to take notes, that was very valuable. A course in art history was wonderful, too. I sort of minored, I suppose you'd call it, in art history.

NOR: In college?

Welty: Yes, that was just out of love for painting.

NOR: What about art courses? You did paint and sketch.

Welty: I was no good, and I found it out when I went to Wisconsin and entered a class. I knew nothing whatever about anatomy or anything, I had no training whatever. I didn't even know enough to know that I couldn't draw the human figure without more knowledge. The teacher told me to go on over to the library and practice drawing on the statues that were over there. To learn how people were made instead of drawing these people in their clothes without knowing how a foot was made or where a shoulder went into its socket or anything. Well, I realized I was in over my head. I took that course and liked it, but I learned that I couldn't do it.

NOR: Did you go practice on the statues?

Welty: Oh, sure. I did all right. I made good enough grades, but he had to tell me I didn't know about the human body; I didn't know it.

NOR: But it seems to me that there is so much of the artist in your stories—the perception of scene and the colors and the depth of the whole scene before you begin to delineate other things.

Welty: I'm sure it helped me to take these courses regardless of whether I was good or bad in them. It helped me to see more clearly. But I, of course, have a visual mind.

NOR: Did any of these special teachers encourage your writing or your art work?

Welty: No, to the art work part, I'm sure. All my teachers thought I did well in composition; I always made good grades. They encouraged me, for instance, or probably put me on the staff of the college magazines or things like that.

NOR: How did you finally come to write a story that was published?

Welty: You mean "Death of a Traveling Salesman?" It was the first one I sent to a magazine. I had written a lot of others and, in fact, I doubt if I would have sent this one anywhere except for Hubert Creekmore. He was my neighbor up the street who was a poet. He was ahead of me in years and accomplishment, and he was getting things published. He had never read anything I had written; I was too shy to show anything. But he said, why don't you send things to magazines? I said, where? Either he suggested *Manuscript* or he told me to go look in the back of *Best Short Stories* and see the list of magazines consulted. I used that all the time to send stories out to. That was the first one I sent off and it was accepted. But I remember writing a story at the University of Wisconsin that was pretty silly. It was a murder story laid in Paris. You know that was about how crazy I was; it couldn't have been taken seriously. Although I wrote things all my life, I was, in fact, a late starter.

NOR: So it was the neighbor who really was encouraging you?

Welty: No, I really wanted to do it.

NOR: But you didn't know what to do?

Welty: I was shy of doing it. I had never shown anybody anything I had written outside of college. You know, nobody. I was trying to teach myself and to learn. In fact, Hubert and some other boys had gotten out a little magazine called *Southern Review* ahead of the real *Southern Review,* which we had published. I helped them work on that, but was I ever asked to write anything? No. I mean, see it was secret, and I worked on the business end and got ads for it and did typing for it, and everything. But I did nothing toward contributing, nor was it ever thought of. And all this time I was writing stories. The stories weren't worth printing, and I hope I destroyed all of them.

NOR: But this friend, Hubert Creekmore, knew you were writing?

Welty: Well, yes. See I read his things; he was getting them published.

NOR: So then you showed him your stories.

Welty: He was always published. Our families were close. We lived right along the street from one another. Later he published seven or eight novels and books of poems and translations from various things, and edited *A Little Treasury of World Poetry* or something like that. He worked at New Directions for a while. You know, he really had a literary life, and I knew he was somebody I could ask. I didn't show him anything, but I asked him.

NOR: He didn't see the stories?

Welty: No, nobody saw them.

NOR: He just told you how to go about doing something about it.

Welty: Just the way children have asked me in class—"How do you go about it?"

NOR: Well, you sent it off to *Manuscript*. Did you send just that one story?

Welty: Yes. No, I didn't. I think I sent the one that came out second, come to think of it. They took two at once, I believe. One I never have reprinted, I've forgotten the name of it. "Magic" or something like that. I believe I did send them both at once.

NOR: Yes, that's it—"Magic."

Welty: I hadn't thought of that in years. If not, they asked me for another one and I sent that. And they took it, they were the first two.

NOR: That was in 1936, and five years later a collection of stories came out. That's fast moving.

Welty: I was writing just every minute and I never revised things. I didn't know enough to. Some of those stories in *A Curtain of Green* were about six years old when the book came out because I was writing one after another and sending them out all the time. See, I would try places like the *Atlantic Monthly* or *Harper's* or something first, trying to get published in a national magazine. Of course, the *Southern Review* had started taking them early and they were a great help because they published so many. But then I got my agent, Diarmuid Russell, after about four years of writing. He had seen some in the little magazines and wrote to me.

NOR: And volunteered to be your agent?

Welty: Volunteered to be my agent; I'd never heard of an agent. He said, "You get all these stories back in from the folds (You know they were all out) and send them to me." And then he sent them out for about two years before the *Atlantic* finally took one. And when that happened, then other magazines of national circulation wrote and asked for things. And some, as you can imagine, took the very ones that they had been rejecting. You know, that always happens. That was my break, when Diarmuid wrote to me. If it hadn't been for him, I don't know if I'd have ever been published. I really mean it, because he worked like everything just because he believed in the stories. And that's the only reason he ever took any writers.

NOR: Everybody says that about him, and I'm sure he was marvelous; but he simply had an eye for what was good material, too. I mean, he knew who should be published.

Welty: I believe he did, and that was true consistently in all of his work. And when he did think you were good, he was tireless and very astute in what he was doing. He never sent a story anywhere when he didn't think the editor would think it was for them, or think it was good. He wouldn't take anybody whose work he didn't like, even very well-known people who tried to get him.

NOR: Of course, that's what makes a good agent.

Welty: Absolutely. Everybody trusted him implicitly, not just his writers but editors. Gee, was I ever lucky. If there were more like him today.

NOR: When you were writing the story "Death of a Traveling Salesman," did you see the whole story as an actual event, or did you see it as an hallucination, or even as part of each.

Welty: I saw it as an event, I saw it as real.

NOR: This man Bowman actually had been sick and he is back on the road from this illness.

Welty: Yes. I think in all my work I try to write things that can be seen and taken as an event. I want them to stand on that solid ground all the way through with anything suggested that might work out of the material as I go. But in that case, that was a first really full-fledged solid story, and I was writing it absolutely like that. I was fascinated with various almost fairytale connotations in it, like go out and "borry some fire." But the reason I used that was that I heard the expression from a neighbor who bought land for the highway department. He had heard somebody way out in the country say "we have to borry some fire." I think that's really why I wrote the story, so I could use that. That's why I used that for what it was worth, you know, that's a little more than an event, but it is an event. I mean, it's got one foot on the ground.

NOR: A friend refers to that act as the Prometheus image of bringing the fire to man, but, you know, that just goes to prove the realism of the legend, rather than the legend in the realism.

Welty: I agree, I've always thought that. I wouldn't use it without its realistic hold on us, I don't think. In my way of looking at things as a writer, I rely on it, that you have one hand on it.

NOR: In "Keela, The Outcast Indian Maiden" there are such dark tones, especially in the ending when Little Lee Roy wants to relate this new episode in his story, and his children will not listen to him. This seems to show a lack of communication; Little Lee Roy is isolated. When the younger man who is guilt-ridden, comes to find him, he fails to see that the past which was so horrible to him is Little Lee Roy's greatest memory. And then the ending is so dark when Little Lee Roy cannot even talk about the day's event with his children. Am I misinterpreting it?

Welty: I'll tell you what I was actually trying to do. I hadn't thought about it like that and I can see how that would apply. What I was trying to do in the story was simply to present three insights into what had happened. One was from the guilt-ridden Steve, and one from the rather callous older man Max, and one from Little Lee Roy. Steve and Max are the ones that are so concerned; they haven't even thought of what he might feel. Everybody is thinking about how *he* feels, Steve and Max and Little Lee Roy, to whom it happened. I just wanted to show how he felt by starting to tell the children. I think it was the children who are the ones that really knew the reality of it, that it was almost too terrible. They knew what it really was, what had happened to him, and they just don't want to hear any more of it—it's just too terrible. It was kind of a sign off for the story, too. The whole thing was just too awful to contemplate, what had been done to this little man. That was all I meant to do. I didn't think about the lack of communication; that is, I think the children knew. It wouldn't be lack of communication, just not wanting to hear it.

NOR: I see. I think that's my own misreading.

Welty: Well, I wouldn't call it a misreading. What you said is perfectly legitimate, but I didn't mean to suggest too much isolation except they were all isolated from each other. But nobody felt it, really, except Steve; he felt that no one understood his feelings about it. Each for his own reasons couldn't really express it, what it was. I have worked on that story. I sometimes read it (I was asked to) and I made it better than it is in the book, to make it clearer what I meant to do. Maybe the way I fixed it, it is clearer—mostly with transpositions of things, revealing things in the right order. That's my greatest failing; I tell something too quick, I mean too early, and it needs to be spaced out.

NOR: The ending of "Flowers for Marjorie" seems dark to me, too.

Welty: That's a poor story; I had no business writing that story. That's a kind of an artificial story that is written about a city. I think I wrote it in New York during the Depression. It's too literary.

NOR: But that oppressiveness that must have permeated the time and place is there. The characters are victims of their time and place. I think it is a successful story.

Welty: I haven't read it in a long time, but the only thing that sticks in my mind about it is a small detail. The thing I think of on hearing its name just now is how he walked up the subway between those heavy, fat, warm ladies. That was oppressive all right.

NOR: In *The Golden Apples,* why did King MacLain run from his twins the first time he saw them on Halloween day.

Welty: Oh, I haven't read these things in so long, I don't remember specifics. Oh, when he comes home and sees them?

NOR: They're all dressed up with their masks.

Welty: He's somebody who comes and goes at will, and I think almost anything could have driven him off. But the sight of those little boys on roller skates with masks on must have been rather scary.

NOR: Because it seemed like an entrapment?

Welty: I think so, but I'd have to read it again to be sure of all the ramifications. He was pretty easy to run off; he's just passing through. I think he came out of curiosity to see what had come of this. I don't think he was even prepared for twins.

NOR: In the ending of *The Golden Apples,* Virgie Rainey is sitting on the steps just outside of Morgana, and the old black woman with the hen under her arm comes by and sits down, too. It's raining and

Virgie thinks of Miss Eckhart and the Perseus as he chops the head
of the Medusa three times. Then she hears the running of the bear
and the other images. Now, I see those as other legends you refer to,
but I see those images also as constellations belonging in a Mississippi
sky in October.

Welty: Good, I think so, too.

NOR: I'm glad to hear you say that. Of course, they are the legends
that have been made into constellations.

Welty: They belong in Mississippi. I really let myself go on that last
page, as you can tell.

NOR: You said in a television interview that you didn't know what
this page means.

Welty: I didn't know what it means in the sense that people ask.
You know, this is supposed to be this and this is supposed to be that,
and the old black woman with the chicken means, as if everything has
an equivalent. I just say that the whole thing was supposed to be a
mesh of suggestions and insinuations that just sort of showed the
whole mysteriousness of experience. I didn't want anything explicit.
I couldn't go into this on the program; in fact, I never have been able
to. What you say is such a key kind of thing that I wanted it to end
up, not in the abstract world of ancient mythology, but in reality. To
Virgie all of this was real, and there was a genuine photograph of the
Perseus and the Medusa. Everything was real along with many connotations. So I'm glad you said that; I'll remember that.

NOR: Somehow I feel with Virgie at the end of the book, and I feel
that she is at last free because she knows who Virgie Rainey is.

Welty: Yes.

NOR: And she is just stopping outside Morgana to assimilate all
this. In the process she is finding her own kinship with humanity, with
everything. And so I see that as the sky.

Welty: That's exactly what I tried to do. I do, too. And she has a
companion in the old black woman who's sitting down for reasons of
her own. This old woman has got something out of it with the chicken.
To me, it all seemed a very natural thing to do. As I remember, she
goes out after her mother dies, after the funeral; she goes out and
swims. She was very beautiful, she was kin to the earth and the sky
and all that. Oh, I think that's fine; I'm delighted to hear you say what
you did.

NOR: I'm glad you agree with it, that it is not farfetched.

Welty: It's so hard to say what you're trying to do with something. *I* know, but I don't know how to put it into any other words than the fiction.

NOR: You've said you intended for your stories to be actual events. In "Old Mr. Marblehall," some critics see Mr. Marblehall as being either an actual life or a fantasy life, with Mr. Byrd as the other. One life is actual, one is fantasy. Do you intend it to be that way, or do you intend that the man is actually leading a double life? Someone has pointed to the title as a reference to the song "I dreamt I dwelt in Marblehalls." Is that not the reference?

Welty: I can't claim that; it never occurred to me. I meant to express the fantastic life of Natchez, Mississippi, which is where I laid it, where all kind of crazy stories about families are always going around. I was trying to write a kind of Natchez fantasy. It, too, was a very early story; I didn't feel too responsible for making everything hang together. But that kind of story could so easily happen in Natchez. I'm sure there are so many double lives going on there.

NOR: I see it as an actual story. Did you use the song as reference?

Welty: I think it *is* an actual story. I didn't know the song.

NOR: It reminds me of the movie "Captain's Paradise," that we spoke of earlier; Alec Guinness leads a double life.

Welty: Right.

NOR: None of these stories ever seem like an hallucination to me, though I see fantasy in them. But more and more critics seem to interpret them as hallucinations or dreams.

Welty: I'm sorry about that.

NOR: It seems to me that what is so real in the story is the fear he has that he will be caught. And that fear can't be real unless there are two lives.

Welty: Well, he *delights* in that fear.

NOR: That's his adventure.

Welty: That's his adventure. "What a thing I'm doing," he thinks.

NOR: He sees himself "netted like the butterfly."

Welty: The story really is crazy, but I loved writing it.

NOR: In several stories, "Old Mr. Marblehall" and "Petrified Man," for instance, you use references to science fiction or detective stories. Both Mrs. Pike and Mr. Byrd read pulp magazines such as

Startling G-Man Tales and science fiction. Do you mean to imply that one's reading influences his life—actions, imaginations, or fantasy?

Welty: No, I thought that *Startling G-Man Tales* would be exactly what would be on the table at home in the stories. I just thought that's what they read. I think probably it was the magazine in that beauty parlor I went to, that they'd be reading.

NOR: It's more the extension of the personalities of the characters than a shaping force.

Welty: It's just what they would be reading.

NOR: A friend recently remarked about your writing in *The Eye of The Story,* that if you had never written fiction, you would still have made your mark through criticism. How does that thought strike you?

Welty: Well, I think I'm a natural fiction writer. I only wrote critical things because they were assigned to me as a job. I never would have normally done it, I think, except I was asked to do book reviews or asked to give lectures, and in order to do these, I would write them. The only piece in that book that I wrote because I just plain wanted to, out of love for something or someone, was the piece on Henry Green, which I never supposed would be printed. For the other lectures, of course, I chose my subject, mostly, and worked hard on what I did. The "Place in Fiction" in the book, I did because I was invited to go to Cambridge University in England on one of those American Studies in English Schools programs, and it was the only subject I could think of that I could possibly speak on with any authority. I'm not a teacher and not a scholar. And the other things were requests like: "Will you write the Jane Austen biography for Louis Kronenberger's *Brief Lives.*" I wouldn't tackle something that didn't strike a congenial note. I liked doing it, but I don't believe I ever would have originated any of those pieces.

NOR: It is rare for someone who tries fiction or poetry to also write criticism. I know a lot of people attempt it, but you write good criticism, not only about other writers, but you have an idea of what it is *you* do that makes a story successful. I'm not sure that most writers have that ability.

Welty: Well, I would have had no idea that I either could or wanted to if I hadn't tried and worked it out. I enjoyed the teaching of myself that writing such pieces made possible for me. I never would have thought I could write anything on writing. Those things I did at Smith

College when I had to give three public lectures about writing, I did
by trying to seize some handle where I already thought I knew
something and to work into it. Well, a lot of it is journalism, then an
effort to support myself with book reviews and lectures, too. It was
what I did on the side to help pay my way. But I've enjoyed what it's
brought to me, and I love, I really *love,* writing about other writers.
But I'm not an analyst in the real sense. I analyze, maybe, my
response to something.

NOR: In responding to it you get right to the heart of the thing
you're talking about.

Welty: I'm glad you say that because that would be its only justifi-
cation.

NOR: On a recent PBS interview you remarked about your story
"Why I Live at the P.O." that you saw the writing of it sort of as a
schoolroom type theme. Can you think of other schoolroom type
assignments that have instigated others of your writing.

Welty: I don't think so; I believe that's the only one. I just wanted
to write a funny story about how I'd heard people talking. I just wrote
that title at the top of the page to amuse myself. I believe that's the
only one that started like that; it is a high school theme thing in the
way it starts.

NOR: How did you think of "Why I Live at the P.O."?

Welty: I don't know. I did see an ironing board behind the window
in some little post office once, and I thought somebody must live back
there. And probably they did.

NOR: I have a theory that Laurel in *The Optimist's Daughter* is a
grown-up version of Laura from *Delta Wedding.*

Welty: There may be something in that. I've never thought of it
because I don't think of people in one novel as existing outside of the
book but probably that sensibility is the same. I can well see that
there is a thread between them, but it never occurred to me.

NOR: It's the same sort of sensibility, but more matured as the
result of having lived through the situation. I thought that sometime I
might pair these two and see what I could do with them. I didn't know
whether it had come to your mind or not.

Some critics have seen "Petrified Man" as a demonstration of how
women emasculate men, and the theory is largely based on that final
line from the child as he runs out of the beauty parlor: "If you're so

smart, why ain't you rich?'' Then, of course, there is the image of the petrified man. Did you intend such an interpretation?

Welty: No, I was just trying to express how people talk in the beauty parlors, and I kind of made that story up as I went, although the freak show next door was certainly talked about in my beauty parlor. And a lot of those horrible quotes, some of which I've cut out when I read it aloud, were really said. But I wasn't trying to say something about men and women except how women talk about men. How *they* talk about them. I wasn't trying to make a statement, and I love "If you're so smart, why ain't you rich?" That's something I've heard all my life.

NOR: I've heard it all my life, too.

Welty: Sure, it's just an old saying that this little three-year-old has just heard. And it fit so well because it was his parents that had gotten rich off the petrified man, and it was Leota who said that they had made all this money from her magazine. And he was pretty precocious anyway, you know, learning about the beauty parlor business. He was the most precocious one in it, and always present; he was the go-between. But I didn't mean anything except the terrible way people talk, and I thought it was funny. I wasn't trying to be horrifying. Someone had said it was the most horrible story they'd ever read. I thought it was funny.

NOR: Well, I always tell my students that such a theory exists, but I try to show them the absurdity of it by saying that someone could equally as well say the story shows how adults tyrannize the children of the world. They see the humor in that. I say that women in beauty parlors do talk about men just as men in pool halls talk about women; that is exactly the same sort of talk.

Welty: I agree with you; I wish I had thought of saying that. At a recent conference I said, as a panel member, that I had not intended such a ponderous statement about the sexes. I just want to quietly assert that. I was just using dialogue to show the extravagant way people talk. It had no more ambition than that.

NOR: So often, especially since the mid-1960's, critics have tended to look for some kind of social statement in works of fiction. I think they picked up on your essay, "Must the Novelist Crusade?" for a sort of license to do this with your work. I tell my students that the comments you make are not just about you, but about all writers, and

that they concern human nature, the universality of the human character and personality, and not on a given situation in a given time and
place. The message is larger than a single event; it's about the
human situation.

Welty: I think they do it, too, and I have answered a couple of
things. This whole year, while talking with students, I often say that
they haven't read anything of my work except the early stories. They
say, why don't you write about things that are happening today? I
explain that I have, but today is not in those early stories. Then I say
that I was always writing about justice and injustice and man's
inhumanity to man, and so on, that those things don't need to be
explained by trends or whatever is stylish to write about. No writer
can write without moral commitments and moral feelings at the very
root. They think that if you don't write about the civil rights movement, that means you don't care about people, that you don't have
any sense of right and wrong or anything. Of course, that's just nuts.

NOR: Maybe it's because we're living in a time when so many
people see morality as an abstract concept which isn't viable in
today's world. They don't know how to handle an abstract concept;
things are relative to them.

Welty: I know it, I know it. They think it's all right to do so and so.
Anyway, I think we are all agreed.

Growing Up in the Deep South: A Conversation with Eudora Welty, Shelby Foote, and Louis D. Rubin, Jr.

Louis D. Rubin, Jr. / 1979

Recorded under the auspices of the Voice of American Forum Branch of the United States Information Agency. From *The American South: Portrait of a Culture*, ed. Louis D. Rubin, Jr. (Baton Rouge: Louisiana State Univ. Press, 1980), pp. 59–90. Reprinted by permission of Louisiana State University Press.

Rubin: I was reading something about George W. Cable, the New Orleans novelist, the other day, and there was a funny remark about Cable by the Scottish writer James M. Barrie. He said, "Don't visit New Orleans. Go into the boiler room and read George W. Cable." I was just thinking that here in Jackson, Mississippi, where the temperature today is about 95°, you could almost say the same thing: "Don't visit Mississippi. Go into the furnace room and read Eudora Welty or Shelby Foote."

I want to ask you to bear with me for a minute while I read a quotation from Ring Lardner, who, as you know, was not from the South. This is from a piece called "Christmas Suggestions"—presents to give one's children. This is "Age 17 and Over":

> When a boy gets to be 17 it is high time he had a good mouth organ. This will not only bring him unlimited pleasure, but will be a blessing to his friends, male and female.
>
> If he is subject to smallpox, a prettily put up box of vaccine will make his Christmas a merry one.
>
> He will be overjoyed with a dog house, particularly if he has a dog.

I think that passage is extremely funny, and I think Ring Lardner is extremely funny, but you could pick that paragraph up and you would know at once it was not written by a Southerner and was probably written by someone from the Midwest. I wonder why?

31

Foote: Well, it has no Southern speech pattern to it, it has no rhythm to it, to my ear, and that's why no Southerner would write it.

Rubin: It doesn't have the rhythm. I hadn't thought of that. But it also has no sense of rhetoric, really, or of the sound of words, or language, or anything like that. The cadences aren't regular. There isn't any of that rhetorical sense. Now why do Southern writers not write like Lardner?

Welty: We don't talk that way. I think Lardner's ear is marvelous, but I think in that case the content even more than the cadences makes it seem non-Southern. Nobody needs a mouth organ at the age of 17. In the South they've been playing since they were two. All those things wouldn't be thought funny by the children, you know.

Foote: There's another thing non-Southern about it: he's not telling a story. I've never known Southerners do anything *but* tell stories.

Welty: Even in that short a space, I imagine.

Foote: "I remember the boy down the block," or something.

Rubin: We are doing this broadcast in the State of Mississippi, which is sort of headquarters for storytelling, I guess. Here is where the biggest storyteller of all comes from, right up the road about 90 miles in the town of Oxford. That passage from Lardner reminds me just a little of the Jason section in Faulkner's *The Sound and the Fury*. He has Jason talking a good bit like that. He's deliberately making Jason talk in that unlovely naturalistic way in order to show that that's the sort of person Jason is.

Foote: An outlander in the land. Characteristic Southern writing, though, does something that Miss Welty calls attention to just by the use of a word; I saw a quotation from her recently in which she spoke of the scene of a novel as being a "gathering-place," which is the best possible description you could give of a scene for a novel. That's what the scene in a novel is: a gathering-place for characters, where something's going to happen. I think that's characteristically Southern, the notion of it.

Welty: I do, too, and not only the notion but the technique of it, from the novelist's point of view: you use it to gather in everything you want to deal with, all of your threads.

Rubin: It's a gathering *place;* not just any old place but a particular place.

Welty: It's where it's happened before and where it may happen again; that's the place.

Rubin: It seems to me that Ring Lardner's stories, for example, could happen almost anywhere. This isn't to say that Faulkner's stories aren't universal, because they are, but I get no feeling of any real sense of place in Lardner—any more than I do in Hemingway—unless he's deliberately setting out to describe a place, such as Paris or a particular spot in Spain, or something like that.

Welty: I think Lardner located his stories within the realms of satire or sports or something; he had a style which was his circle that he put things inside. His style was the circumference of where these things happened. And he wasn't interested, as you said, in the place as a place, as I think perhaps we are. Shelby, don't you agree?

Foote: Yes, I do. Another thing about Lardner: he had a marvelous ear, but he had an ear for the quirky, the strange, in everyday speech. He would speak of someone's girl friend's boy friend. He liked the sound of things like that. It had very little to do with the natural rhythms of speech, which I don't think interested him much.

Welty: That's why he was so wonderful also in the letters he wrote, which are 10,000 miles removed from speech, but on purpose, because his people were writing letters to sound different from the way they talked.

Foote: And they were satire, especially a story told by a middle-aged Illinois businessman on vacation, who calls his wife "Mother."

Rubin: If you were going to draw up a literary map of Mississippi it would be a series of places—you would have northern Mississippi where Faulkner grew up, and you would have Oxford, Greenville, and the Delta, where you, Shelby, and Walker Percy grew up, and Elizabeth Spencer in nearby Carrollton, and here in Jackson would be Eudora Welty, and in Natchez, Richard Wright. And where did Tennessee Williams live in Mississippi?

Welty: Columbus.

Rubin: That's quite a collection, you know. You could legitimately work up a book and call it *Mississippi Writers,* and you wouldn't be dealing with any little provincial reputations at all; you'd be dealing with major currents of 20th century American literature.

Foote: One of the characteristics of Mississippi is that there are at least seven very distinct areas, each different from the other six. I suspect most states are like that; I know Tennessee is. But Mississippi does seem to me to have diversity. And it's not because part of it is mountains and part of it is flat, because there aren't any mountains in Mississippi. The Gulf Coast is the Gulf Coast because it is, and the Delta is the Delta because it is; the Jackson area is the capital of the state; Faulkner's area is in the hills. But there's not a huge geographical distance, the way there is in Arkansas, for instance. It goes back to history. The Black Prairie region was settled by a certain kind of people in a certain way at a certain date, and the same with other parts of the state, especially Natchez and the Delta.

Rubin: Mississippi has the most wonderful names. I really don't know any other state that has names like Senatobia . . .

Foote: There again you get that enormous variety. There are Indian names, there are German names, there are French names, there are Anglo-Saxon names. It's not like Pennsylvania, where half of them are Dutch, or something. There's just everything in the world in Mississippi.

Rubin: They all seem to be created, too. I get the feeling that places in Mississippi were all consciously named. I mean, they didn't just say "Let's call this place 'Brown's Corner,' '' or something like that. It's as if someone went out and said, ''I'm going to call this place 'Senatobia.' ''

Welty: Or ''Midnight,'' or ''Coffeeville,'' for a good reason. Of course those are extreme.

Foote: There's a funny story about names. There's a British cricket player and a man who didn't know cricket. There is a certain kind of delivery that is called a googly and the man asked the cricket player, ''Why is that called a 'googly'?'' and the player took his cap off and scratched his head and said, ''I honestly don't see what else you could call it.''

Rubin: Shelby, you grew up in Greenville, and Walker Percy was a close friend of yours when you were in high school together, and Walker's uncle was Will Percy, who as a literary figure is not well remembered now, though I think most people remember *Lanterns on the Levee,* the book of memoirs he published in the 1940s. Eudora, did you know Will Percy?

Welty: I never did get to meet him; I wish I could have.

Rubin: He was a remarkable man. You knew him, of course, Shelby.

Foote: I knew him very well indeed. I was over at Walker's house about as often as I was over at my house. Will Percy single-handedly is responsible for anything literary that came out of Greenville. Not by having a literary coterie, or anything like that. He did it by example and by a sort of teaching that you didn't know was going on. He was a man who had travelled widely throughout the world. He had good music in his house, which very few of us had. He had a formidable library—just the fact that it was there—plus the fact that he published books of poetry, actually published books. It was quite a thing to be close to. I guess there are at least 15 published writers from Greenville, and practically all of them are due to the presence of Will Percy. Not a direct influence, just his presence.

Rubin: There is usually somebody like that, or else a school teacher. Have you noticed that there will be a particularly good high school teacher somewhere, and for this reason there will be a group of writers in that place?

Welty: Absolutely.

Foote: Well, Percy was there for that reason. Carrie Stern, a teacher there at home, was the one who fostered Will Percy when he was a boy.

Welty: I'm so glad you said what you did about Will Percy, because I think those things need to be said, and I was awfully glad. Louis, did you read the new preface that Walker Percy wrote for *Lanterns on the Levee* for the LSU Press? I thought it was a marvelous thing for him to have done, because it's sort of a translation for people who couldn't perhaps comprehend the exact background or the measure of what Will Percy did.

Foote: Walker spoke in there of something that's very true—about how Will Percy was one of the greatest teachers he had ever known; simply by the way he presented what he wanted you to know, he made it attractive, in the way a great teacher can, and didn't detract from it by boasting about it or leaning on it too heavy, or anything. He really knew how to do it.

Rubin: Eudora, did you have a teacher, a particular teacher, whom you found when you were in grammar school or in high school . . . ?

Welty: Oh, sure. We were talking about that the other day—about my particular high school class. It wasn't in high school, it was in grammar school—the principal of the grammar school was Miss

Lorena Duling. We were trying to wonder why nearly every one of
our little class—it was the year that they added a year on, so it was a
very small graduating class, 60 people—managed to do something
kind of special in whatever we chose. And we all said it was Miss
Duling. I think she was from Kentucky.

Foote: It could well be true.

Welty: It could really be. I remember there was one Sunday when
there were seven people from Jackson represented as reviewers in the
New York Times Book Review. They weren't all still living there, but
we'd all grown up under Miss Duling. It was very funny. One was Bill
Hamilton, from Duke; they were scattered about.

Foote: It's a real talent, and you find it everywhere. Thank God
you do.

Rubin: You usually have a teacher in every one of your books,
Eudora, one way or the other.

Welty: I'm sure I do, because it meant a lot to me. Also, my mother
was such a teacher, although she didn't teach me, but I heard her
tales of school teaching in the mountains of West Virginia. She was
the same kind of soul that these other teachers were.

Rubin: I guess Faulkner didn't have a teacher like that, did he? I
guess he had Phil Stone.

Foote: I'd be willing to bet anything he did; I never knew anybody
who didn't.

Welty: I never knew anybody who didn't.

Rubin: I know I had one, a Latin teacher, even though I flunked finally.

Welty: Yes, it doesn't matter about the subject so much.

Foote: I had an English teacher, her name was Lelia Hawkins, Miss
Hawkins. I think teachers in those days made about $80 a month, and
what they got was the respect of the community, which they certainly
deserved. Miss Hawkins never gave me a high grade—oh, it would be
a great day or month when she would give me a B, because she would
always tell me, "You can do much better than this; I am not going to
give you anything over a C."

Rubin: I remember distinguishing myself with my Latin teacher in
South Carolina my senior year in high school by turning in a paper
which came back with a 17 on it; he went through the answers in class
and I found he had failed to give me credit for one correct answer, so

I brought the paper up at the end of the class and he changed the 17 to a 19, and said, "That makes a great deal of difference, doesn't it, Rubin?" He was a fine person and one of the greatest teachers I ever had. He taught me a great deal, a sort of respect for learning, as this sort of person always does. It's not just what he teaches but how he or she makes you think that there's something fine about knowing things.

Welty: About learning, and that it's in the *thing*—not to beat somebody, but *it*.

Rubin: The dignity of it, as such.

Foote: I've found the common characteristic of all the good teachers I ever had was that they could communicate to you their enthusiasm for their subject. They did it in many different ways, but that was always what it came down to. And others gave you an example of a life well lived, that the values that she (usually) lived by were indeed worth living by because you saw the result of them in her life. If I were able to do it, I would write about Miss Hawkins, for instance, who lived what you might call an empty, lonely life, but it was one of the best lives I've ever seen—a great life, and everyone knew it, too.

Welty: I think children are very much aware of integrity; when they see it, they know it, though they wouldn't know the word.

Rubin: Well, this certainly has been one of the things you've written so much about. I was just thinking of Miss Eckhart in "June Recital," and the teacher in *Losing Battles,* and then you have a teacher in *The Optimist's Daughter.*

Welty: It always takes me aback to realize that I repeat myself this way; I don't realize it, I just don't know that I do it. But I think we all do this kind of thing—there are patterns in our minds.

Rubin: The teacher in *Losing Battles* is Miss Julia Mortimer, and at the end of the story when Gloria and Jack go to the graveyard where she's been buried, Gloria says, "Miss Julia Mortimer, she didn't want anybody left in the dark, not about anything. She wanted everything brought out in the wide open, to see and be known." But Jack says, "People don't want to be read like books." I guess it's that kind of tension between the need to know and the instinct, almost the animal instinct, I guess, to hide, that is one way of representing the human condition, or something like that. And writing about a teacher is an awfully good way of showing that.

Foote: I've thought back about Miss Hawkins, and it's a wonder any of us ever reads Shakespeare again after being exposed to him in high school, and now that I look back on it with my vast wisdom I can see that Miss Hawkins didn't know a great deal about Shakespeare, either, but she loved Shakespeare and that is what came across. And it was up to us to get from it what she had somehow managed to get. It was a very real communication.

Rubin: This sort of person is like the outside world coming into the community. Here's the community with all its patterns and its doings and its own values . . .

Foote: Will Percy did that, and in a good way. He had been to Japan, he'd been all over South America, he knew Europe quite well, and to hear him speak of these as real places was quite different from reading about them in a book or hearing some tourist tell about the day he or she went to Brussels and Paris all in one day, or something. It was a real experience to hear somebody speak of it the way he did.

Welty: You know another thing about what Louis was saying, about the pattern in the South of the teacher, is that it also applies to the way we all lived in those days, of not moving around much in the South, so that the teacher knew the generations and the generations knew her. And that made another web.

Foote: That could really be extended. There was a woman named Miss Lee who taught my mother in the first grade, she taught me in the first grade, and she taught my daughter in the first grade. That's three generations she taught in the first grade.

Rubin: I remember in 1931 or 1932 we moved to the town of Summerville, right outside of Charleston, for a couple of months—my father was ill—and I went to the public school there. I must have been in about the second grade, or maybe the third grade. I'd never seen the teacher before, but she returned a book that my aunt had lent her 25 years before!

Foote: I was interested in reading Dan Young's biography of John Crowe Ransom, *Gentleman in a Dustcoat*. To think of Ransom teaching in a little Mississippi town. He spent two years there, in some little country town, living over the stable or boarding in somebody's house. He was so young when he finished at Oxford, and this was between Vanderbilt and Oxford, wasn't it? Or was it between years at Vanderbilt, because he didn't have enough money to go back?

He was only about 17 or 18 years old. He finished high school when he was only about 15, and was in college at 16, and then took two years off to make some money.

Rubin: They commonly did that: go to school for a couple of years and then go off and teach. And of course in the rural South most of the teachers were not college graduates.

Welty: You were trying to get to be one; that's why you were teaching.

Foote: It's so strange to think of Ransom going off to teach, to make some money. He was probably making about $18 a month teaching.

Rubin: And probably saving $12 of it.

Foote: Right. There was nothing to spend it on.

Rubin: We were talking about Will Percy, and of course Will Percy was a planter and the son of a U.S. Senator and the grandson of another Senator, wasn't he?

Foote: Of a Confederate colonel.

Rubin: And he was a person who had been all over the world, highly sophisticated, and so forth. And a figure like Will Percy meant a great deal for the town, as you say. But when you read Will Percy's poetry—and for some reason I've been acquainted with Will Percy's poetry since I was about 12 years old; I just happened to have come across it—although this man was living through a great deal of the most interesting events and periods and so forth in Southern history, when he wrote poetry, almost none of this ever appears. There's almost no attempt on his part to describe Mississippi, or to show his time and place, in his poetry. His poetry tends to be sort of world-weary, end-of-century-ish, like Dowson and the *Rubaiyat,* langorous subjects, the death of the gods, and things like that. It's as if his cosmopolitanism, and his generation's cosmopolitanism, in terms of literature at least, wasn't turned into any real scrutiny of their own time and place. This wasn't true at all of the next generation of Southern writers.

Foote: Well, they had what I consider a bad misconception, that there were certain areas of experience that were fit for poetry, and certain areas that were not. Will Percy did write some regional poems, of course.

Welty: Remember the one called "Home"? In that one he said he was sick of the rest of the world, and he described the levee and the river at Greenville.

Rubin: Did he write about the levee and the river as if they were at Greenville, in terms of the actual levee at Greenville, or did he make it seem as if it were a levee of the Nile, or something?

Foote: Only in his lyrics did he write about his home. Any time he sat down to do some serious writing he took it to Greece or the Children's Crusade, or as far away as he could get. But he did write local lyrics. Probably his best known poem is about a flowering bush that's only down there. He wrote a nice poem to his dog, "To Rip Who Died Mad"; that's a good poem. But Will Percy was not a poet, he was just somebody who wrote poetry. I don't think he ever came to grips with his art, so far as being a poet went. That's why he was never truly good at it. *Lanterns on the Levee* is a lot better than his poetry.

Rubin: Do you think this has anything to do—I'm trying to use Will Percy representatively, of course, rather than just as Will Percy—with his time and place?

Foote: Yes, almost everything to do with it. When I mentioned definitions of fit subjects for poetry, I meant that the group subscribed to that notion. But Mr. Will was cut off from what happened to poetry in a direction that he was not taking. He didn't like Ransom's poetry, for instance. He thought that "Bells for John Whiteside's Daughter" was rather silly and inaccurate and he said, "Geese don't move like that; that's not real." I didn't know what to make of his not liking Ransom. I didn't see how anybody could not like Ransom, but he didn't. He had no use for Eliot. Faulkner he didn't like because Faulkner came down there and played tennis once and got drunk on the court and wouldn't take the game seriously. He objected very much to that.

Rubin: Faulkner tried to write Percy's kind of poetry; Faulkner's early poetry was very much like that. Eudora, did you ever write poetry?

Welty: No.

Rubin: Not at all, not even as a young girl?

Welty: Well, I wrote some in high school, but not since I've grown up.

Rubin: It's a lot harder to deal with the texture of everyday experience, to document the world around you, in poetry than it is in prose, don't you think?

Foote: I don't think anything's harder than prose.

Welty: I don't, either.

Foote: Nor as satisfying. I envy poets sometimes. I began, like every writer I ever knew, as a poet, but it really didn't satisfy me. I couldn't spread-eagle enough in it. It held me in ways I didn't want to be held and didn't turn me loose in ways I wanted to be turned loose.

Welty: When was this?

Foote: At the very beginning, in high school. I haven't written a poem in 30 years or more.

Rubin: When I studied poetry in high school in the South—I don't know about you-all in Mississippi; I was in South Carolina—the poems that were taught to me were things like "The Building of the Ship."

Foote: That's when the New Englanders dominated poetry.

Rubin: I mean, nobody would have thought to teach me anything about a poet as recent even as Carl Sandburg.

Welty: Oh no, never.

Foote: By the time I came along in Greenville, the American literature textbooks had poems by Eliot and Sandburg at the back of them.

Welty: Well, you're that much younger.

Foote: They were taught, too. Miss Hawkins taught it to us. She pointed out to us that it was very sensitive poetry, not coarse, crude stuff, especially Eliot's. It was good to come in contact with. And Sandburg came by and gave a reading once. Vachel Lindsay came by and ranted and raved for two days.

Welty: I think he came by home, too. I didn't realize that was poetry, I guess.

Foote: The school was where it was available. There was another quality to it. I grew up in a town that in my boyhood went from a population of about 10,000 to 14,000, somewhere in there. (Greenville is now about 55,000 or 60,000.) There was one high school. I have to correct that by saying there was one *white* high school. In any case, every white person in that town between the ages of 14 and 18 was in that one building five or six hours a day. And we all got to know each other in a way that it's not possible to know somebody by any other method. So that in Greenville, Mississippi, in those days when nobody left and nobody moved in, everybody in that town knew each other in a way very different from the way you would have known each other in a larger town.

Rubin: How big was Jackson when you were growing up, Eudora?

Welty: About the same size, from 15,000 to 25,000.

Rubin: One high school for Whites and one for Blacks, or were there more than one?

Welty: There was one senior high school for Whites and two junior highs.

Rubin: You were much more advanced than we were in Charleston. We didn't have any junior high schools. We just had grammar schools and high schools.

Welty: I don't mean junior high schools. We had junior high schools, but our class didn't go to them. There was one in West Jackson and one in North Jackson. There's West Jackson and North Jackson just because Jackson is made that way—two extreme ends. There was only one high school where everybody had to go, and one black high school, I guess. It's awful that people my age didn't even really know the conditions of the black schools. We knew the black colleges, where they all were.

Rubin: Well, we had in Charleston, which was a city of 62,265 (we all had to memorize the 1930 census), one white high school for boys and then one white high school for girls . . .

Foote: There's segregation!

Rubin: . . . and then a black high school. I don't think the black high school was segregated, though it may have been.

Welty: Ours wasn't segregated, I mean sexually.

Foote: My son is 15 now and he's never been to school with girls, and I don't see how he's ever going to learn to respect them the way I did because they were all smarter than we were, and he won't know that.

Welty: Miss Duling, of whom I was speaking, had a girls' side and a boys' side to the recess yard, just as there were two different basements and toilet facilities. We watched each other play, but a sidewalk went down the middle.

Rubin: You didn't play together?

Welty: Well, supervised play we did, you know, "physical training" or whatever it's called, but at recess we clustered each in our own yard, but in full view of the others.

Foote: We did that too, Eudora, and one time there was a boy who kept wandering over on the girls' side, and three girls caught him and put a dress on him one day, and when they turned him loose he tore the dress all to pieces and ran back to the boys' side, and he never went over there again.

Rubin: You say in Jackson there was a West End and a North End of Jackson. Did this carry social distinctions too?

Welty: Maybe I was just so dumb, but I didn't know that it did. We found that *they* had a chip on their shoulders when we were forced to meet for that one little class I told you about. There were 30 from each selected to graduate, and we were all furious. We wanted to keep our own group—they wanted theirs, we wanted ours. It didn't last more than a month once we were mixed up in the classes, which was done on purpose, and that's all it took. There wasn't any sense of "across the tracks," or that kind of thing that you read about.

Foote: There was in Greenville, because the grammar schools were regional, and there were people who lived near the gypsum mill and their folks worked in the gypsum mill, which was a dreadful thing to do—working in the mill.

Welty: Well, we didn't have any of those.

Foote: It was a bad situation, but quickly corrected when they all got together in high school.

Welty: Exactly. The children corrected it, and that's all it needed.

Foote: The good thing about that grouping was that, of your two best friends, one might be the son of the garbage collector, and the other the son of the president of the bank, and you were very close friends, the way you are in high school. Education is in pretty bad shape today. They're all shaken around, teachers are not used to new methods, and the schools are pretty bad in Memphis, for example. It's a powerful argument for a boy going off to a good prep school where he will get a good formal education. He can still get Latin, and even Greek if he wants it, and so on, which you can't in Memphis. But I can't face up to my son not spending his adolescence in his home town. It just seems horrible to me to grow up in a cubicle in a prep school. I see the advantages, and not only the educational advantages, but still it just seems terrible to me for a boy not to experience his 15th, 16th, and 17th years milling around. And some-times, too, get up and have a bacon and tomato sandwich and a Coca Cola for breakfast. That's a great breakfast.

Rubin: You've been talking about Greenville, with a population of 12–15,000 when you were growing up there, and Jackson, with about 25,000. I grew up in Charleston, South Carolina, and the population there was, as I say, about 62,000, and that was within 4,000 of the population of Charleston at the time of the Civil War. I suspect that the population of Jackson was probably no more than twice as large as it was at the time of the Civil War.

Welty: Oh, heavens no. And it's the only city in the state, you know.

Foote: There was a time, I'm sure, when other places probably made the same claim, but I remember hearing in the 1940s sometime that Jackson was the fastest growing city in the United States, and it was doubling and doubling and re-doubling.

Welty: I know it. Meridian and Vicksburg used to claim with us, which was going to win out, and so on. And of course it's just a pure matter of circumstances. But Mississippi is really, as I'm sure Shelby will agree, a rural state with small courthouse city-towns, like Green-ville. That's its structure. We didn't really need a city like Jackson. I wish we'd stayed like we were.

Foote: And Greenville, too. Greenville's 60,000 now and it used to be I knew every dog in town, not only every person.

Welty: You did, and everybody's car, too.

Rubin: You know the old joke about the two largest cities in Mississippi being New Orleans and Memphis.

Welty: That's true, and Jackson was half-way between.

Rubin: What I was getting around to was this: these places—these Southern towns and Southern cities in which you grew up—were still rather small communities in which there was a considerable amount of defined stratification. You knew who everybody was and everybody knew who you were, and all this sort of thing. I'm not talking now about caste and class, I'm just talking about a sense of a very tightly knit social community, for good or for evil. These school teachers we were talking about were, in a sense, the harbingers of the change of all that. They were bringing in that outside world.

Foote: They were exempt from any notion of class. They were outside it, like the third or fourth estate or something. But I'll tell you something interesting, about the Delta in any case. Nobody could afford to look down on anybody else, and nobody needed to look up at anybody else, because everybody had been up and down so fast with that easy credit in the Delta. I don't know of anybody, friends of mine, who didn't have somebody of considerable consequence in his immediate ancestry, no matter how poor they were now. And no matter how rich they were now, you'd know they were apt to be broke within a couple of years. All it took was a bad crop. But the glorious thing, Louis, the really glorious thing about growing up in a Mississippi town, is what you got from it that you could use as a writer. I'm in the egocentric predicament of looking at it from that direction. When you are thoroughly aware of the ins and outs and vicissitudes of the family who lived two doors down the street, what their grandfather had done (and everybody knew perfectly well he had done it, and shame on him for doing it) and then the tragedy that came on his children and then the glorious recovery of what the oldest boy managed to do when he opened the Buick agency, and so on—those things are of enormous value to a writer and I do not see anything that could take their place. I wouldn't swap it for anything.

Welty: I wouldn't, either. And it's what gives you a sense of narrative and a sense of the drama of life. Everything has a consequence and everything has a root.

Rubin: You know where everybody comes from. I can remember all the new people that came into my class when I was a child.

Welty: Sure, I can, too.

Rubin: And where they came from.

Welty: Absolutely. I can remember the first Yankee that came into my class; we were in the fourth grade and he was from Indiana and he said "cor-dju-roy." We used to say, "Say 'corduroy.'" Can't you remember *every*thing about them?

Rubin: I used to go up to visit my relatives in Virginia, and that seemed like I was going to the North. I really thought I was going North, going to Richmond. And they used to make me repeat words. They used to make me say "late date at eight" and I'd say "let debt at et." You know, I still had that deep Charleston pronunciation, which I've almost completely lost. But these teachers that we were talking about sort of stood for that outside world, and they were telling you all, "Listen, right out beyond the city limits is not where the world ends."

Foote: They didn't necessarily know the geographical outside world, but they were certainly aware of the world of art in a way that other people were not.

Rubin: I was thinking of things like history, and geography, or anything you want. And the way you look at things, in the sense that you don't judge everything by the people involved in it, because there's another world out there. And that's what these teachers represented, in a sense. They had been out there in the world, if only to the normal school, to learn to teach.

Foote: Or one quick trip to Europe when they were young. And they lived on it forever, remembering.

Rubin: The outside was breaking in, then, and now you look around there and you say, "Greenville is gone. It used to be 15,000 and now it's 60,000." Of course I think part of that is just a basic sort of nostalgia.

Foote: It's pretty heavy to look out where you used to go bird hunting and see subdivisions and what looks like miles and miles of little houses. You can't think it's good, and it's not good. It's a vitiation of what was a good thing.

Welty: The road on which we drove out to this radio station, which I had to find the same as you did, was our old blackberry-picking road when I was a child. And right next door down here—it's called "Hanging Moss Road"; it used to be just called the "Pocahontas Road," its real name—there are trees with hanging moss on them, and one little lot that they haven't torn down. I guess they left it to interest real estate people. That's the way this whole country used to look. And the sight of it just gripped me. I thought it's like a slice out of the past looking at me, just one block long. As for all the rest of it, you could be anywhere in this state, or Indiana, or anywhere else.

Foote: A Wisconsin historian named William Appleman Williams summed it up in a good way. He said, "Better highways don't make better picnics."

Welty: Absolutely.

Rubin: Well, on the other hand, you can still find in Jackson neighborhoods which are just like the neighborhoods where you grew up, can't you?

Welty: Not exactly.

Rubin: Pretty close to it?

Welty: No, they've torn everything down. We've been ruthless here.

Foote: What's left is in tatters, you see. If for some reason it got overlooked, boy, did it get overlooked! You can find somebody's estate which they've still got the money to keep up, but it would be a very tight enclosed thing and what was going on around it would not be good. No, it's gone.

Welty: It's really gone.

Foote: In a lot of ways it deserved to be gone, but I'm talking about for my purposes and my pleasure, not making a judgment as to whether it justified its existence or not except for my use.

Welty: Not just because it's old, but the first things they got when they began tearing up old neighborhoods were the most worthy. Now there are petitions to save such-and-such, which nobody really wants, because they think they should have saved something.

Foote: They grabbed the best first, like when they tore down the old depot in Memphis. That was the thing they really should have saved. And when it was gone, everybody said, "My God, we must save, we must save," because it was gone.

Rubin: And they try to hold on to it, but all they're really holding on to is a facade, isn't it?

Foote: They have some very strange ideas. They've come up now with the idea that when you put on something it has to have a theme. In Memphis now the old fairgrounds is Liberty Land, and there are Walt Disney characters wandering around in costumes and everything. It's not near as much fun.

Welty: It's so unreal.

Foote: Right. They're going to restore Beale Street, and they're going to do something down on the riverfront finally, but they've got to call it "The Mark Twain," and they're going to have imitation steamboat runs, and things like that, and it won't work. What they really ought to do is what they did at the start. Get the very best architects you can afford and tell them to do the very best job they can, and see what you come up with. But they'll never do that.

Welty: The sad thing is that when they call something "The Mark Twain," the young people will grow up thinking, "Is that all it was?"

Foote: That's right.

Rubin: In Charleston harbor there's an old boat which is made into a restaurant. I think they built on the facades for the paddle wheels, and in large letters on the side it says, "The Scarlett O'Hara." With all the historical things that went on in Charleston, they have to sell a restaurant by calling it "The Scarlett O'Hara," and I don't think Scarlett ever put a foot in Charleston. They could at least have called it "The Rhett Butler"—Rhett Butler came from there.

Foote: I remember Faulkner telling me once—we were driving through one of those subdivisions and they all had picture windows and what they were looking at was each other right across the street there—and he'd look at one of those picture windows and not know what to make of it. And he said, "I know what it needs. It needs a *Gone with the Wind* lamp in it."

Rubin: How much of your literature is built on just that sense of all this changing, though? I don't mean in terms of subject matter, but in terms of your relationship to it.

Foote: I'm sure a great deal, but I wouldn't be able to analyze that. I write mainly about what it was before it changed, because I liked it before it changed.

Rubin: Would you be writing it, though, if it hadn't changed?

Foote: Maybe not. It's just like you don't ever know your homeland until you get away from it.

Rubin: Don't you know that what on the surface, on the obvious level, is nostalgia, in a good deal of Southern writing gets below that level of nostalgia and looks at the pros and cons, and that it's out of the tension between those two that a good deal of the impulse to write about it comes?

Welty: I don't think nostalgia in itself is a very serious reason for art; it means something, but it's sentimental, I guess, in essence, when it comes to material for art or to conceiving it. But I think, if I understood what you meant, that's true of all we do when we write, isn't it, to try to get the fountainheads of these things—why things change?

Foote: I think that when something *has* changed, and you believe you have seen the end of something, then you're able to assess it, because you're aware of its beginnings and you have seen its end, and therefore you can deal with it. So in that sense, yes.

Rubin: But we all always see the end of things in that sense. I'm not saying that all times are relative, because I don't think they are. And I do think that a good deal of what Southern literature is today is built on a particular time and place and a particular change. But nevertheless a sense of change. One of the most beautiful passages I know is in a writer that I know you admire a great deal, Shelby, and you do too, Eudora—Marcel Proust. It's the passage close to the end of *Swann's Way* when Marcel tells about going back to the Bois de Boulogne and he sees the people in their fashions, the fashions of the 1910s, and he thinks these people don't know what beauty is. If they'd seen Mme. Swann come along here, the way she was dressed with a different kind of hat. . . . Then he says that what he is really looking for is not a *place* at all but a *time*. Nostalgia, which seems to be memory of a place, is really memory of a time. But how much *had* the Bois de Boulogne changed? All of us have this built in us, don't we, in a sense?

Foote: Well, he began by looking at the automobiles and the women's clothes, and his reaction was, specifically, "Oh, horrible!" And then he says regret for a particular place is regret for a particular moment, just as you say.

Rubin: And when you've got this particular moment built in to the change from a small town to a much more eclectic, cosmopolitan, modern society, then you've got a powerful, looking-back involvement, haven't you? It seems to me that our first reaction to anything like that is this sort of nostalgia: Isn't it nice to look at these old photographs and think about these days and remember this and remember that? But when we get to thinking about it more, there's something real about that that doesn't seem real, imaginatively, about contemporary experience. That is, we sort of anchor it.

Foote: I was looking last week at some photographs Eudora took during the 1930s . . .

Rubin: Her book of photographs, *One Time, One Place.*

Foote: Yes. And I was saying how differently these same eyes see those pictures 30 years later from how these eyes saw those pictures then. They seemed perfect pictures of things that were happening; now they've taken on an oddness, they are encrusted by time. It's very strange what time can do to things. That's what happens, what Stendhal called an encrustation has built up on them—a crystalization.

Welty: And that's what gives the pictures any value, I think. That's why I thought they could be published after all this time—because now we look at them through that knowledge of what's happened between then and now.

Rubin: Let me ask you this. When you took those pictures in 1935 or 1936, did you have the sense at the time that you were preserving something?

Welty: Oh, no, indeed not. I took them because something appealed to me in the form that a story or an anecdote might have—to capture something. I just did it for the moment.

Rubin: You didn't have any sense of being a recorder?

Welty: Oh, no. I think that attitude probably would have ruined everything. They were utterly unself-conscious.

Foote: It's not only that you look at them with a more knowing eye, later on, but that mystery gathers. It's not only knowledge, but it's un-knowledge. They get an added mystery. Someone said once that you could take a pretty junky doll and bury it in damp ground for a couple of weeks and dig it up and you'd have an authentic mysterious object because of what has happened to it in the ground there. It would be very strange looking. And some of that gathers, too; as well as the knowledge, the mystery gathers. Somebody's arm being in a particular position can be very strange in a photograph.

Rubin: To me one of the most mysterious things about old photographs, when they involve things that I knew, is what was right off the edge of the photograph that didn't get in.

Foote: Nobody did that better than Vermeer, a long time ago.

Welty: That also is connected with the storytellers: the sense of what is impending, what is threatening.

Foote: That's what Vermeer could do. He would never tell a story in a picture, and yet the picture is surrounded by story, but not on the picture itself. Nobody's sighing over anybody or anything.

Welty: No painting can afford to tell a story.

Foote: Very bad ones have.

Welty: And I don't know that my photographs tell a story. It's just that I felt the story possibilities. . . .

Foote: All around the frame.

Rubin: Did you travel up and down the state doing those, or just around Jackson?

Welty: All around the state. It was the first time I'd ever seen it up close; I'd just seen Jackson.

Rubin: Did you print your own pictures and everything?

Welty: Yes, in the kitchen. But I did not develop the negatives. I couldn't do that, I should have.

Foote: What picture-taking I did, I did the same thing. I'd send the negatives off and make the prints.

Welty: And then enlarge them and play with them.

Foote: Have fun with them. Print them very dark or very light.

Rubin: When you have the picture, though—here's a photograph of two people sitting on a bench, say, and this photograph was taken 25 or 30 years before. Now you remember when you took that photograph that your car was parked over here, and let's say it was a 1932 Ford V-8, the first Ford V-8, for example. But that's long since gone. Now you know your car was over there. If you could somehow open the picture frame up . . . that's the strange kind of sense I get about pictures, old photographs: the frozen time involved in it and the way that by freezing it in time you liberate the place and everything around it and so forth.

Foote: I have a sort of postcard picture of me at the age of two standing by a cart to which a billy goat has been hitched, and I'm required to hold the thing, and I'm terrified of the billy goat, looking at me with his yellow eyes. It's a very spooky picture of a kid holding a billy goat.

Rubin: How much of this that we've been talking about would have been true if, instead of you and me and Eudora sitting here, Richard Wright had been sitting here?

Foote: We would talk about different things, probably; I mean, talk about additional things. But I don't know that there would be all that much difference.

Welty: I can't think there would be any sense of inhibition or something; I don't think so. That isn't probably what you meant. Do you mean subject matter?

Rubin: No, I mean talking about the good old days and how things were so much better when they were smaller.

Foote: I think he would share every good old thing we remember. He would remember some horrible injustices, how could he not? But he would have some of the same feelings that we have, I'm quite sure.

Welty: I've talked to other people of his age and color and it is exactly that. You share many things. I've had letters from people—I had a letter from a black friend of mine when something had happened to me, and she said, "I don't know if you remember me, but my mother was your mother's wash-lady, and I used to come to your house on the express wagon"—this would have been when we children were six or seven years old—"and we used to play together." It was when my mother died; she had seen it in the paper. And she said, "She was a nice lady and you were a nice girl. And my daughter and I think of you." She said she was now the wife of a professor at a college somewhere, but she often thought of those days. Now this was completely spontaneous on her part. But that's what you remember. She shared something when she read that about my mother. She thought, "We have memories in common."

Rubin: That's what I was hoping you'd say, because that's the feeling I have. I think one of the difficulties in dealing with black American literature and black Southern literature is that so few white critics think of the black community as having its own complete life, and the black community in the South, even in the worst of time, as not being defined by its relationship to the white people at all, but having its *own* integrity, its own identity. And that experience—however in this area or that area, politically, socially, or economically it may have been very much underprivileged—was real. And the relationship of the writer to it is not just in terms of political issues or things like that.

Foote: I know the Negroes had integrity under those circumstances, and some of it was pretty militant, too. If I went back in the kitchen and got in the cook's way I was committing a very serious offense and I'd get run out of there fast, maybe with the flat of the bread knife.

Rubin: Well, I would say that what you've both been talking about—for the past 45 minutes we've been going all around Robin Hood's barn—but what you are finally getting down to really, is that you've lived in a time and a place that have a very palpable kind of identity, and that you wouldn't be what you are as a writer without that particular time and place.

Foote: No, indeed.

Welty: Absolutely.

Foote: It has to be understood, about these things that we're talking about, that everybody's integrity was well understood to be not only important but precious, and people respected it. I'm talking about from this level down to that level, or from that level up to this level. Everybody knew perfectly well that everybody else had his integrity and it wasn't to be sneered at or fooled with. There could be serious consequences of doing that, including getting shot off a horse some day out of a bush, and you didn't do that. The broader the social separation, like plantation owner and sharecropper, the more formal the relationship was. It was as if everyone perfectly well understood that this thing is not to be shaken around by any heavy-handed person. There were people who did it, and it was disastrous. They had no tenants. Nobody would put up with it. And you couldn't put up with it. You were finished in your own eyes when you did. So nobody required you to put up with it. There was a great deal of very real courtesy in relationships between people.

Rubin: In towns and cities?

Foote: Just as much in towns and cities as in the country. There was a quite formal relationship between my aunt, for example, and her cook. They were close friends, but it was perfectly well understood that each had to treat the other with a certain kind of respect as part of that friendship, and it was a very real thing. Now it's true the cook was making $7.50 a week.

Rubin: That would have been pretty good wages in Charleston.

Foote: It was pretty good wages there, but it was an outrageous wage, and that was one of the things that was wrong with it. But that's been corrected now, with a vengeance. You see, she was making $7.50 and she was worth about $40. Now she's making $60 and she's worth about $40.

Rubin: So the more it changes, the more it remains the same.

Foote: Something like that. I'm really joking about that, I hope you know.

Rubin: Of course. We'll make sure your aunt's cook doesn't see a transcript of this. I think we should say something noble and interesting that would end this conversation, but I can't think of anything noble and interesting. You've done exactly what I wanted you to do which is to talk about everyday Mississippi. I didn't want you to have a literary discussion, because we can read those by the dozen.

Foote: I think that was a good ending.

Eudora Welty's Garden of Triumphant Simplicities
Henry Mitchell / 1980

From *The Washington Post,* 10 June 1980, Sec. B, 1, 11.
Reprinted by permission of *The Washington Post.*

"Oh, you're famous now, Eudora, sure enough," someone greeted
Eudora Welty, the Mississippi writer, yesterday after she had ac-
cepted the Presidential Medal of Freedom from President Jimmy
Carter.

"I think so," she said, pleased as a dog with two tails.

"Give you a lot of money too?"

"No," she said, "and I don't need any with what I got."

She opened a polished walnut box, and there, against white silk,
was the gold (not "real gold" in these economical and, to be plain,
cheap times) and red enamel medal with five eagles standing around
the outside stretching their wings, the whole suspended on a blue and
white ribbon.

"And with it you get a little one, too," she pointed out. Bill Smith,
the poet, told her he recently got a distinguished medal in Budapest
and it, too, had a tiny version, and he asked what the miniature
was for:

"To wear on your pajamas," he was told.

Welty may or may not wear hers to bed, but it pleased her to get it,
partly because, she said, "it was not just a representative sort of
thing—I felt the citation sincerely reflected the president. [It spoke,
among other things, of Welty's 'triumphant' humor.]

"They give you lots of things to take home," she went on, opening
the blue leather folder lined with watered silk that held the presidential
citation honoring her for her fiction and other dandy works.

Home is, of course, Jackson, Miss., to which she is returning to get
on with her work.

"It's a story I've been working on in my head. It doesn't seem to
quite fit as a short story, but it's not at all something I want to make
a novel of," she said.

54

"Well, once people start reading," she was encouraged, "they won't mind going on another few minutes. I hate to think you'd start throwing things out just because they didn't fit a short-story space."

"If they fit, fine. But that's the problem. I'm not sure they do. I may just file it. Or I may throw it away."

With Welty, the task is for the work to emerge perfect, very like Athena from Zeus' head—organic, powerful, lovely and reasonably immortal. It's not a question of just batting out a nice story. It has to be monumental and easy, too, for that writer eschews on-the-cuff nobility. The nobility her readers mark in novels like *Losing Battles* and short stories like "A Worn Path" is built in, not stuccoed on.

As a result, everything takes her forever. She once delivered some lectures upon considerable urging, and it takes her several months to write a lecture.

"So now I've written all the lectures I know, and therefore I can't deliver them any more. They've been published, and it would be a rip-off if I delivered one now, now that anybody can read them in a book.

"But I do like to read some of my things to young people. We have question-and-answer sessions. Sometimes when I read a batch of stories at colleges, I am amazed at how bright young people are. At that age, I could never have written anything as good. They master the hard short-story form so quickly."

"When you get back home, people will leave you pretty much alone to do your work, won't they?" she was asked.

"Yes. I learned a long time ago not to try doing everything at once. I divide my time into working, at home, and then I spend other time reading at colleges or traveling. I don't try to work when I'm gone.

"Spring in Mississippi was strange this year. Cold, then lots of rain. The yellow banksia [a rose that's a great favorite of Southerners] came and went in a flash. It was the same way with irises."

"It's that way every year in Washington," she was reminded. "Up here people don't count on settled weather till the end of June. That's why they're increasingly up to their ears in day lilies, that only bloom in full summer."

"Same with me," she said. "More and more day lilies. I like the ones that bloom at night and smell good. Still (thinking back on the spring) you feel cheated of part of your life."

Welty was dressed in a pale green dress that showed off her snowy hair nicely. Asked to say something wise, she ignored it and went on with her reflections of spring:

"My mother was the real gardener," she volunteered.

"Yes. Even after she was sick," someone observed.

"Even after she couldn't see," Eudora corrected.

One of the most complicated of all English words is, of course, the word "see."

"She used to hate the combination of magenta thrift and bright yellow daffodils and azaleas. She used to say, 'Now don't let's drive down that street, they have all that thrift there,' so we'd drive another way.

"But I don't know, I don't think it bothers me so much any more. I used to worry about tangerine azaleas mixed with those fuchsia-colored ones."

"Still," she was interrupted, "you have to admit they clash well."

"Clash well. Yes. I suppose you might say all flowers are meant to bloom together."

"This may sound insulting, but perhaps you are mellowing. The tangerine and fuchsia and thrift and those things no longer drive you mad?"

"Mellowing," she said. "Oh, don't say that."

Eudora Welty is celebrated, among her admirers, for grace but not for accepting outrageous combinations of things.

"Is the world the same or worse or better or what?" she was asked. She has, after all, seen a lot of young people.

"About the same, isn't it? With me, it's just that it took so long to begin to understand it. To understand how complicated things are."

Complex, one is almost tempted to volunteer, rather than compli-cated.

Her art, after all, appears always to have been aimed at grand simplicities, not usually found at the first flirtation with a typewriter, but not all that complicated, either. It takes years, perhaps, to learn what is simple and what is right.

For example, in one of her books she includes a common enough rural scene, in which a family sit on a porch and watch the young men of the family come up from the valley for supper. The sun has commenced to fall, but in the half-light the old folks can still see the youngsters' white shirts. Then, they can't really even see the shirts, but they know they're there and know the young men are coming on up, so they still "see" them. Welty uses a phrase, "their love outlasting the light" or something similar. They still see the young guys climbing the hill, even if technically the light is too far gone for the eyes to register literally.

As Eudora's mother still saw the garden, even after she couldn't see.

It's this kind of thing in her stories, so simple and in such accord with what everybody knows to be true, that has given her a reputation for accuracy, even if it's all made up.

Of course, there has to be something that lights up the kids' climb, when the eyes are none of the best and the very shirts are hid in the darkness, and in Eudora's story—that particular one—the thing that lets the old folks see is simply love.

But to convey it convincingly, and with grace and humor, is something that takes Welty a lot of time and energy.

It's nice, in a way, when she notices people like the stuff that she is at such effort to turn out.

"Triumphant," as President Carter put it, and you didn't hear all that much argument and nit-picking (for a change) over his choice of language.

Eudora Welty

Charles Ruas / 1980

From Charles Ruas, *Conversations with American Writers* (New York: Alfred A. Knopf, 1985), pp. 3–17. Copyright © 1984 by Charles Ruas. Reprinted by permission of Alfred A. Knopf, Inc.

Eudora Welty was recognized early as a master of the short story in the Southern tradition. *The Collected Stories of Eudora Welty,* published in 1980, reveals the whole range of her artistry over four decades of writing.

Our meeting was set for four o'clock in the lobby of the Algonquin Hotel. I recognized her stepping off the elevator, a pale woman of medium height with white wavy hair. She walks carefully, due to a touch of arthritis. Her greeting is gracious— friendly, but reserved. The strong Southern lilt in her voice places her vividly in Jackson, Mississippi, where she has always lived.

We selected an out-of-the-way corner of the dim paneled lounge to settle down undisturbed. Eudora Welty was uneasy about being taped but readily entered into the conversation. Her melodious drawl, reminiscent of the dialogues in her stories, created a sense of spontaneity. There was also in her attention a great perspicacity. She weighs her words, pausing to select a nuance or else to edit herself. When she is absorbed in a moment of thought, her expression is that of someone completely absent, but when she speaks, her eyes become luminously intelligent. In laughter her face is illuminated by the afterimage of the young woman and the child she must have been, so open is her merriment. It reminded me of the way she described herself in *One Time, One Place*: "My complete innocence was the last thing I would have suspected of myself." Her recollections of childhood, her family, and her artistic maturation are the subjects of *One Writer's Beginnings* (1984).

CR: You've just brought out your collected short stories. The last pieces are from the mid-sixties, and you've been writing novels since. What are you working on now? Can we expect another novel?

EW: I'm working on something, I don't know exactly what. Since the last of these stories, I've written two novels, a book of criticism, and a collection of essays. Short stories are my favorite form, though, and most of the novels have become novels accidentally. I'll lead myself into them thinking they'll be short stories, and then I have to go back and work on them as novels.

CR: If the material determines the form, don't you project a final form when you begin writing?

EW: Well, I'm just not smart enough. I think the short story is my natural form. That is, the long short story, about the length of "The Demonstrators." When I realize that it has the scope of something I should explore further and really treat differently, then, of course, I'll recast the whole thing totally. It was a waste, it was a delusion on my part to think it was a story. That has happened nearly every time I've gotten a novel. But I love the short story and I intend to go on writing them. This is not the end. But I was very glad to have the book done.

CR: It must be satisfying to see them all collected in one volume.

EW: It just made me feel very good that my publisher wanted to do it.

CR: So many critics see you as a regional writer, because your stories are set in the South. That doesn't differentiate between your particular vision as a writer and your subject matter.

EW: I think it's probably because there's a long history behind me of Southern writers, and people want to fit me into that frame. Of course, I grew up in that. I don't "classify" myself, naturally. What I'm trying to do is write about life as I see it, and I have to define it. I set a stage within the framework I see around me, which I think I would do wherever I lived, whether it was Norway or Tokyo, because I feel there is a close connection between fiction and the real world. No matter how far you might range in fancy or imagination, I feel that your life line is connected to the real life around you. I couldn't take off without a firm base, so I do use the real world as well as I can. It helps me, defines things for me, and makes me understand my feelings about life in general. Unless any story connects with life, it doesn't have an impact on anybody, does it?

CR: Does this intimate connection also entail a responsibility towards the culture?

EW: I don't think so. In the South a lot of times people say, "Oh, we're so glad you're writing, because you're doing this for the South." And I say, "No, I'm doing it for the story."

CR: That sort of generalization is so self-conscious that I think the speaker doesn't connect with the artist or the culture. Do you find

that the idea of the Southern writer is becoming more abstracted as
the phenomenon becomes less true?

EW: I believe that it becomes less and less true for the simple
reason that the great founders are dying off, I'm sorry to say. I'm
thinking of Katherine Anne Porter, who just died last week [18 Sept.
1980], the poet Allen Tate, Faulkner, and some of the great figures
who are no longer here. Of course, in Mississippi they always say,
"What about you and Faulkner?" It was just a coincidence that we
lived there. I am happy that I came from the same place, but I can't
see any other connection.

CR: Regional distinctions have, sadly, all but disappeared nowadays.

EW: I think the whole country is much less a matter of regions now
than it used to be. The distinctions are much less easy to define. I
happen to think there always will be a Southern character or feeling,
which may not even be definable when a town looks like Illinois or
anywhere else. It's an attitude towards life, a way of looking at things
that may not last long, but I think it will last longer than other places,
except possibly New England. But the sense of family which gives
you the sense of narrative and drama, that's where we draw our
stories.

CR: You draw on the custom of family histories and storytelling.

EW: I think so. Then, also, the fact that you are able to follow a
person's life from beginning to end, almost. You know the people who
went before him, and you know the result of all his actions, and what
happened in the end. You don't just know people in little segments, or
minutes, or only under certain circumstances. You know them under
all circumstances. It can't help but develop your sense of narrative,
the continuity in history of the life there. I think that will persevere
somehow in the Southern attitude, but maybe not in the form that you
were asking about, the old, absolute Southern regional variety. It's
much more connected with the world, and I'm glad of it.

CR: As the old order disappears, I think people turn to their artists
to keep the culture alive. Do you think that's what people look to find
in you and your work?

EW: It intimidates me so, that anyone wants me to speak for a
culture. I'll leave that to those other girls [Carson McCullers and
Flannery O'Connor], and they can't speak now. Some group was

doing a seminar on the three of us, and they sent me a tee shirt on which were drawings of Welty, O'Connor, and McCullers [*laughs*], so I guess that's what they want. I don't know why we are combined, except that we are all females and come from south of the Mason-Dixon Line. I think that all of us as writers knew what we wanted to do. Part of it was the time when we were all alive and working at the same time. But I'm not very good at seeing connections anyway, just at reading people's work. Then I feel in direct touch with the writer.

CR: Since you're often compared to them, let me ask, were you aware of the works of Carson McCullers and Flannery O'Connor at the time? Did you ever meet?

EW: I met Carson McCullers when we were both given fellowships, I guess you'd call it, to Bread Loaf [Writers' Conference]. Carson had already published her first book [*The Heart Is a Lonely Hunter*], and I was just beginning on my stories. We were up there for a week at the same time. We never were intimate, and it never came about that we were later. Flannery O'Connor I only got to meet, I am sorry to say, towards the end of her life, when we both worked at giving college readings, and we corresponded some. I was crazy about her, and I wish I could have known her better. It took me a while to realize the things I didn't know about her work, the spiritual force of them. I wasn't acquainted with the Roman Catholic Church and concepts like grace, I had to find out. Of course I loved her stories on any level. I didn't realize how much more was in the stories until I got it from her, hearing her lecture and talk. Terrifying power, and so true to the idiom, the way she's got those Georgia country people down.

CR: Paul Theroux thinks that a regional writer has to leave his place of origin to acquire the perspective to know his material. I know you studied in New York. What made you decide to return to Jackson, Mississippi?

EW: I knew I wanted to be a writer, but I went to Columbia Business School because my father was very practical and down to earth. He said, "It would be fine to be a writer, but you still have to earn a living." At that time most all that girls could do was either teach school or go into business. I knew I didn't want to teach school, so I spent over a year in New York going to school. I didn't get any kind of business degree. All I did was take courses in business so I could apply for jobs. But that was when the Depression came along, and my father became ill and the next year died, and life was changed. I had thought that I could get a job supporting myself in advertising in New York, and go to the theatre and everything else, and write at the same time—a dream. I'm glad I didn't get caught up in any of that. I did get jobs, but they were back home, they were part-time, and they happened to be jobs that showed me a lot about Mississippi, about which I didn't know much at the time, except for Jackson. I traveled all over the state.

CR: Was that part of your work with the WPA?

EW: I was a junior publicity agent. I wrote about it to explain those photographs in *One Time, One Place*. I went on from there and just sent stories to magazines and did everything by mail. That was very lucky for me. I don't know what I might have turned into if I stayed up here. But I still love New York.

CR: When you say you don't know what you might have turned into, does that mean you've thought about "the road not taken"?

EW: No, I'm sure I would have written stories, but I don't know where I would have laid the stories. Later I wrote one story set in New York, which I don't think was successful since I didn't even know enough about my own home grounds, much less a vast city. You can't tell what you might do. But I know I would have written stories.

CR: Did the Depression affect the way you saw things and wrote about them?

EW: I hadn't really started then except for myself. In fact, the Depression in Mississippi could hardly be told from the normal way of life. It was already so poor. But I was seeing it for the first time. If you've seen those photographs, you'll know what I mean. We've always been so poor in that part since the Civil War. It was burned from one end to the other and there was nothing left to start on, and recovery was very slow. As Walker Percy says, "There was no Marshall Plan for the South after the war."

CR: Your interest is in psychology also, so that a story such as "Why I Live at the P.O." is a comedy of hysteria. The humor comes out of a pathological behavior.

EW: No, I tell you I don't think of them at all as being pathological stories. I know Katherine Anne Porter refers to the girl as a case of dementia praecox in the introduction [of *A Curtain of Green*]. She believed I thought so, but it's far from what I was doing in that story. I was trying to show how, in these tiny little places such as where they come from, the only entertainment people have is dramatizing the family situation, which they do fully knowing what they are doing. They're having a good time. They're not caught up, it's not pathological. There is certainly the undertone, you're right, which is one of wishing things would change. Even though Sister goes and lives in the post office, she'll probably be home by the weekend, and it could happen all over again. They just go through it. I've heard people talk, and they just dramatize everything—"I'll never speak to you again!" It's a Southern kind of exaggeration. There is something underlying it, needless to say. That's what gives it its reason for being.

CR: But the current beneath the humor is despair, isn't it?

EW: I know in those early stories I have a number of characters where something visibly is wrong, they're deaf and dumb. Although I didn't think about it, it was a beginning writer's effort to show how alone some of these people felt. I made it a visible reason which is, of course, inside everybody. I must have chosen that as a direct, perhaps oversimplified way. I was not aware at the time that that was what I was going—for instance, the story about the feeble-minded girl, Lily Daw. Nearly every little town had somebody like that in that part of the world, and the whole town made it their business to take care of her. They wouldn't usually send her away to the Institute for the Feeble-Minded unless they really reached an emergency, which they felt this was. Everybody takes care of everybody to the point where it's not taking care at all. You could see the futility of what they were doing. It was something I observed, just as I observed how people talk in exaggeration. All these things are rooted in a reality which I can use for the story, but I didn't invent it.

CR: "The Wide Net" is a comedy of misunderstanding between newlyweds. The young wife threatens to kill herself, and the husband calls the community together to drag the river for her body. Your description of the forest in autumn is elegiac, knowing that all things must come to an end, and yet inevitably return.

EW: That's exactly how I felt when I was writing. They were going on an excursion. Old Doc says, "The excursion is the same when you go looking for your sorrow as when you go looking for your joy." Young love is a mysterious thing, and anything might have happened.

Things could have been very terrible. William Wallace, who was so inarticulate, could fish and dive down to the bottom of this water. That's part of it, because they wanted the presence of mystery and the possibility to be there. That's about the season of the year, the fall and the changing times.

CR: Young lovers acting out the drama in the fall reminded me of Chekhov, and I wondered if he influenced your concept of the short story.

EW: He certainly was my ideal. I didn't consciously try to base things, although that is an acknowledged method of teaching yourself. I guess I never thought I could base anything on a master like that.

CR: Did your reading determine your direction?

EW: I'm sure it must have done it indirectly, but not directly. I feel that when I'm really working on something, I'm not aware of anything but the story. I'm not thinking of myself, or of another writer. I'm just trying to get the story the way I want it. Those things can certainly help and bear down on me, but it's done at other times. Then they are worked out in the story without my conscious knowledge.

CR: When you began writing, did you identify with the Southern tradition?

EW: I'm self-taught, so I really didn't. I just wrote stories. I was befriended by Robert Penn Warren and Cleanth Brooks, who published me in *The Southern Review;* I met Katherine Anne Porter fairly early; and they were already long-established writers, but we had no group. We're all such individuals, I hardly see how we could. I'm thinking of Walker Percy and Peter Taylor and many more. We all met in the course of things without seeking one another out, just meeting as life opened and enjoying each other.

CR: Katherine Anne Porter was a lifelong friend, and I wondered if she was involved with the direction of your writing.

EW: I don't know that I would have known how to take any kind of direction. What she did for me that was so great was to believe in my work. This was like a bolt of lightning from the sky, that people whose work I loved thought well of mine. It made me feel that I was really in the world, that I had understanding and some readers. That's the greatest thing you can do for somebody.

CR: You have this independence in your work. Does it carry over also to publishers, because they are at such a geographical distance?

EW: I don't think about that end of it when I write. All I want to do is write that story, and I had such a long wait before stories appeared. I began writing six years before a story appeared in *The Atlantic Monthly,* which was my first national magazine, but from the beginning they were welcomed by university and college magazines. I was published, which gave me a sense of reaching somebody. I don't know what would have happened to me if I'd waited to be published to write the next story. One blessing about living at home—although I imagine I would do it anywhere—is that I write just the way I want to, and when I want to, until I get it nearly as I can to what I want. Then its fate is up to the other end. I've always been blessed with wonderful editors and agents. I didn't even realize how extremely lucky I was.

CR: How would you interpret the development of a writer such as Truman Capote? He began by writing stories and novels set in the South. Then his later works change completely and become a synonym for all that is most urbane and sophisticated.

EW: I think he is a man of great talent, but I like his talent in his earlier work. I truly can't subscribe to, and I don't think there is such a thing as "faction." People are free to do whatever they wish, but then I think it stops being fiction. It becomes whatever it is, and I like it so much better when it is purely in the world of imagination. The introduction of real people, especially when it's blended with other motives than the imagination, to me detracts from what can be done. I would not want to do it myself. I would feel like I was amputating something of myself, taking away the main equipment I work with. It's such a waste. Why have you worked all these years to try to develop this tool that you just keep wanting to use better, if you can, and then just deny it? I don't understand it—that's my real answer.

CR: You have such a strong sense of what you want to accomplish in your writing. Having just seen the film version of Flannery O'Connor's *Wise Blood,* I wanted to ask if you were interested in other media?

EW: I think there is a definite connection between short stories and films. The methods of making them are similar, the use of flashbacks, for instance, the seeing of a town, being able to show what people are thinking or dreaming, things you cannot show on stage but which you indicate in a story. You have that much freedom and even more in a film, it's much more fluid. You can use shading and speed the way a short-story writer does. But it's in the abstract I'm speaking.

CR: What was your reaction to seeing your work adapted for the stage?

EW: I was interested because the forms were so different. One form needs to take off from the other and have a life of its own. Once I was prepared for that, I enjoyed it. I can see lots of other ways *The Ponder Heart* could have been treated. In fact, a film is the way I would best imagine it.

CR: You said that the Depression was scarcely different from normal circumstances in Mississippi when you began writing. Was it the Second World War and Hiroshima that was the major shock to you as an artist?

EW: Oh, yes. I was at the age where my brothers were in the war, and all the men and boys I knew. Everybody was personally caught up in it—before the atomic bomb was dropped—just the war itself. I went to the wedding of some friends. We didn't know it, but on the day of the wedding was Pearl Harbor; we just turned from the celebration to the whole world engulfed in war overnight.

It's hard for young people today to conceive of how the country felt about the war. It was not like the Vietnam War in any respect. Everybody honestly believed we were trying to save the world from Nazism. We believed in our country; well, I still believe in my country. It was a very pure kind of wish to accomplish this victory, and we were in it heart and soul. Members of our family were over there fighting. My brother was in Okinawa, and my friends were in the landings in Normandy and Italy. That was a terrible time to live through. I couldn't write about it, not at the time—it was too personal. I *could* write or translate things into domestic or other dimensions in my writing, with the same things in mind.

CR: In contrast to the Second World War, the civil-rights movement and the war in Vietnam brought dissent right to your doorstep.

EW: Of course, that war's another world. At home we have a good small amateur theatre, and one of the things we've done is programs on different songwriters, such as Cole Porter and so on. We did one on George M. Cohan, who wrote "Over There." I would go and watch the rehearsals. It was so hard for the young people to realize that all these songs were really ardent and meant. It was a strange thing to realize that belief had evaporated in the young.

CR: In the time span of your volume of collected short stories you've seen the South become part of the mainstream. There has even been a president from the South.

EW: Mississippi is very conservative, and I'm surprised that they gave their vote to Carter in the first place. Reagan carried the state because he came down there and he talked about "We'll be having states' rights" and a whole lot of things like that. You know, that was very wicked of him. A lot of old conservative die-hard elements think that indeed he is going to turn back the clock, whereas Mississippi as a whole, I think, has really done very well in its adaptation. We have a far better [civil-rights] record than up north. Once we did it, we did it. [Race] relationships, as far as I know, and I know something about living in Jackson, are on the whole sound and fluent. We have things come up that are bad, but nothing on the scale that happens in the big cities. We now have a progressive upcoming governor, and his whole idea is to connect Mississippi with the rest of the world. We're part of the Union or we can't live.

CR: Your stories "Where Is the Voice Coming From?" and "The Demonstrators" are about desegregation and the civil-rights struggle. You've written about suddenly understanding the assassin of Medgar Evers.

EW: Well, I knew the situation because I lived there, but it had never occurred to me that I could write something about it from within an assassin's mind. At that point any writer putting himself or herself into another person was sticking his neck out, but I had been so put out by stories I had read written in a synthetic way about Southerners and their attitudes. They were so "simplistic," as people say now, with no distinctions made between one kind of person and another. They lacked understanding. I knew many people who came down and helped work for civil rights, and I was a friend of theirs, and I knew they were good people. But journalists and other people would telephone me in those times, because I was a writer—they didn't know me. "Why aren't you going out there and writing about those devils you live with down there?" Nobody made any distinctions of character. I thought, I know how bad this man is, and I'm just going to try to imagine what it would be like to be in his skin, because I ought to know. They don't know. It was a story writer's challenge.

CR: You've captured his voice, and I was wondering how you would read it as compared with your well-known readings of Sister and your other characters. You've experienced all these transformations around you.

EW: It's been interesting to watch all of this. I have had an opportunity to know some of the people bringing these things about, because I've lived there all my life. For instance, no one thought our new governor [William Winter] could ever be elected, except he was defeated before by a scoundrel, so when he ran again, for the third time, I think everybody thought, Well, look what we got when we didn't vote for him. When he had his inaugural, he invited leaders in different fields from all over the country, who were either born in the state, or had lived there, to come present a symposium on what Mississippi should do to connect herself with the rest of the world. I was part of the team, so was Margaret Walker, a black writer who lives in Jackson, and Leontyne Price came down and sang for the inauguration. It was all so joyous. Everybody just thought, the top rail is on top instead of on the bottom, where it had been for so long.

A Visit with Eudora Welty

Anne Tyler / 1980

From *The New York Times Book Review*, 2 November 1980, 33–34. Copyright © 1980 by the New York Times Company. Reprinted by permission.

She lives in one of those towns that seem to have outgrown themselves overnight, sprouting—on reclaimed swampland—a profusion of modern hospitals and real estate offices, travel agencies and a Drive-Thru Beer Barn. (She can remember, she says, when Jackson, Miss., was so small that you could go on foot anywhere you wanted. On summer evenings you'd pass the neighbor's lawns scented with petunias, hear their pianos through the open windows. Everybody's life was more accessible.) And when her father, a country boy from Ohio, built his family a house back in 1925, he chose a spot near Belhaven College so he'd be sure to keep a bit of green around them, but that college has added so many parking lots, and there are so many cars whizzing by nowadays.

Still, Eudora Welty's street is shaded by tall trees. Her driveway is a sheet of pine needles, and her house is dark and cool, with high ceilings, polished floors, comfortable furniture and a wonderfully stark old kitchen. She has lived here since she was in high school (and lived in Jackson all her life). Now she is alone, the last of a family of five. She loves the house, she says, but worries that she isn't able to keep it up properly: A porch she screened with $44 from the *Southern Review,* during the Depression, needs screening once again for a price so high that she has simply closed it off. One corner of the foundation has had to be rescued from sinking into the clay, which she describes as "shifting about like an elephant's hide."

But the house seems solid and well tended, and it's clear that she has the vitality to fill its spare rooms. Every flat surface is covered with tidy stacks of books and papers. A collection of widely varied paintings—each with its own special reason for being there—hangs on wires from the picture rails. One of them is a portrait of Eudora Welty as a young woman—blond-haired, with large and luminous eyes.

Her hair is white now, and she walks with some care and wears an Ace bandage around her wrist to ease a touch of arthritis. But the eyes are still as luminous as ever, radiating kindness and . . . attention, you would have to call it; but attention of a special quality, with some gentle amusement accompanying it. When she laughs, you can see how she must have looked as a girl—shy and delighted. She will often pause in the middle of a sentence to say, "Oh, I'm just enjoying this so much!" and she does seem to be that rare kind of person who takes an active joy in small, present moments. In particular, she is pleased by *words,* by ways of saying things, snatches of dialogue overheard, objects' names discovered and properly applied. (She likes to read technical manuals and diagrams with the parts labeled. Her whole face lights up when she describes how she heard a country woman confess to a "gnawing and a craving" for something. "Wasn't that a wonderful way of putting it?" she asks. "A gnawing and a craving.")

Even in conversation, the proper word matters deeply to her and is worth a brief pause while she hunts for it. She searches for a way to describe a recent heat wave: The heat, she says, was like something waiting for you, something out to get you; when you climbed the stairs at night, even the stair railing felt like, oh, like warm toast. She shares my fear of merging into freeway traffic because, she says, it's like entering a round of hot-pepper in a jump-rope game: " 'Oh, well,' you think, 'maybe the next time it comes by. . . .' " (I always did know freeways reminded me of something; I just couldn't decide what it was.) And when she re-read her collected stories, some of which date back to the 1930's: "It was the strangest experience. It was like watching a negative develop, slowly coming clear before your eyes. It was like recovering a memory."

A couple of her stories, she says, she really had wished to drop from the collection, but was persuaded not to. Others, the very earliest, were written in the days before she learned to rewrite ("I didn't know you *could* rewrite"), and although she left them as they were, she has privately revised her own printed copies by hand. Still others continue to satisfy her—especially those in *The Golden Apples*—and she laughs at herself for saying how much she loves "June Recital" and "The Wanderers." But her pleasure in these stories is, I think, part and parcel of her whole attitude toward writing:

She sees it as truly joyful work, as something she can hardly wait to get down to in the mornings.

Unlike most writers she imposes no schedule on herself. Instead she waits for things to "brood"—usually situations from her own life which, in time, are alchemized into something entirely different, with different characters and plots. From then on, it goes very quickly. She wakes early, has coffee and sets to work. She writes as long as she can keep at it, maybe pausing for a brief tomato sandwich at noon. (And she can tell you exactly who used to make the best tomato sandwiches in Jackson, back during her grade-school days when everybody swapped lunches. It was Frances MacWillie's grandmother, Mrs. Nannie MacWillie.)

What's written she types soon afterward; she feels that her handwriting is too intimate to re-read objectively. Then she scribbles revisions all over the manuscript, and cuts up parts of pages and pins them into different locations with dressmakers' pins—sometimes moving whole scenes, sometimes a single word. Her favorite working time is summer, when everything is quiet and it's "too hot to go forth" and she can sit next to an open window. (The danger is that any passing friend can interrupt her: "I saw you just sitting at your typewriter. . . .")

Describing the process of writing, she is matter-of-fact. It's simply her life's work, which has occupied her for more than 40 years. She speaks with calm faith of her own instincts, and is pleased to have been blessed with a visual mind—"the best shorthand a writer can have." When she's asked who first set her on her path (this woman who has, whether she knows it or not, set so many later writers on *their* paths), she says that she doesn't believe *she* ever did get anything from other writers. "It's the experience of living," she says—leaving unanswered, as I suppose she must, the question of just how she, and not some next-door neighbor, mined the stuff of books from the ordinary experiences of growing up in Jackson, Miss., daughter of an insurance man and a schoolteacher; of begging her brothers to teach her golf; bicycling to the library in two petticoats so the librarian wouldn't say, "I can see straight through you," and send her home; and spending her honor roll prize—a free pass—to watch her favorite third baseman play ball.

And where (she wonders aloud) did she get the idea she was bound to succeed as a writer, sending off stories on her own as she did and promptly receiving them back? How long would she have gone on doing that?

Fortunately, she didn't have to find out. Diarmuid Russell—then just starting as a literary agent—offered to represent her. He was downright *fierce* about representing her, at one time remarking that if a certain story were rejected, the editor "ought to be horse-whipped." (It wasn't rejected.) And there were others who took a special interest in her—notably the editor John Woodburn, and Katherine Anne Porter. (Katherine Anne Porter invited her to visit. Eudora Welty was so overwhelmed that she only got there after a false start, turning back at Natchez when her courage failed.) A photo she keeps from around this period shows a party honoring the publication of her first book: a tableful of admiring editors, a heartbreakingly young Diarmuid Russell; and in their midst Eudora Welty, all dressed up and wearing a corsage and looking like a bashful, charming schoolgirl. She does not admit to belonging to a literary community, but what she means is that she was never part of a formal circle of writers. You sense, in fact, that she would be uncomfortable in a self-consciously literary environment. (Once she went to the writers' colony at Yaddo but didn't get a thing done, and spent her time attending the races and "running around with a bunch of Spaniards." She'd suspected all along, she says, that a place like that wouldn't work out for her.)

Certainly, though, she has had an abundance of literary friendships, which she has preserved and cherished over the years. She speaks warmly of Robert Penn Warren; and she likes to recall how Reynolds Price, while still a Duke student, met her train in a pure white suit at 3 A.M. when she came to lead a workshop. But some other friends are gone now. Elizabeth Bowen was especially dear to her. Katherine Anne Porter's long illness and death have left her deeply saddened. And Diarmuid Russell, she says, is someone she still thinks of every day of her life.

In a profession where one's resources seem likely to shrink with time (or so most writers fear), Eudora Welty is supremely indifferent to her age. She says, when asked, that it does bother her a little that there's a certain depletion of physical energy—that she can't make unlimited appearances at colleges nowadays, much as she enjoys doing that, and still have anything left for writing. (Colleges keep inviting her because, she claims, "I'm so well behaved, I'm always on time and I don't get drunk or hole up in a motel with my lover.") But it's plain that her *internal* energy is as powerful as ever. She credits the examples she's seen around her: Elizabeth Bowen, who continued full of curiosity and enthusiasm well into her 70's; and V. S. Pritchett, now 80, whose work she particularly admires. In fact, she says, the trouble with publishing her collected stories is the implication that there won't be any more—and there certainly will be, she says. She takes it as a challenge.

She does not, as it turns out, go to those ladies' luncheons with the tinted cream cheese flowers that she describes so well in her stories. (I'd always wondered.) Her life in Jackson revolves around a few long-time friends, with a quiet social evening now and then— somebody's birthday party, say. Her phone rings frequently just around noon, when it's assumed that she's finished her morning's work. And one friend, an excellent cook, might drop off a dish she's prepared.

Nor is she entirely bound to Jackson. She loves to travel, and she positively glows when describing her trips. "Oh, I would hate to be confined," she says. Her only regret is that now you have to take the plane. She remembers what it was like to approach the coast of Spain by ship—to see a narrow pink band on the horizon and then hear the tinkling of bells across the water.

When she talks like this, it's difficult to remember that I'm supposed to be taking notes.

Is there anything she especially wants known about herself— anything she'd like a chance to say? Yes, she says, and she doesn't even have to think about it: She wants to express her thankfulness for all those people who helped and encouraged her so long ago. "Reading my stories over," she says, "brings back their presence. I feel that I've been very lucky."

Eudora Welty: One Writer
at Home
Thomas Fox / 1984

From the *Commercial Appeal* [Memphis, TN], 29 April 1984,
Sec. H, 3. Reprinted by permission.

Near the end of a spring day in Jackson, Miss., with the sun reduced
to a russet brushstroke, the mosquitoes were making their first runs
from the azalea banks to plant a hit on an exposed arm or to tickle an
ear. A magnolia from central casting dominated the grassy stretch
before a white-columned extravagance of brick and wood. There was
scattered talk of the sudden heat, and of literature. Southern literature. The literature of Eudora Welty.

Inside, the "small gathering" filled three large rooms, with waiters
rotating in from the kitchen offering trays of white wine and champagne and a selection of cheesy tidbits in the shape of the home state.

A knot of friends, fans and literary groupies gathered around Miss
Welty, the guest of honor, who sat wearing the biggest orchid someone
could find, holding a glass of champagne and carrying on with admira-
ble stamina. "Gracious" is a word everyone uses to describe her and
it is difficult to imagine her in any other pose. Another word is "shy."
She is known as a writer who guards her privacy and close friends
proudly let on that they hold her unlisted phone number.

The day before and most of that one, she had spent at nearby
Millsaps College, where a literary festival had been called to examine
the values of Southern fiction and to honor Eudora Welty on her
75th birthday.

With full dark, the affair would migrate from mansion to campus
for a "British view of Southern Fiction," and then to a reception in
the Academic Complex, where there would be another crowd, a cake
and an admirer who would offer Miss Welty the gift of a peacock
feather.

This hometown treatment for one of our best writers was being
echoed by the publishers. Her latest book *One Writer's Beginnings*, a

74

rich, slender goldmine of autobiography, was enjoying best-seller status. The University Press of Mississippi had just released *Conversations with Eudora Welty,* a collection of interviews.

One Writer's Beginnings grew from a series of lectures she gave last year at Harvard, and is essentially a book of discoveries, a guide to looking at life as a setting for literature. Through it runs the "continuous thread of revelation," the process of linking time and imagination and memory. For one of the rare elements of the author's craft, consider the simple act of homecoming as the family returns from a summer visit with relatives:

"Back on Congress Street, when my father unlocked the door of our closed-up house, I rushed ahead into the airless hall and stormed up the stairs, pounding the carpet of each step with both hands ahead of me, and putting my face right down into the cloud of the dear dust of our long absence. I was welcoming ourselves back. Doing likewise, more methodically, my father was going from room to room re-starting all the clocks."

The remembrances paint a long-ago era, when the after-dinner entertainment might include taking a telescope into the yard for a check on the progress of the planets and stars, when no lady would travel without a hat, when children learned big words by reading the subtitles at silent movies. She learned "somnambulist" from watching the early horror film *The Cabinet of Dr. Caligari.*

In the Welty home the living room was called the "library." A big event in the year they moved into the house where she lives now was the arrival of the latest edition of the Britannica. Her mother "read Dickens in the spirit in which she would have eloped with him." And books were Miss Welty's passion before she came to master their words:

"It had been startling and disappointing to me to find out that story books had been written by *people,* that books were not natural wonders, coming up of themselves like grass. Yet regardless of where they came from, I cannot remember a time when I was not in love with them—with the books themselves, cover and binding and the paper they were printed on, with their smell and their weight and with their possession in my arms, captured and carried off to myself. Still illiterate, I was ready for them, committed to all the reading I could give them."

Her two-story Tudorish home on Pinehurst, the one her father built in the 1920s across from the campus of Belhaven College, is a shaded, sturdy place of sensible colors and comfortable furniture. In front are pines and a hovering oak; on bright mornings the sound of school-age laughter drifts through the windows.

Despite having been out past midnight, Miss Welty is up and ready to be interviewed and then chauffeured to Millsaps for another round of readings and panel discussions. She moves with deliberation through the arranged clutter of birthday mail. There are flowers on almost every surface, the latest addition being a splash of lilies of the valley from a friend in Oxford. "Everything is so disorganized," she says, settling into a seat by a window.

The subject of age comes up, as it has so often during the past days: "I never think of age, neither mine nor anybody else's," she says. "I have always had friends of all ages. Now that it has been brought upon me, I think 'girl, you had better start thinking, adding up.' I just don't think about it because I am thinking about other things."

She still drives and still doesn't care for the rush of interstates, which she once compared to the jump rope game of hot pepper. "It's like trying to enter an egg beater."

Her memory is remarkable, and her conversation is precise and alive with the wonder of discovery. This awareness is "part of my imagination, which is my equipment for work and I guess I have kept it in pretty good exercise throughout my life . . . You stay aware and observant just by nature.

"All I claim are good eyes and I used to have good ears, but I don't hear overheard remarks as well as I used to. It's a great loss . . . I think part of it is nervousness. There is this nervous feeling that I am not going to be able to understand some profound remark made in the distance."

She says she keeps no writing schedule, but "when I am working on something I like to work as long as I can without a stop. I had been writing stories—that's what I think is my real work—but I stopped to write the lectures that went into this book, which has taken about a year. So I want to go back to what I was doing before that. I am glad I did this—I didn't mean to sound resentful—but your mind doesn't work the same."

Still on the subject of her writing, she says all of her novels have started as short stories. "But of course once I realize it is a novel I've had to scrap the story because that's not the way to approach a novel—the story has sort of expanded in my mind beyond its natural limits . . . then I have gone back and written it as a novel. But I don't think of myself as a novelist. When I begin to work I think I am writing a short story. Anyway, they are all fiction; that's the way my imagination works.

"I feel the whole thing is in the germ of a story, its beginning and development and its destination. That usually remains even in a novel, but I allow myself to expand it and have time to develop different aspects. And it grows so it is no longer a story. But I do know I couldn't begin it unless I knew the content of it—a whole in my mind.

"I don't usually start unless I think it is a pretty viable idea. I can usually tell when something has a life of its own, a strength to it. That's what makes me start it. I don't think I would sit down to something very frail; in the first place it doesn't have its own direction and destination. I have made mistakes in my work. I have found there are some things I can't handle, and I put them aside and try them another way later. But the idea itself, I wouldn't start. I think I would know right at the start if it wasn't worth it."

She is a writer who seems totally at ease with the demands of her profession and says she has never experienced writer's block. "I haven't reached a block, but I have reached what has the same effect. I can think of too many ways to do it, and the only way to handle that within a novel is to try the different scenes. To make the same point, you can try it under different circumstances." At that point, invention can offer too many possibilities. "That is why I am not a natural novelist."

She has lived briefly in other cities and has been traveling since those summer trips with her family, but Jackson has remained her home, the center of her territory, the place of friends and memories.

"Since I really like to write about human beings, I don't think it matters where you set your story. The important thing is to be so familiar with it that you don't have to stop and say, 'what would be blooming there in July?' I know. It sets my stage and then I can push off from that base. I think story writing is a dramatic concept; it really is like a stage, where you have a scene and a setting and you know the kinds of people who would be there and just what kind of speech they would have. All of that is something you can rely on to start with and don't have to worry."

"This," she says for the second time that morning, "is just my way of thinking."

With a copy of her latest book before her, and with gifts and cards in neat stacks among the bursts of flowers, she lowers her pale blue eyes and considers for a moment the event her birthday has become.

"This has been a strange experience. Of course it is unique in my life, both being 75 and having so much attention paid to me. It is going to take me some time to sort of come to terms with all that has happened to me this week. I have never felt as honored, in every way. You can see what a good hometown I have. It is humbling and moving. I can sort of hear my mother saying, 'I think you have had just a little bit too much attention.'"

A Visit with Eudora Welty

Barbara Lazear Ascher / 1984

From the *Yale Review*, 74 (November 1984), 147–53. Reprinted
by permission of Barbara Lazear Ascher.

She's worn a pretty hat for the occasion, an occasion she says she has
dreaded ever since she decided to make an exception to her rule, no
interviews. Her smile is shy, her voice soft and hesitant: "You look
like a Virginia girl." She reaches for my bag, but I protest—after all,
she is seventy-five. Her hair is white. She is slight and walks with
slow care in a shiny new pair of loafers. Her azure knit dress is the
color of her eyes. The next day, when we have settled into pants and
comfortable shoes, she tells me, "I would have worn pants to the
airport, but I thought, 'She'll think I'm some sort of hick!' "

She eases herself behind the wheel of her car. She's tired. "I've
been on the go ever since the first of the year. And this weekend I
signed 400 of those Harvard books for a limited edition. Are you going
to use a tape recorder? I always think I sound as if I don't know what
I'm talking about on tape. You'll have to excuse me if I don't hear
you. I don't hear as well as I used to."

The book to which she refers is her autobiographical *One Writer's
Beginnings*. It was developed from the Norton lectures she gave at
Harvard and was, she says, "the hardest thing I've ever had to do.
First there were the lectures. I don't know why they wanted me. I'm
no scholar and I hate to lecture. I much prefer conversation—a back-
and-forth exchange. I've always had to reach to supplement my
income, but I think if I had to do it again, I'd do something completely
different. Not different from writing. Different from teaching. I think
I'd do something mechanical, something with my hands."

"Such as plumbing?"

"Such as painting chairs. You paint a chair in the morning, and
there it is in the afternoon."

In talking more of the book, she says, "It was amazing to discover
that nothing is ever lost. Thomas Mann was right, the memory is a
well. In writing this book each memory uncovered another. It was

probably important for me to remember these things, but it was very
hard. I kept thinking, 'If only I'd known then what I know now.' Or,
'If only I'd said . . .' And I'm so sorry I never had the chance to tell
my father how I felt about him. We were a very reserved family.
But passionate.''

Given the reserve, it is no surprise that in *One Writer's Beginnings*
part of her self remains in shadow. She tells, for example, of her
father's death and the blood transfusion that was a desperate attempt
to avert it, but what is left unwritten is how she felt. ''I originally had
it in the book,'' she says, ''but I took it out. I thought it would be too
self-indulgent. What I remember is that there were venetian blinds in
back of me, that the heat of the sun was coming through the slats and
onto my back. I suppose that was my creeping horror. That's what a
person remembers—the physical sensation. I'd never seen anyone die
before. Have you?''

She often asks such questions. ''Don't you?'' ''Can you imagine?''
''Don't you find that to be true?'' It is her attempt to bring you into
the circle, to include you. It goes beyond Southern hospitality and
seems to be a complete turning over of the self to another's sensibilities. ''Are you warm enough?'' ''Are you hungry yet?'' ''Land! You
shouldn't have spent so much money on that book. I would have given
you a copy.'' ''I worry about you.''

It is not possible to capture on paper the rich melody of her accent,
but there are certain words that, once you have heard her pronounce
them, seem unmistakably hers. ''Buzzard'' and ''sinister'' are two of
them. As we drove along the Natchez Trace, the setting of many of
her tales, two birds were spotted weighing down branches atop a dead
tree. ''Buzzids,'' she shuddered, ''I hate buzzids. I always knew,
when I was coming home on a train, when we had entered Mississippi
because you would see buzzids out the window.'' She notes the
cypress swamp beneath their perch: ''Isn't it sinista?''

Because the Natchez Trace is what we think of as Eudora Welty
country, it is jarring for me to leave it behind and drive into Jackson,
a city of 300,000. Jackson's population is up 297,000 since Eudora
Welty's parents settled there as a young married couple—her father
from an Ohio farm and her mother from the mountains of West
Virginia. The grand homes that once graced State Street have given
way to Cooke's Prosthetics and Cash-in-a-Flash Pawn Shop. The

architecture is that of any town in commercial, suburban America. "I
used to play in all these yards," she says, pointing to parking lots.
"And that is where the insane asylum used to be. Imagine—it said
'Insane Asylum' on the gates. That's what they were talking about in
The Sound and the Fury when they said they were going to send
Benjy to Jackson. In those days Jackson meant the loony bin."

Her own street, back from State, is quiet and slightly elevated. Her
father chose the site in part to ease her mother's homesickness, but
"my mother never could see the hill." Her childhood home, a 1920s
Tudor designed by her father, is solid and graceful. "I feel awfully
selfish living here alone, and I can't afford to keep it up the way I
should, but I can't imagine moving. And it's home." The lawn is full
of pine needles and is dominated by a huge oak tree. "The builder
told my parents to chop down that tree, but they said, 'Never chop
down an oak tree.' They were country people. I guess that was
something country people say. Well, they were right. That's the only
one left—all the pine have died."

We enter through a vestibule. "My father was a Yankee. He thought
all houses should have vestibules." There is a living room to the left
and a library to the right. Between is a solid mahogany staircase.
Books are everywhere—they've overrun bookshelves and have moved
to tables and desks. There are books by friends—Walker Percy,
Reynolds Price, Elizabeth Bowen, Katherine Anne Porter, Elizabeth
Spencer, William Jay Smith, and Robert Penn Warren. There are the
diaries of Virginia Woolf and a new biography of Ford Madox Ford
("Can you imagine that he held a chair for Turgenev?" she asks).
There are Seamus Heaney, Barbara Pym, Chekhov, and all of Henry
Green, one of her favorites. On the mantel is a Snowden photograph
of V. S. Pritchett, looking spry and amused—she's cut it from a
magazine and mounted it. A similar photo is on her desk—"for
inspiration." The desk is in the bedroom, where she has always
worked. "When there were five of us here it was the only place I
could work," she says, referring to the days when her parents and
brothers also occupied this house.

She is generous in her praise and encouragement of other writers.
"Anne Tyler was a whiz from the time she was seventeen!" she
exclaims. She laughs as she recalls that "Reynolds Price had Anne
for one of his first students. He thought, 'Teaching is going to be

great!' He thought *all* his students were going to be like Anne.'' She thinks the title of Tyler's latest novel, *Dinner at the Homesick Restaurant,* is ''inspired,'' and that the last sentence is a tour de force. ''If I had written that sentence, I'd be happy all my life!''

When asked about another prize-winning writer whose works she has reviewed, she says, ''I wanted so much to like her book, but I found some of it impossibly precious. I did not put my misgivings in the review because it was the first book by a young writer and I couldn't hurt somebody like that. She was a bit self-indulgent, which is perfectly natural for someone of that much talent. I tried to point out the parts that I thought were marvelous.''

Although she enjoys talking of writers and books, she warms most to speaking of the act of writing itself. ''I love the function of writing—what it is *doing.*'' (She offers to pour us some Jack Daniels—''what Katherine Anne Porter called 'swish likka.' Just a jigger. This is powerful stuff. Whenever Red Warren is coming he calls and says, 'Eudora, get out the Black Jack, I'm comin' to town.' '') ''Elizabeth Bowen, in her marvelous notes on writing a novel in *Collected Impressions,* pointed out that dialogue is really a form of action. Because it advances the plot, it is not just chatter. She was so succinct in what she said. I think television may have ruined that for us. If you watch serials and talk shows, you would probably think that one-liners were the answer to conversation. That is what has hurt Broadway so; dialogue has been sacrificed for the one-liner. That's putting it too extremely, but the building of a conversation is designed to gradually reveal something.

''Elizabeth was a marvelous writer about writing and very helpful to me. So was E. M. Forster's *Aspects of the Novel.* I don't think that can ever be outdated. It's important to read these books, but you can't teach a person how to write. That has to come directly from inside the writer.

''What I try to show in fiction are the truths of human relationships. But you have to make up the lies of fiction to reveal these truths— people interacting, things beginning one way and changing to reveal something else. You *show* a truth. You don't tell it. It has to be done of itself.''

She feels the same way about moralizing in fiction. ''A writer has to have a strong moral sense. You couldn't write if you yourself didn't have it and know what you were doing. But that's very different from wanting to moralize in your story. Your own moral sense tells you what's true and false and how people would behave. And you know what is just and unjust, but you don't point them out, in my view. I don't think it works in fiction because fiction is dramatic. It's not a platform.

"That worried me in the sixties because I was asked so many times by strangers why I didn't come out for civil rights, something I'd worked for for years. They would call me in the middle of the night, mostly from New Jersey and New York City. They would say, 'Eudora Welty, what are you doing down there sitting on your *ass*?' I just told them that I knew what I could write and what I couldn't. That I was doing the best I could in my own field. I would be so shaken up that I couldn't sleep the rest of the night."

Glasses emptied, we depart for dinner at Bill's Burger House: burgers by day, native redfish by night. She is welcomed more like a football captain of a local, undefeated team than a literary eminence. Bill grabs her hand and tells me with Greek-accented gusto, "Everybody love this charming lady." And for the final flourish, "God Bless America!"

A pretty young woman approaches our table. "Miss Welty, you honored us by gracing our wedding tea. I just wanted to say hello." After she leaves I'm told whom she married. The parents and grandparents are identified, as are the members of the family who are Yankees. I begin to understand what she meant when she told me that she agreed with Walker Percy's response, "Because we lost," when reporters asked him why the South had so many fine writers. "Since we never really industrialized—reconstruction saw to that—the pace is slower," she explains. "People don't move around as much. You know who a person's mother is. We're more introspective, interested in the psychology of people."

The next morning when we meet she shares the mail with me, mail that keeps her awake at night because "I feel so guilty that I never have time to answer it." This morning's includes a letter from a sixteen-year-old, Christine from Georgia who writes, "I really loved 'Why I Live at the P.O.' because it is so true to life. My brother and sister are always trying to get me in trouble." Then she asks whether the narrator of the story "will come back home, and do you think her parents will take her in if she does?

"Of course." The answer is as natural as though we were speaking of a flesh-and-blood neighbor. "These people *live* by dramatizing themselves. She'll come home, they'll take her in, and it will start all over again."

There are letters asking for explanations. "I think that bears a lot on the fact that young people—students and children—are not taught and don't understand the difference between fiction and nonfiction. I recently heard about a student who, having found my name in a directory, said to his teacher, 'It says here that Miss Welty lives on Pinehurst. I thought she lived at the post office.' Well, after all," she says, pretending this is perfectly understandable, " 'Why I Live at the P.O.' *was* written in the first person.

"[Students] are not taught. They don't *experience* what a story does. They just try to *figure it out*. I think that television has something to do with that. People don't believe events. I remember when man landed on the moon, I called my cleaning woman in to watch it on television. 'You should see this,' I told her. And she said, 'Now Miss Eudora, you know that ain't true.' "

She tells of a phone call received shortly after publication of *The Ponder Heart*. "The phone rang and a voice said, 'Miss Welty?' 'Yes?' 'This is Officer Ponder.' He was a policeman. 'I'm standing on the corner of State and Manship. I understand you've written a history of my family.' I explained to him, 'Mr. Ponder, that was a story. I love my characters. But they are not real.' Ponder. Isn't that a wonderful name? So he said, 'Oh. Well. If you ever need me I'm here at the corner of State and Manship.' "

That her characters have names similar to or the same as her neighbors' is no accident. "It must always be a name that people really name their children." Even when that name is chosen for mythological significance. "Of course I knew what that meant when I named Phoenix Jackson, but it was also a name that was common among old black women. White owners often gave their slaves mythological names, so we have lots of Homers and Ulysses and Parthenias. Also, poor people in the South tend to give their children beautiful names. They think, 'Well, at least I can give her a pretty name.' And they do."

Asked about Old Man Fate Rainey in *The Golden Apples,* she says, "The South is full of Fates. It turns out to be short for Lafayette who was a real hero down here." And Miss Ice Cream Rainey? "I learned that in Wales they give people names like Tree-Chopper Jones to distinguish him from the other Jones. My dancing-school teacher was called Miss Ice Cream McNair because her husband owned the ice cream parlor. Of course we never called her that to her face."

In a sense these names are found poetry. From obituaries, the telephone book, memory, bus rides, and conversation come Old Mrs. Sad-Talking Morgan, Miss Billy Texas Spights, Mr. Fatty Bowles, Stella-Rondo, Homer Champion, Miss Snowdie MacLain. All characters existing in the nimbus of Welty's love.

"I loved all my schoolteachers. And I loved everybody in *The Golden Apples*. The good ones and the bad, the happy ones and the sad ones. I loved them all." I bring up Phoenix Jackson again, the old black lady in "A Worn Path" who makes death-defying trips to town for her grandson's medicine. "I worried about her so much," I said. "I still do," she murmurs.

Of course there is the famous exception—the character she created out of anger rather than love the night that Medgar Evers was shot. The similarity was so striking between the arrested suspect and the imagined murderer, the narrator of "Where Is the Voice Coming From?" that changes had to be made before the story appeared in *The New Yorker*. "There was concern that it would be like convicting him before the trial. Of course I didn't know him. I just knew the type of person who might do that and I got inside his head." The title was chosen because she "really did not know where the voice was coming from that was telling the story.

"It's so queer. Your material guides you and enlightens you along the way. That's how you find out what you're after. It *is* a mystery. When I'm not writing, I can't imagine writing. And when I'm writing, it doesn't occur to me to wonder. Sometimes I feel like a completely split personality. I think the really true self is probably the one that is writing. But the other self is trying to protect me. Sometimes I think, 'While I'm out at the Jitney will be a good time for me to retype this.' That is, that my daily life will leave me alone to do my work." She pauses to consider this, then laughs shyly, "They're really going to think I've lost my marbles if you print that."

She speaks of other aspects of the work. "Your ears should be like magnets. I used to be able to hear people in back and in front of me and on the street. I don't hear as much as I used to. It's so *maddening* not to overhear remarks. I hate that. When you're working on a story it's always with you. You hear somebody say something and you know that is what one character is going to say to another." Her friends delight in bringing her snatches of dialogue. Reynolds Price recently came bearing what she considers a treasure. "Reynolds was coming here from the airport in a taxi. He said that the driver told him that the reason the reservoir keeps flooding is because 'That dam is done eat out by crawfish.' Isn't that marvelous! 'Done eat out by crawfish.' " Eager to contribute, I tell her something I overheard earlier in the day. "Maybe you could use it," I jest. "Or it could use me," is her serious response.

"The fictional eye sees in, through, and around what is really there," she writes in her new book. As she and I stood staring into the silent gloom on the cypress swamp in the Natchez Trace, I asked her, "How would you describe that color?" I was referring to the water's strange shade of beige beneath the darker brown of tree shadows. "Oh, sort of blue. Like an ink wash." Blue? Ink wash? What was she talking about? And suddenly there it was. She had seen the color of the air.

My Visit with Eudora Welty
Gayle Graham Yates / 1985

From Gayle Graham Yates, *Mississippi Mind: A Personal Cultural History of an American State* (Knoxville: Univ. of Tennessee Press, 1990), pp. 141–59. The interview was conducted on 26 February 1985 in Jackson, Mississippi. Reprinted by permission of the University of Tennessee Press.

Eudora Welty's picture and name are everywhere in Jackson. The city public library in the old Sears building is named the Eudora Welty Library. The portrait of Eudora Welty painted by prominent Jackson artist Karl Wolfe can be seen at night from the street, spotlighted on the second floor of the Millsaps College library near North State Street. At the state Department of Archives and History, a photograph of her in dark-rimmed glasses, pen in hand, bent over her writing desk, is placed over the reception desk in the entry. The display case in the state Department of Archives and History, during the year it had a Welty scholar-in-residence, showed pictures of her and photocopies of precious letters to and from her. A 1936 letter from John Rood at *Manuscript* accepts "Death of a Traveling Salesman" and asks to see more, telling her "various publishers will be interested." One letter from Robert Penn Warren, at the *Southern Review,* dated 13 January 1937, speaks of "Flowers for Marjorie" and "The Petrified Man" and says of his editors' response to her stories that they "have been on the verge of publishing two of them." Displayed there, too, was a much-revised page of the *Losing Battles* manuscript stuck together with safety pins.

Eudora Welty is much admired and loved in her home city and in the world. I am one of those admirers and joined the fortunate few of them who have been able to meet and interview her. While there exist a number in the hundreds of interviews with her in print and on tape, in recent years, because of the fame that came after her best-selling memoir *One Writer's Beginnings,* there have been thousands more hopeful interviewers who have wanted to meet and talk to her. Long admired by writers and readers of serious fiction, she now holds celebrity status with a much wider audience. I was invited to visit her only through the intercession of my greatly revered college history professor and her friend, Ross Moore.

Gayle Graham Yates: I know that place is an essential category for you as you work in fiction. Is the place that you invent in your mind grounded in Mississippi, nourished by Mississippi?

Eudora Welty: Yes, it is. But I feel it really comes from the fact that I am a fiction writer and that wherever I happened to be I would do the same thing. I think it didn't start out because of Mississippi, but because of my wish to write. I don't want to claim that I am a spokesman for the state in itself. It's just that it happened that I was born here.

And I love it. And it has taught me a great deal. But it is for the selfish reason that I realize that I needed that to write my stories within to make them reflect life as I saw it. I nearly always write from the point of view of the stranger or the traveler because that is the only way I could vouch for what I say.

Gayle Graham Yates: Let's talk about some specific places that you invented. For example, in the town of Banner in *Losing Battles,* you brought your outsider voice, or brought in a narrator who is an outsider, to create the place. You actually have several regions of Mississippi in your writing. Banner is what?

Eudora Welty: North Mississippi. Near the Tennessee line. That was chosen for specific reasons. I like to try something new for all my books, though probably the outside world does not think there is any difference between one and the other, but to me they are always different. I wanted to see if I could write a story, as I thought it was going to be, without introspection being described in it, that is, going inside the characters' minds. I felt I had been doing that maybe overly, that I had gotten too contemplative and slow-moving, so I thought I would see if I could do something altogether in action and conversation and still show the same thing, still show what was going on, but to do it in the way a playwright does, by action and voice.

And, so to do that I needed a place where the action could be rather in primary colors, that is, a place where whatever people do normally shows things, so that is action. And I also wanted to write about what the poorest people in the world would probably always have to depend on, which is the family and subsisting on their own devices. And, so [for the time period in *Losing Battles*], I got the epitome of that in the Depression when people didn't have anything, wouldn't have, anyway. In the Depression and that section of the state which never had any riches, never did. And where the family would just be starkly out there. And I was so aware that life can be very rambunctious. People living as the family did in Banner where everything is overt. I did it through a family reunion so everybody would talk. I couldn't have ever laid that story in the Delta or the Mississippi Gulf Coast.

Gayle Graham Yates: Because the people in the Delta and on the Gulf Coast are more affluent?

Eudora Welty: Yes, they are just brought up differently, too. They had more and they expected more and they were more aware of the rest of the world.

And in *Delta Wedding,* it was to be my impression of the Delta. I don't know too much about either section of the state except as a visitor or as somebody driving through it, but I know many Delta people. You are from Wayne County?

Gayle Graham Yates: [Yes,] Wayne County.

Eudora Welty: That's south.

Gayle Graham Yates: Southeast.

Eudora Welty: Southeast.

Gayle Graham Yates: About a hundred miles from the Gulf Coast.

Eudora Welty: Just the opposite from the Delta. That is what I was about to say, but I wanted to be sure. (Laugh) Anyway, I wanted to set that novel at a time when there was nothing except the family again that you have to deal with. And all the men had to be home, so there couldn't be a wartime, any war. It couldn't be a floodtime, for that is another crisis. So I set it in the 1920s—1927 was the terrible flood—I couldn't have it that year. It just sort of came down to the fact that I had to set it in this time in the 1920s when I wasn't really very old myself. So I had a little girl enter the story on the train and everything was revealed to her.

Gayle Graham Yates: The little girl is the outsider that you can bring the knowledge to. In your discussion of those two novels and their locations and the need for those locations because of the story you had, you talked about the value of the family in each one, of your wanting to show family values. It seems to me that in *One Writer's Beginnings,* you talk about your own social values and their origins as a basis for your literary values, one of them being respect for the family and joy in the family. And another being cherishing friendships. And another being—well—tolerating eccentricities or diversity among people. But abhoring or rejecting cruelty or human unkindness. You suggest in *One Writer's Beginnings* that the origin of those values is in your own family, in where you were brought up or how you were brought up. Though, even in *One Writer's Beginnings,* your own voice is the center. You are not the outsider.

I was interested especially in your attention to values as you focused that book or that set of three lectures [that compose *One Writer's Beginnings*]. Was [attention to family values] at all central to your creation of that book, *One Writer's Beginnings*?

Eudora Welty: I think so. It is like the opposite of your question about place because I chose the place to fit what I wanted to say. In my case, it was the family life and the way I was brought up that taught me what I wanted. I am interested in human relationships. That is my true core. That is what I try to write about. Certainly it begins in the family and extends out and out. Of course, all these things are hindsight. I never thought of anything like this when I was writing the stories. Not in an analytical way. I was aware of what I was doing, but not analytically. What I had undertaken to do was to try to see what in my life produced certain things.

Gayle Graham Yates: Yes. I understand from Ross Moore [her friend, the Millsaps College historian] that you were reluctant to undertake that assignment.

Eudora Welty: I was. If it hadn't been for Ross I probably wouldn't have done it, because he had called me on behalf of David Donald [the Harvard professor who commissioned the lectures]. All he asked was that I would talk to David Donald.

Gayle Graham Yates: Talk to David Donald?

Eudora Welty: Talk to David Donald. Which, of course, I was delighted to do. But I don't know if I ever would have undertaken lectures at Harvard. Still it seems to me amazing that I had the temerity to do that. If it hadn't been—well, I met him [David Donald] after Daniel Aaron who was already a friend of mine had really suggested where I might catch onto a handle to it. I said I don't know anything to tell graduate students at Harvard—you know, I am not a scholar, I am not anything like that. He said, well, there is one thing you know that they don't, and that is you know about what in your life made you into a writer. And that *is* the one thing that I could have talked about. So between the two of them they were very receptive and helpful. I am very grateful to Ross for setting the ball rolling for me.

Gayle Graham Yates: You enjoyed it when you got started?

Eudora Welty: I didn't enjoy it until I had done the first lecture. I was petrified—I enjoyed the *writing* of it. But *delivering* it in the form of three lectures was very frightening because I couldn't imagine whether or not anything I had written would communicate itself to the audience I was reading to. Also, it was a different time, a different place, a different everything. But they were receptive [in the audience for the first lecture], and after that I drew a deep breath for the first time! After the first one.

Gayle Graham Yates: And then *One Writer's Beginnings* has been number one on the bestseller list for just weeks and weeks and weeks and weeks.

Eudora Welty: Isn't that amazing?

Gayle Graham Yates: I think that's marvelous.

Eudora Welty: Harvard was as staggered as I was!

Gayle Graham Yates: I understand that it is their first bestseller. Harvard University Press hasn't had another one.

Eudora Welty: That's what they say. Isn't that funny? I mean, it is amusing. As if that were what they strove for. Or me, either.

Gayle Graham Yates: Well, if I might move to a short story. My all-time favorite story of yours is "Livvie." I have read it with students again and again. And I am curious [about its source]. Do you remember where any of those people came from in that story? How they came to you. Livvie or Cash or Solomon or Miss Baby Marie?

Eudora Welty: Not as a story. In a very limited way—it was the place really. And it was the bottle tree that made me write it.

Gayle Graham Yates: Ahhh! I love that image. Tell me about that.

Eudora Welty: Well, there used to be—you have no doubt seen them—I don't know whether they have them in Wayne County.

Gayle Graham Yates: I haven't seen them. I have seen pictures of them.

Eudora Welty: Well, there are hardly any anymore because of the highways. You know, the interstates have come through. I have tried to find some of the old bottle trees down on Highway 49 where they used to be and where the old houses used to be that had them. They have vanished now. Access roads to the interstates have just come in and just plowed them up. So there probably still are some away back in somewhere. But there used to be a number of them that I could get to very quickly from Jackson. You know, drive down there.

None of the people—characters that I invented for my story—were people that were where the bottle trees were. In fact, I almost never saw any. I saw one. An old man. The one that lived with the best bottle trees. The ones that I really used. There was an enormous avenue of them. And the little peach tree that I put in the story was blooming at the time with these beautiful blue Milk of Magnesia bottles, you know—

Gayle Graham Yates: Oh, my goodness.

Eudora Welty: —and the peach tree was blooming. So, this old black gentleman came out one of the times I passed there to look at it. And I asked him if I might take a picture of his beautiful bottle trees and he said that was fine. I wasn't using color film. I didn't know how at that time. I am sorry I didn't get that. So then I said—I don't remember how I asked him—but one of the things that had puzzled me was that he had an altar built in there. It looked more like a speaker's podium with a slanted desk top—like a dictionary stand or something was standing there. That did puzzle me. I did ask in a polite way if the bottle trees were anything besides beautiful. Are they here for beauty or for what? Because somewhere I got the idea that they were sometimes built to contain the spirits of unfriendly or evil spirits that might try to get into the house. I may have put that into the story.

Gayle Graham Yates: I think that is in there.

Eudora Welty: He said he didn't want to talk about that, though. I was trespassing. When I asked him, I realized. But I figured that it had to be an old house—and a very dignified person that would live there. He was dignified, but he wasn't my man, wasn't Solomon. When I pictured a spring story, I had to have a young man come down the Trace, the Old Trace, I used to call it, deep down. But I saw a man in a zoot suit on Farish Street in Jackson that I copied, that I put on Cash. That was a real outfit. I couldn't have made it up. Those were the times of the zoot suit. Nobody now knows what they are. Your students would—

Gayle Graham Yates: —have to look it up.

Eudora Welty: I have to tell them. When I read that story. Be prepared for something called a zoot suit. It is a very simple story. It is about old and young, spring and winter, changes.

Gayle Graham Yates: I remember as an undergraduate being taught to look for symbols in a story. And in a lecture that you gave—it was a marking point in my literary education—you talked about how items in a story that could be interpreted as symbols just came. You didn't think, "I'll put in a symbol."

Eudora Welty: No.

Gayle Graham Yates: But in that story there is so much that can be interpreted symbolically.

Eudora Welty: And, correctly. Yes.

Gayle Graham Yates: Cash.

Eudora Welty: But, also what I would always like to say if I say anything about symbols is that they have to occur organically or they don't mean anything. You know, they have to be a part of the story. But, there are people in the [news]paper whose names are Cash. Of course when I saw it I was galvanized and stored it away so that when I needed it it came. But I wouldn't have made up that name Cash if I had never seen it used anywhere.

Gayle Graham Yates: And similarly Livvie?

Eudora Welty: Yeah. There was a girl that went to camp with me when I was thirteen years old whose name was Livvie. And it never occurred to me that it was probably for Olivia. I just thought they named her Livvie. That's all I know about her. That was intriguing. And there are lots of old people, as you know, old black people, whose names are Biblical and Greek. And Solomon could be—So all these things have precedents in real life.

Gayle Graham Yates: The names fit organically.

Eudora Welty: The people were more than the names.

Gayle Graham Yates: You have several times mentioned people, or life, being your inspiration. I interpret your work as saying a lot about society. I think your fictional truth corresponds to what a lot of good sociologists write about society.

Eudora Welty: Is that so?

Gayle Graham Yates: And the society that you have created that I think is most complex is Morgana in *The Golden Apples*. I came late to *The Golden Apples*. I hadn't read *The Golden Apples* until recently. And it was as if someone had given me a new classic.

Eudora Welty: Oh, how wonderful!

Gayle Graham Yates: I was just amazed. And loved it. And I have appreciated all the things of yours that I have read, but I think it rose to the top. Or the near-top!

Eudora Welty: That gives me a lot of pleasure because I most loved writing that book.

Gayle Graham Yates: Oh, did you?

Eudora Welty: I just *loved* writing it. And it was opening up to me as I wrote. I didn't realize the stories were going to be connected. You probably read my comments on this if you have been reading some of these because a lot of people ask me, Isn't it really a novel? Which it isn't.

Gayle Graham Yates: Yes.

Eudora Welty: But I just *loved* it! And I don't know any time in my life I ever felt so embedded and so carried away by the story. I just loved writing it.

Gayle Graham Yates: That shows. You loved the story. And you loved the people. And you loved the language. I think I could read it without paying attention to the story one time around and just paying attention to how lyrical and marvelous the language is, but the story is—the stories are—quite profound. But, how did you make up Morgana? I am thinking of my earlier question about society.

Eudora Welty: It evolved, too. Because I didn't even realize when I began writing the stories that they were connected. And I think Morgana came to me in one of the stories. I saw it was right because all the characters, as you know, were living under dreams or illusions or even obsessions. I wanted to get a name that would unite all of them. And then I chose Morgana because [of] "back to Morgana" and all those things that you have read about the illusion of the genie on the ocean.

Gayle Graham Yates: No, I don't know.

Eudora Welty: You don't know that? Well, it's in stories and things, fairy tales—maybe it's true that there is an illusion from the fog or something at sea. But it has fooled sailors. But I thought again that it was organically right. Because you know how the Delta has so many place names named after people?

Gayle Graham Yates: Yes.

Eudora Welty: And so, it was named after the Morgans. It was Morgana. So that fit it and everything came together. I thought it helped unite all the stories.

Gayle Graham Yates: Yes. And the people's lives all overlap and they interact with each other. They have a mythic connectedness with each other as well.

Eudora Welty: Of course, I had all this thing about the Greek myths at the time. Had I foreseen how critics talked! [Laugh.] I just made free with it! Because I just did whatever came to my mind. Not only Greek, but Irish and every other kind of myth. And people have written me all these abstruse questions about what I was trying to do and what the—. I'm glad I didn't take it too [seriously].

Gayle Graham Yates: I love hearing you talk about the liberties you took—you took with the myths!

Eudora Welty: That's the only way to write, anyway.

Gayle Graham Yates: Yes. Yes.

Eudora Welty: There are a lot of things. I realized it when I was reading proof on the *Collected Stories*. I hadn't read most of those things since I wrote them. I just read the ones I use when I give readings in colleges, a small handful. And I thought, Heavens, when I think of the questions people have asked me on some of those stories! It would have made me self-conscious. I would have hesitated before I did some of the things I did. [Laugh]

Gayle Graham Yates: Yes.

Eudora Welty: I don't intend ever to hesitate, but I didn't realize what I was stepping into.

Gayle Graham Yates: Well, it is a good thing you didn't have those critics' questions!

Eudora Welty: It sure is! It sure is!

Gayle Graham Yates: [Let's] return to my interest in Eudora Welty's Mississippi. I read a quotation from a review of *The Golden Apples* by Hamilton Basso. He wrote, "I doubt that a better book about the South has ever been written."

Eudora Welty: Bless his heart!

Gayle Graham Yates: Do you think it [*The Golden Apples*] is *importantly* about the South?

Eudora Welty: I think it is important in that if you are not true to the place you are writing about, it won't be true for life. And I think it follows that if you are very true to what you might try to get, things really revealing of human beings in relation to where they live and their time, then it will apply to anywhere.

Gayle Graham Yates: It has to be both/and. It is both about the South and about life.

Eudora Welty: That's all right. But I was proud of that little Hamilton Basso. He died young. But he was from New Orleans, and he wrote some good novels. One was called *The View from Pompey's Head*. And he reviewed books for the *New Yorker*. I was proud of his saying that because he knew what he was speaking of.

Gayle Graham Yates: You also celebrate relationships, friendships, family. Maybe we could talk about one more work [considering] relationships, *The Optimist's Daughter*. That novel has an inside-outsider, an outsider coming back. Laurel has lived away and comes back for the death of her father. In the character of Laurel, in her having her roots in Mississippi but having to go away and come back for a kind of mature self-realization—Is there something different or unusual about that set of relationships in that story from your other stories?

Eudora Welty: It occurs to me that it penetrates in ways I had not tried before. And it would take another facet. You know the facet of law. And yet the other characters have fully as much value as she [Laurel] has if not more.

Gayle Graham Yates: Yes.

Eudora Welty: And she knows it. I mean, she takes that secondary place, both by my wish and hers—it wasn't just what Laurel thought that mattered—I mean, that is the way it comes through. The point of view that I used. But I think more is shown of all the other characters through the scenes in the book than of her. I tried a sort of multiple thing.

Gayle Graham Yates: What was that?

Eudora Welty: I tried to show many of the characters in more depth than I usually try. Nearly the whole thing is introspective, except for one or two rather garish scenes [laugh]—which were necessary. The whole thing. I hoped to see the interiors of nearly all the people in it, like—well, everybody. I was just interested in all the people. I wanted to show how much there was to them.

Gayle Graham Yates: They are different in that they come from different social backgrounds, different experiences.

Eudora Welty: Yes. And yet they all were worth knowing. Even Fay. [Voice changes to lower, confiding tone] I must say I really did hate her.

Gayle Graham Yates: You really did hate Fay? [Both laugh]

Eudora Welty: I really hated her. I couldn't help it. I tried to be fair to her by bringing her family. [Both laugh again] I really did! I thought they would explain her! But, anyway, I hate what she stood for.

Gayle Graham Yates: Yes.

Eudora Welty: I don't mean she was a symbolic character, but the one who doesn't understand what experience means. And doesn't learn anything from it. You could scratch the skin and there wouldn't be anything under it, the way she would see things. And to me, that is horrifying and even evil, almost sinful. And I may have gone overboard in that case. I have been accused of it. But the point was I did want to show—in a quiet way, I wanted to show more of life than I had been able to with some of the others. It was a smaller cast and a direr situation.

Gayle Graham Yates: Yes.

Eudora Welty: Well, I wrote it at a time when I was feeling rather dire. It was soon after my own mother's death. It is not about my own family, but the character of Becky is a little like that of my own mother. She has her background, West Virginia; but I was not writing my mother. You know. But the judge is totally made up. I wanted a man who was—you know that kind of Mississippian, I am sure, like Judge McKelva. And you know there are many men like him. I've known many. I mean of his background and substance and so on.

Gayle Graham Yates: Yes.

Eudora Welty: It was necessary for each one to have what—to have the weight they have. What I tried to do was to give it to them. I don't know whether I succeeded, but that is what I tried to do.

Gayle Graham Yates: I liked it. And I am glad that Laurel left the breadboard.

Eudora Welty: Me, too.

Gayle Graham Yates: Let me ask you a few last questions about other interests and influences, other than the novels and stories of your own. What about other art forms? You write wonderfully about music, but say you are not a musician.

Eudora Welty: No, I am not. An extra benefit by Belhaven's being over here [the college with a good music program, across the street from her house where we were talking]. In the days before air conditioning, everything came through the window. Right over here to me at my window!

I love music. I love painting. I know more about painting than I do about music just because it is easier to. It has been more accessible to me. When I went to college in the Middle West where you are, in Madison [at the University of Wisconsin], I used to go down to Chicago and go to the Art Institute. It was wonderful to get acquainted with the French Impressionists that were early. So I had more opportunity to [learn about painting]. I minored in art, as a matter of fact. I took art history and things like that. I was better educated in it.

Gayle Graham Yates: Do you suppose that your wonderful visual imagery has been influenced by your art education? Your enjoyment of art?

Eudora Welty: It could well be. I am a visual person. I mean, I don't know whether that got me interested in painting or painting got me interested in it. Who knows? That is, I feel I have learned more through my eyes than my ears. I love photography, and it taught me a lot, too.

Gayle Graham Yates: It was a combination of the historical moment—and the job that you had.

Eudora Welty: Right. That's what it came out of. But when I went to write this book about—*One Writer's Beginnings*—I suddenly realized what a good photographer my father had been. You know. All these pictures turned up, pictures he had taken before he had ever married my mother. When he was traveling on his—I don't know how he ever managed to do that—up in Canada and out West and everywhere. Wonderful pictures! And just the mass of them simply staggered me. I didn't know he had done all of that. He and Mother used to print them at home. So I grew up with picture taking going on all the time, but I didn't even realize it.

Gayle Graham Yates: Yes. Well, as a final kind of question: Who would you say of people—teachers or family or whoever—most influenced you? You don't have to pick one.

Eudora Welty: To be a writer?

Gayle Graham Yates: To be a writer and to develop the kind of life that you developed. Which is one and the same, isn't it?

Eudora Welty: Yeah. Well, my mother was always very much for my being a writer. But my father died when I was only—twenty—and

I had not written anything then except school things. Let's see, he died the year after I had been at Columbia. I was twenty-two when I came home. So he never knew if or what I could write. But together they made, as you know from my book they made such a home with respect to [literature]—I mean, they loved the arts and they loved reading and they loved things like that. I am sure it put the mainsprings of my imagination working which is what it is. And I always had good teachers. I have been so *lucky* all my life. Teachers and literary agents and editors. I didn't know that everybody didn't have all these things. Until I hear of the other kind. I have been very much blessed. And I know it. I don't think you can put it on any one thing. Just the combination of wonderful people. They have encouraged me and understood my work.

And Jackson is just wonderful to me. You know, they're almost too wonderful!

Gayle Graham Yates: What Jackson times have you most enjoyed? I mean the ceremonial ones like speaking at the William Winter inauguration or the seventy-fifth birthday party for you at Millsaps?

Eudora Welty: I deeply felt the honor. But I also felt on the spot! [Laughter.] To produce. It is hard for me to do anything in public. It really is. I am basically pretty shy. I can talk about work or something that I care about, especially to a friend, but it is *hard* for me to do things in public.

Gayle Graham Yates: Well, thank you for letting me come to your home and for talking with me.

Eudora Welty: I have enjoyed it. I knew I would enjoy it.

A Conversation with Eudora Welty

Albert J. Devlin and Peggy Whitman
Prenshaw / 1986

From the *Mississippi Quarterly*, 39 (Fall 1986), 431–54. Reprinted by permission of the *Mississippi Quarterly*.

AJD: Peggy and I want to start by thanking you for what is obviously a kind gesture. We're very appreciative.

EW: Well, thank you. I'm honored by the issue you're getting out. I just didn't know how I could help. You said earlier that you were pleased with the contributions.

AJD: Very much so. They're intense and varied, I think, and yet they have a point where they all meet. It's the evidence of the great pleasure the contributors take in your writing.

EW: I'm glad to hear that word, "pleasure."

AJD: Pleasure just shines through. Some of the essays are rather technical, and perhaps at times we try to say highfalutin' things, but there's a deep pleasure, so strongly felt, in all of them.

EW: That's very reassuring.

AJD: I wanted to tell you that.

EW: I'm glad you did at this point, too, because it makes me feel more comfortable. [laughter]

AJD: Miss Welty, this interview was a wonderful excuse for me to reread several authors and stories that I know you love, and which I do too. In reading I found myself very much aware of your presence, both in my mind and in the text too, it seemed. It was a comforting and yet challenging presence.

EW: What stories were you reading?

AJD: Oh, I was reading, for example, Katherine Mansfield's "Prelude," and *To the Lighthouse.*

EW: You felt my presence? That's extraordinary. That's wonderful of you to say. Do you mean, you could understand how I responded to them?

100

AJD: Not only how you responded, I felt your values and your perceptions, and your authority as well. Perhaps that's how real literary community is founded or formed today. Individuals meeting in texts like that.

EW: You remember what Henry Green said—I know it, I've quoted it myself—about prose. "Prose is a long—

AJD: "—intimacy"

EW: "—intimacy between strangers. It uses terms that neither knows." I would like to quote it exactly, but that's the sort of thing you were saying. That it's a connection, a communication that doesn't depend on knowing the same people or speaking the same idiom or anything like that. I was thrilled when I read that passage. It's like what you're saying, only I didn't at first recognize how it was meant.

PWP: In writing an essay for this issue, on *One Writer's Beginnings* and Elizabeth Bowen's *Seven Winters and Afterthoughts* and *Pictures and Conversations,* I also read *Collected Impressions* and *Bowen's Court.* As I read, I saw much in Bowen of what I felt would have appealed to you, would have excited you, especially the wonderful visual, material quality.

EW: She was a marvelous lady, a responsive person, you know, to mood and place, and she was so happy, so delighted by things in life. And very apprehensive too. It was an Irishness, a sense of your surroundings, very sensitive to what you can feel all the time.

PWP: You met her first in Ireland or in England?

EW: I met her in Ireland first. At Bowen's Court.

PWP: What was Bowen's Court like? What was it like to visit there?

EW: I met Elizabeth during my first trip to Europe, which was Holy Year, as I remember. I sailed late in the fall of 1949. This was on a Guggenheim and I was trying to make it last. I was in France and Italy for much of the time, but I decided I *had* to go and see England and Ireland. I had always wanted to see Ireland, though I didn't know anyone there. I went over on the ferry, first to Dun Laoghaire, and then I just walked around Dublin, looking at all the places I'd read about. It was just heavenly. I'd go out in the country and walk on these little roads and get under the hedge when it rained. I just wanted to see it for myself, just to be there. I loved Dublin. And then I thought—someone had told me in Paris that they'd seen Elizabeth Bowen at a party and Elizabeth had said something about my work.

She was reviewing then a lot. And so whoever it was told her that I
had been in Paris lately, and she said, "Oh, I wish I had met her."
Well, I had never in my life looked up anybody that I didn't know.
But it kept tempting me, like a fantasy almost. I thought that Bowen's
Court was in Dublin; I didn't know it was a long way off. I wrote
Elizabeth a note and told her that if it were possible, I would like to
pay a call on her during the next week or so. And then she telephoned
me at my hotel and told me that she was in County Cork and for me
to come down that weekend. This turned out to be very typical of
her. So I went down and she had me met in a car at Cork and we
drove to Bowen's Court. It was my first sight of the South of Ireland,
the real South. Later on I saw that still further south there were palm
trees and fuchsia hedges and pink and blue plastered houses that
made you think of Savannah or New Orleans. It's almost tropical. At
any rate, Elizabeth is a *Southerner*. She said that wherever she went,
in the whole world almost, the Southerners were always different
from the Northerners. She always felt the congeniality.

PWP: She had lived in Ireland when she was young, but she left
when her father was so ill.

EW: Those were the "seven winters" of her book. Then she went
to school in England. When I saw Bowen's Court, she had moved
back into it, and as she could, she was restoring all of the rooms.
Some were partly done and some were not. I had this wonderful
room, it was on the second floor. You know what the house looked
like—huge, stone, three story, perfectly straightforward.

PWP: Utterly rectangular and balanced on either side.

EW: Yes, Georgian, with a porch and steps out front where everyone sat in the summer afternoons. As far as you could see was the
demesne. And a group of elms out there on the lawn. Elizabeth said
that when she was growing up, they used to call this the lamb's
drawing room, because the little lambs would come there and browse
in the afternoon.

PWP: Isn't that the setting she uses in *Last September*?

EW: Yes, she does. It was so lovely to be in that house, and I
immediately fell into the way things were done. Elizabeth worked in
the morning, which is what I like to do, and at about eleven o'clock
you could come downstairs if you wanted to and have a sherry, and
then go back to work. Then you met at lunch, I mean to talk, and the

whole afternoon was spent riding around, and the long twilights coming back. There was usually company at dinner time. And evenings, just a few people, or maybe more, easy and—We liked to play games. Eddy Sackville-West was visiting her once when I was there and we all played "Happy Families," a children's card game—it's just like "Going Fishing" where you try to get all of a family in your hand by asking, "May I have?" except that it's done with Victorian decorum. The cards are designed with Dickens-like illustrations and names like Mr. Bones, the Butcher, and Mrs. Bones, the butcher's wife, and Miss Bones, the butcher's daughter, and Master Bones, the butcher's boy, all with huge heads and little bodies. What you do is say, "May I have Mrs. Bones, the butcher's wife?" and I say, "*Sorry, she isn't at home.*" So you've missed your turn. There are more thanks and a whole lot of politeness. [laughter] I would get the giggles to see Elizabeth and Eddy being so unfailingly *courteous* to each other. So we'd sit around the fire in the evenings, drinking whiskey and playing "Happy Families."

PWP: I read several times Bowen's "Notes on Writing a Novel," and it struck me that there's a certain sympathy between her views and some of the things that you've done and talked about, for example, place in fiction.

EW: I learned from her. I think she had the best analytical mind of a writer, about writing, that I've ever come across. She had a marvelous mind, you know, all aside from imagination and the sensibilities you need to write fiction. I know they felt that in Oxford, where she and her husband lived for a time. She was such marvelous company in the evening for these Oxford people. She was not in the *least* academic, but their minds could play together.

AJD: I'm sure you remember the fine introduction that she wrote for the Vintage collection [1956] of Katherine Mansfield's stories.

EW: Oh, yes, and it was so needed, wasn't it? Katherine Mansfield was going unappreciated.

AJD: One passage in particular reveals that "marvelous mind" for me. Bowen writes of Katherine Mansfield reaching her maturity as a writer shortly before her death. She goes on to say that "it is with maturity that the really searching ordeal of the writer begins. Maturity, remember, must last a long time—" Isn't that wonderful?

EW: That's marvelous. No escaping it once you've got it.

AJD: "—and it must not be confused with single perfections, such as she had accomplished without yet having solved her abiding problems."

EW: Isn't that marvelous? It's just the very seed of things, isn't it? The very core.

AJD: So often, I think, your own criticism works on much the same high level of perception. I especially admire the Cather and Porter essays—they're extraordinary, and they certainly belie for me the overly modest statements that you've made at times about your criticism.

EW: I'm glad to hear you say it, but if you think so, the reason is that I won't even try something about which I don't feel a great empathy. I turn down so many things because I can't feel close to them.

AJD: Well, isn't that a good lesson in itself for critics?

EW: It's the only way I feel halfway equipped. I *can't*—I'm not much good at destructive things. One person I tried to destroy once. But the thing that you feel you love about your work is overpowering, and that's what teaches you, I mean me, that's the way I learn. It's my ability, imagined ability maybe, to enter in by imagination. I find criticism very, very hard to do.

AJD: I know that you find it hard to think about your own work.

EW: I don't think of it analytically. I can't because the process of writing a story is different, taking the opposite direction.

AJD: I'm fascinated by what seems to happen to your work in *Delta Wedding*. For me it's your most valuable book.

EW: I wonder why—I mean in my case—if that's true.

AJD: I sensed that you had addressed those "abiding problems" that Bowen mentions, whatever they may be, and in a very decisive way.

EW: I would have been lucky if I had, because the way I happened to write *Delta Wedding* was almost accidental. I was writing short stories, and I sent the story "Delta Cousins" to Diarmuid Russell, my agent, who was very astute. He read it and said this is chapter 2 of a novel. It challenged me when he said that, and then I had a good friend, John Robinson—this was war time, you know—who was in the Air Force overseas. He came from the Delta and had introduced me to it. So as I wrote *Delta Wedding,* I sent it to him chapter by chapter. I just made it up as I went; part of it was to entertain him, and part of it was to try to do something Diarmuid thought I could do. [laughter] It was the most ill-planned or unplanned of books. I was just writing about what a family is like, trying to put them down in a place where they could just spread themselves—that's also why I set *Delta Wedding* in that special time, the twenties. It's what I've always done, I guess, the whole time.

PWP: I don't think I've ever heard you read from *Delta Wedding*.

EW: I haven't ever read from the novels—this is reading for a living, I mean. This means reading short stories, of which there is just a handful that I can use.

AJD: What strikes me about *Delta Wedding,* Miss Welty, is that in Ellen Fairchild you discovered or shaped someone who is unlike any character in your earlier stories.

EW: That's certainly true.

AJD: She's a richly imaginative character and she's in part at least the outsider.

EW: That's true. I think that was probably my first conception of that figure in my work, when you come to think of it. I realize I have used outsiders in fiction from time to time since; it gives you a point of view, a place to walk in. It gives you the outside view of what you're writing about. And I have to have that.

AJD: There's a wonderful moment at the dance—after the wedding which takes place in about a line—when Ellen sees each of her children individually, and then sees them together, inseparable, "in a turn" of India's skirt. Ellen's imagination seems to be bringing together powerful forces in your world. It's a thrilling moment, and it seems unlike earlier ones in your fiction.

EW: I'm glad I did that, I'm glad I could. And I thank you for telling me this. You know what you try to do, but not what you—

AJD: Was Ellen Fairchild a difficult character to show?

EW: She was easy, in fact she was the only one. I was writing about people I didn't know, I didn't know Delta people, only the surrounding of this one family. But I'd been up there sometimes—this was in the old days with cotton and all that when the Delta really was a different world—I'd been up there to visit this friend's family, while he was away. They had lots of old diaries that they let me read, which gave me a feeling of the background of the Delta. You know what a *short* history it's had. It was the wilderness till just about yesterday. And I hadn't realized any of these things. When I wrote the story "Delta Cousins," it was what I had gathered over the years about the kind of mood that abided there and the kind of people that made the Delta families. But I had to have a character that was not of the Delta, that I could kind of latch onto. It was Ellen showing me. That's my feeling about her, as I say. I used several outsiders, young ones, and in a way the hero's an outsider, George. But I didn't reduce them, I didn't call them outsiders or anything like that.

AJD: They certainly weren't outside your novel.

EW: No, but you have to compose the inside out of all that world's different colors and moods and varieties of viewpoint. I loved writing about all those children.

AJD: I thought you did. The games you gave them were so boisterous.

PWP: And that novel is so full of voices, but it also has the poetical and mystical side. I guess that all of the family, except for Ellen, are the busy talkers. She brings the reflective and meditative side.

EW: The only one that does. I loved the names I got for the people too. Some of them I had heard but my characters weren't at all like the people. I loved India—that's a Southern thing to give people such exotic names.

PWP: I have a cousin named China.

EW: Exactly. I knew a girl named India, a lady named India. But of course, not this girl. And I like Bluet; I knew a girl named Bluet one time. And a Battle. They all seemed to me very Delta names. Do you think so?

PWP: Oh, I think so.

EW: That was so much fun, you know, finding the thing that you needed to help you along. I was happy about the names.

PWP: The first time I saw any of the typescripts, when they became available at the archives in Jackson, it was exciting to discover that you had changed the names of characters sometimes.

EW: When I first began writing I didn't realize the importance of names. I would just name characters anything. And then I realized how much it mattered, for cadence, and for example, how families name their children in a kind of pattern, you know, everybody's name beginning with a B.

PWP: By the alphabet.

EW: Well, you've got to get people to sound like brothers and sisters. The same parents. By the way, there are *still* wonderful names to be found in the Mississippi newspapers. The other day I was reading in the *Jackson Daily News* the list of people arrested for drunk driving. There was this man whose name was Quovadis something. "Quovadis, whither goest thou?" [laughter] It's just wonderful. They'd once heard of somebody else named Quovadis, I'm sure. It surfaces from no telling what kind of history.

PWP: I wanted to ask about your visit to Cambridge, when you gave the "Place in Fiction" lecture.

EW: Can you imagine?

PWP: Well, yes. It's an extraordinary essay and many readers like me have certainly learned from it.

EW: I worked a year on that. It was three lectures to begin with, I combined them to make the published essay. I think it was the first time I'd been invited to lecture anywhere. How could I turn down a free trip to England, with a year to work on it? Did either of you ever take part in one of those exchanges? They brought American teachers over to talk to British teachers of American subjects. The six-week session was held in the University, though the University didn't do anything but provide a place and entertainment. Cambridge was a lovely host. I was the only one who was not a teacher. No, Jack Fisher, who was editor of *Harper's,* also went. This was the year of the McCarthy hearings and the first question any Britisher asked the lecturer, no matter what your subject, was "What do you think about McCarthy?" The University program lasted five years. I was the first woman invited. And I was the first woman ever to cross the threshold into the hall at Peterhouse College, where they had a special dinner. Women weren't allowed there. They were so dear the way they told me: they said, "Miss Welty, you are invited to come to this, but we must tell you that we debated for a long time about whether or not we should ask you. No woman has ever crossed the threshold, including Queen Victoria, who *demanded* to and was refused." And I thought, well now, what would be the correct thing for me to do, they having given me this leave? And then I thought, I'm going to do it. They've already decided that I can, and I think to back out would sort of

demean the *greatness,* the *momentousness,* of this invitation. Besides, I was curious.

AJD: Isn't it interesting that Cambridge intellectual life, which in
large part officially excluded Virginia Woolf, is now so often remembered by us through her reflections?

EW: Absolutely. Just extraordinary. Forster was still alive at the
time, by the way, when I was over there, living in Kings College, and
he invited me to lunch. He was writing *Marianne Thornton.* I love
that book. And Dadie Rylands was still alive. All these people that
show up in Woolf's diary.

PWP: You have spoken of Katherine Anne Porter as having a gift
for—or of valuing the gift of—making people feel at ease. Elizabeth
Bowen and you, too, in spite of having a writer's solitary life, have
spent much of yourself with people.

EW: I enjoy people, and I think there's a great difference in that
respect between Katherine Anne and Elizabeth. Katherine Anne
might enjoy having a circle around her, but there she really remained
within herself. Elizabeth was the opposite; she was an in-taker. She
just took everything in. She was curious and fascinated by most
people she met, and she really wanted to know. She had a wonderful
curiosity, too, but it was more outgoing. She was very sharply aware
and very cognizant of what was going on. She quickly got the feel in
a room. She could come in and she would know that there may have
been two people at odds just about ten minutes before—she could get
the feel of everything. And she was always in command. That sounds
as if she were authoritative. I mean, she was in command of herself.
She had the best time; she loved gaiety and dancing and she loved a
party. Loved to give one. She loved to go to the movies. Over and
over and over. She thought that the cinema and fiction were much
alike, which was instructive to me. I think that's true, too, don't you?
I went with her one time in New York to see *Breathless.* She just
loved that movie. I went with her and Howard Moss. Elizabeth had
already seen it, of course, several times. She could drop off to sleep
in the movies, as she often did, and wake up and point, "That's his
brother." Howard said, "Elizabeth is *wired* to the screen." [laughter]
Not much escaped her that was going on, even while she was asleep.
She traveled a great deal, she knew this country well. She'd been here

three or four times, I guess. She liked being in the South. I always
enjoyed coming together.

PWP: I have heard a friend mention that you and Elizabeth made a
trip to Longwood and saw a ghost.

EW: We did see a ghost. I found this out weeks later, after I was
back in Jackson. And Elizabeth was a little disconcerted because she
believed in ghosts, but never had seen one. Do you want me to tell
you? Well, this was not the tourist season in Natchez. I wouldn't have
taken her down there then. This was right around Hallowe'en. I
remember a huge moon came up and Elizabeth said, "That's the
biggest moon I ever saw in my life." I took her to see Longwood
because I thought that would amuse her. We got out of the car on a
Sunday morning and walked up through the woods. I knew she loved
strange houses, I knew she'd be fascinated by it. We were walking
around it and this man came out of the woods from beyond and said,
"Would you like to see the house? I can take you over it if you'd like
to," and Elizabeth said, "Very much." So we went in the house and
he said, "Would you care for a drink?" [laughter] It was about ten
o'clock Sunday morning and we said "Thanks, no, not now." So he
took us all over the house—a very garrulous old man. He explained
that the reason he knew the house so well was that he lived in it as a
caretaker for all these years. After I got back to Jackson, I was talking
to a friend about seeing Longwood and I said, "The caretaker took us
over." She said, "Oh, he couldn't have, he was killed in an automobile
accident about three months ago." She said he was driving down that
little winding road that runs to Longwood and was hit by something
coming the other way, and killed, and that now there was nobody in
the house. There *was* somebody at the house.

PWP: Do you take it to have been a ghost?

EW: I don't know. I told Elizabeth it was due to her—she didn't
too much like that.

AJD: I know that you've tried your hand at one ghost story ["The
Purple Hat"], and maybe others would qualify too. Is it hard, do you
think, for a writer to get the supernatural into a story?

EW: I don't think it would be hard to get it in. It's probably harder
to employ it correctly so that the reader will accept the thing. I have
a very strong feeling about there being something—I don't mean
ghosts or bogeymen, not that kind of thing, but the sense of a

personality. I think those things can hang about a house, for instance.
I don't see any reason not to think so if you should feel that. It doesn't
bother me, that is.

AJD: Can you help me with a passage in *Losing Battles*?

EW: If I can.

AJD: It's that meditation of Vaughn's.

EW: The one time I get into somebody's mind.

AJD: He seems perplexed throughout that passage, and then Granny's invitation seals his perplexity and sends him to the barn. I'm not
sure how to understand, or how to react to, the nature or cosmos of
that passage. Vaughn is listening with ears that "stick out like fun-
nels"—I think that's your image—but is it the intention of that nature
to speak to him? Is it a nature that wants to communicate itself?

EW: I don't know, but I think it's his nature to want to. He thinks
there's something else besides the voices he's heard all day. He feels
that everything may have a voice. But he's *in* the world, he's in this
strange, blue-lit night, and he feels—what I was trying to say—that
there's so much more than what he's been listening to all day. I don't
know whether I conveyed that. He is the introspective one; he's
questioned so many things that the others don't, and he's also young
enough not yet to have got that armor over him. I think I just tried to
express an awareness that there was something over and beyond the
circle of the family that was still capable of being understood. It was
just my one chance—I never meant to have anybody at the reunion
betray introspection all the way through. I wanted to show everything
by action and speech, but when I got to that part, and when it was
night and everything had been so strained, I succumbed.

PWP: Vaughn was the perfect one to choose.

EW: The only one.

AJD: Miss Welty, do you by any chance remember Virginia Woolf's
little essay, "On Being Ill"?

EW: I'm trying to think—I haven't read it recently.

AJD: She describes illness as a time of reflection when we become
"irresponsible and disinterested" in our ordinary lives, and can see,
"perhaps for the first time for years," the extraordinary performance
of the sky—its "endless activity" and plunging experiments with
color. And the she goes on to say, "Divinely beautiful it is also
divinely heartless. Immeasurable resources are used for some purpose

which has nothing to do with human pleasure or human profit." Does this help to explain Vaughn's perplexity and the apparent distance between him and the marvelous performance of the sky? You say he could neither "stop" nor "out-ride" the great "wheel of the sky."

EW: I don't think so. I think he feels very close to what's going on. He sees the acrobatics of the falling star, like the feats he's been hearing about all day. No, I think he is a little frightened, but I think he accepts all that just the way he's accepted everything he's heard all day. I mean, it's all part of the world and part of life, part of living. I know he had no philosophical attitude. When Virginia Woolf wrote that essay she may have been going through strange phases—you know, when the birds spoke Greek, and the world was very much apart from her in her illness. Maybe there were different phases and stages of that feeling that she had, which would be likely with such a consciously learning mind. But, of course, Vaughn didn't have anything like that, just the sensitivity.

PWP: That moment for Vaughn is the same sort of experience, a moment of deepening insight, that Laura has in *Delta Wedding* at the conclusion.

EW: They're probably all about nine years old.

PWP: I think that's a special age, about nine years old, just coming out of childhood. There are those beginning sparks.

EW: I think so too. I thought so at the time, didn't you, that nine was wonderful. I used to write N-I-N-E, nine, nine, nine, all the time, as if it were something magical.

PWP: I was always so eager to be a little older. I was always short a year or two, I thought, of happiness—if I could only be eleven, when I was nine.

EW: That's right, you're always reaching ahead—"In two years I'll be a teenager." [laughter] That's a very frightening statement.

PWP: Recently, I had occasion to reread some historical romances that I had loved when I was about eleven or twelve years old. Also, I was reading Elizabeth Bowen's *Collected Impressions,* anticipating our conversation today. She's quite stern in her view that one should never go back and read the books one has read as a child. She talks about Dickens, saying she could never go back and read Dickens, that he was "used up" for her.

EW: I heard her talking about Dickens here in this room. It was the

time she met my mother. They had Dickens in common because they
both loved reading him in childhood. I had to confess that when I was
little I was so perverse that when my mother said you have to read
Dickens—"I read Dickens when I was your age"—I wouldn't read
him. I said I guess I'll have to go on and do it, and both of them said
it's too late. [laughter] It's too late now. You have to read Dickens
when you're very young, they agreed on that. That's when he's a
master. Elizabeth thinks that he's a wonderful writer, but that the
time when he really breathes something in you that you never forget
is when you're young.

AJD: Peggy and I were talking earlier about a story of yours that
you're not too fond of, "The Burning." I think Peggy agrees, in part
at least, with you.

PWP: No, I said I thought I understood the objections you had to
the story, the reservations that you had.

EW: I think I stuck my neck out.

AJD: I like the story very much.

EW: You do? Well, I haven't gone back to read it, but I had a
feeling—this comes from the questions people ask me in letters—that
I didn't do at all what I wanted to. I think it's too elaborate, too
impressionistic.

AJD: I felt freedom in the gaps in the story. I thought they were
purposive, they invited me.

EW: That interests me. I think I'll go back and read it. I was
ashamed to because I thought I would see everywhere I fell down.

AJD: You said in an earlier interview—you'll probably rue this—
that you wrote historically and you shouldn't have done that.

EW: That's true, because I don't like to write things that I could
not have experienced—I mean, a life that I haven't experienced in the
world where those things happen. I don't like to write historical
stories, though I did a couple of other times.

AJD: I guess you did in part in *Delta Wedding* by filling in the
middle distance with ancestors and Civil War stories.

EW: Yes, that's true, but as they were handed down; they weren't
going on during the story. The reader and writer weren't present in it
in the way they are in "The Burning." I used Aaron Burr in "First
Love," but I made the story told through a deaf-and-dumb boy
because I didn't know what Aaron Burr would have said, since he

was a real person. So I had to make it understood by the deaf boy, who then could say what he thought. I never could understand how people could write historical novels with real people speaking. I would feel very inhibited. Don't you feel that you would always be aware of the great chasm?

AJD: Isn't that what a certain kind of writer tries to do, though, to dare that chasm, to bridge it?

EW: I know it is, but it's something I'm not equipped to do, I couldn't do.

PWP: You did "Circe," though, wonderfully.

EW: Yes, but "Circe" is not really historical. I had so much fun writing that story. That was on my first trip to Europe. I never thought I was going to write anything. I was looking. I didn't write anything till I got home. We were passing Sicily and all of those other islands where Circe was supposed to be. And I thought, "What would it be like to be condemned to live forever?" To see everybody that you love die and not be able to feel anything about mortality or the preciousness of the moment. That must have been what she felt.

AJD: I thought that "The Burning" was also a daring kind of experiment. For lots of reasons, I think it's still hard to write about that plantation world and the effect of civil war upon it. There's a residue of ideology and partisan romance that's ready to intrude on a writer, but I thought you warded that off and found the human core.

EW: Well, thank you. That's the only way I could have entered into a story about which I knew so little, as I would almost any other story of a murder or a suicide that came about through a hopeless situation. You know, I don't like reading anything about the Civil War, that's the truth. I hate the Civil War. I hate it. I never have read *Gone with the Wind*. I'm totally ignorant about the Civil War. I mean, I had people on both sides, being half-Yankee, and half-Southern. [laughter] But I just hate it, all those hideous battles and the terrible loss.

PWP: We're only just now beginning to get beyond it in Mississippi.

EW: I know that. It's something that Elizabeth Bowen understood too, because she said in Ireland scenes of Cromwell's destruction, the burned churches and abbeys, are still standing, and people look at them all day long. They can be in your yard. And it's the same way in the South. You still have the physical memories of things that happened on your property, in your homeplace. That's one reason why it's so hard to forget.

PWP: I remember in John Crowe Ransom's "Antique Harvesters" one of the characters says, "On this spot stood heroes and drenched it with their only blood."

EW: Yes, and they say of the Archbishop of Canterbury, "Right here is where he was murdered." Blood stains in Canterbury. No, it's just too much.

AJD: May I asked a related question that begins on a personal note of sorts? I became interested in politics in the early 1960s, and I found both President Kennedy and the Civil Rights legislation of '64 and '65 to be inspiring. Maybe I deceived myself, but I felt a sense of unity then and also a national purpose. Today I have no idea where we are, either nationally or more individually. You've seen this over a longer period of time, do you have a sense of perplexity too?

EW: I do, I feel that the perplexity is all over the nation. I don't feel that the answer is *this* anymore. And I also loved John F. Kennedy; I thought something wonderful was going to happen in the world when he was elected. And that really vanished with his assassination and with the thing that happened after that. When I was growing up here, politics was everywhere, but there was not any kind of glorification of politics in my family on either of my parents' sides. There were Mississippians like Bilbo and Vardaman who were almost unbelievable. And that is the kind of thing that a lot of Jackson who were on the wrong side of Civil Rights hark back to: "What we need is somebody like . . . !" So that's where their ideals led them, an idiotic return to something that was not any good in the first place. Well, that's not anything to place too much confidence in. I can't talk. Such a tremendous—I do feel that private relationships between blacks and whites have always been the steadying thing. I believe in private human relations anyway, for understanding. And I've always had faith that they would resolve problems. And I think by and large that that eventually has happened here in Jackson. It was last Christmas, or maybe the Christmas before, that the President of Tougaloo College had a wonderful troupe of mimes and medieval music players who came and did all the early Church music. I went with some friends from Millsaps. And it was an interesting thing to see because Tougaloo, you now, had always been very congenial with Millsaps—

teachers would go back and forth and we always went to each others' lyceums—but during the worst of the Civil Rights times Tougaloo barred its doors, severed relations. Then last year the President said to a very large half and half, black and white, audience, "This is a free evening, it's Tougaloo's Christmas gift to Jackson." That was so spontaneous. Have you ever been in that college? It started out as a kind of Northern missionary project and it was needed. It was a private school to educate black students. In the old auditorium there are pews brass plated with names from New England, donors' names like Alcott and Peabody. They had given these pews to the college and now they were inhabited all alike by the black and white citizens of Jackson. It was something spontaneous and solid and *convincing*. Of course it was Christmas, but I still found it convincing. Because I am a writer people come up and speak to me sometimes in the Jitney or the library. Many are black and they may say, "I'm a teacher and I've read all of your works," and so on. And then we have conversations, straightforward conversations about what I've written. I think they feel they can trust me when I write stories about black people, many black people.

PWP: My black students have read your short stories. Many of them, of course, come from the Jackson area. They have read them in high school.

EW: Of course, the stories go back in time, such a long time, for them.

PWP: Most of these students, in fact, have no memory of the 1960's. And there are not many stories being told now about the '60s, much less before.

EW: You know what Patti Black said when she put on the Civil Rights exhibition in the Old Capitol. The whole history of what happened on the home scene was there in photographs and newsprint. And classes of students were taken to look at it. Patti said she would go and listen to the children, and a lot of them didn't even know anything about segregation, had no family memory or race memory of it.

PWP: Some don't believe it.

EW: Here was this evidence, and the children didn't know what it was. They were pretty bored, too. So strange. Patti said, "But they should know it! It's so important to know what happened, both white and black. To know what we did.''

PWP: My students read Richard Wright's *Black Boy,* and many question it—black and white alike. They don't believe such times happened. They take it to be gross exaggeration.

EW: I put some of the blame for that on the fact that we've become so dependent on television. People believe what they see on the screen, which has happened today. And they have no sense of a perspective of time, of things growing and changing and becoming something. It's never brought to mind. Never brought to their attention. It worries me that there's not going to be any memory someday. People will have these things stored up on a computer if they need to use them. [laughter] Another thing that is related is the way we travel now. You know, from airport to airport, with no sense of the country that you're flying over and no sense of the difference between one place and another. Just airports, the same *strip* along the road. You know, I was thinking this morning of a birthday party I went to the other night in my family. I said to the honoree, who was thirty-nine, [laughter] "I remember the day you were born because I was in San Francisco then, and I got a telegram from your parents." I always remember that exactly. And Mittie, my sister-in-law, said, "Do you know, people don't know what *telegrams* are anymore." Nothing in a telegram was ever tranquil, the most dramatic messages, sad and happy, always came in telegrams. I thought about writing an article titled, "Daddy, What Was a Telegram?" [laughter] It would show a lot. The arrival of messages used to be important. There was suspense, drama, in everything.

PWP: Even the way the movies depicted the receipt of telegrams, that was always high drama.

EW: They came on a bicycle and rang your doorbell. If it was a death message, there were three stars on the envelope to prepare the recipient.

PWP: Oh, I didn't know that.

EW: Well, that's what they told us they did. So that you wouldn't tear it open, expecting something good, only to find: "Susie died." Three Stars. [laughter] The telegraph carrier wore a uniform and was supposed to wait if there was a death message, just to be sure that the family *took* it all right. They felt a certain sense of responsibility. You didn't get telegrams from strangers that said, "Congratulations, you have just won a free trip to the Virgin Islands! All you have to do is . . ." You know, one of those ads that mimics a telegram. Honest telegrams were *serious*. In fiction you're trying to convey living life, but so many of the old daily trappings now are meaningless to readers. In many respects you have a new vocabulary that you have to write with. I think we have to do it.

AJD: Were you trying to find a new vocabulary in *One Writer's Beginnings*?

EW: That was unlike anything else I'd ever written. My mind was entirely on what I was trying to convey, but I never have written about myself as myself. Non-fiction to begin with is hard for me. But I'm glad I did it—I at least learned what the writing of it taught me.

AJD: Terms like memoir, autobiography, or non-fiction seem so inadequate to describe the feel of that book. It's so intensely imagined.

EW: I think it sort of created itself when I was writing it because I wrote much, much more than I used. It was three lectures, and there's more there than in the book. I didn't think it was fair to assume that people attending a lecture had necessarily read my books. I was so frightened when I went. I did it because Dan Aaron invited me to do the Massey lectures. I told him I could not possibly lecture to graduate students at Harvard. "I'm not an academic. I don't know anything they don't know better." He said, "You know one thing, and that's what in your life you think made you become a writer." And I started thinking about it and it rather interested me. Everything began to come in. I've got a pretty good memory, at least so far, and I thought of, remembered, so many things that I just didn't know where to take hold of them. Then I hit on a construction I could make, the simplest one. And then everything was magnetized; the things that didn't magnetize I threw out. But it was so much fun putting my life together, so much enlightenment. I advise everybody to do it.

AJD: We began, Miss Welty, by talking about a special kind of literary community that's founded in stories, one that brings strangers together before dispersing them for the rest of their lives. The values of that community are not inconsiderable. I seem to be making a speech, but that's really one half of a question. The other half concerns a call that we hear increasingly in our political forums.

Secretary of Education Bennett lectured last week in Columbia, and
he called for Americans to recover the virtues of a moral citizenship,
which he roots in a Judeo-Christian heritage. On the one hand is a
literary culture which is terribly private, even anonymous, on the
other, this national entity, whatever it is. Do you have any faith or
hope that the two are continuous, that they meet at some point?

EW: No. I don't think literature—I'm talking about fiction now—I
don't think it can exhort. Or it loses every bit of its reality and value.
I think it speaks to what is more deeply within, that is, the personal,
and conveys its meaning that way. And then one hopes that a person
made alert or aroused to be more sensitive to other human beings
would go on to look at things on a larger scale by himself. I wouldn't
like to read a work of fiction that I thought had an ulterior motive, to
persuade me politically. I automatically react the other way. Is that
just perversity? I think things should be written to persuade, but
openly as a column or an editorial or a speech. But perfectly on the
up and up. That's because I understand as a person, not as a motto.
This is not to say that I condescend to such writing or think of it as
less important. It's just that I don't think the two meet, except
accidentally in something in the composition of the reader. But there
are no rules. Anybody can exhort us that wants to. And I don't think
anybody should be censored or held down. But a lot of people are
open to inhibiting others. Smearing people, shutting people up. Killing
all the people who have AIDS, you know, just get rid of those who
give us trouble. It's scary the things that you read that are written in
cold blood in the paper.

PWP: It does seem that we're embarked on a new era of dogmatism.

EW: I think so too, and it scares me, it really does, but I can't let
that apply to what I do with fiction. Which does not mean that I don't
often in stories use such a character as a fictional creation who speaks
for himself *in* the story. He shows a reader what he is, out of his own
mouth. I'm not advocating, but I'm *presenting* it as honestly as I can.
My stories tried to do that sometimes in the days of the [Civil Rights]
troubles. I may not be answering your question.

AJD: It was probably more a reflection than a question. It seems
that our intellectual and cultural life attempts to create intensely
personal virtues, almost as Bloomsbury did, as Virginia Woolf, if I'm
not reaching too far afield.

EW: Yes, I know, but you see what that led to. I guess the thing I don't really like is any kind of group existing for its own sake. I could never have belonged to anything like Bloomsbury. There wasn't any danger! Everything aside—qualifications aside—I just wouldn't have flourished as a writer in a closely interknit group like that, all talking to each other. I'm just interested in people as individuals and caring for individuals so much.

Eudora Welty: A Writer's Beginnings

Patricia Wheatley / 1986

An unpublished transcription of a videotaped interview conducted by Patricia Wheatley in spring 1986 in Jackson, Mississippi, for the BBC Omnibus series documentary, *Eudora Welty:
A Writer's Beginnings*. Subsequently telecast in Great Britain
and the United States. Copies housed in the Welty Collection of
the Mississippi Department of Archives and History. Permission to publish the transcription granted by Patricia Wheatley
and the British Broadcasting Corporation. Edited by Peggy
Whitman Prenshaw.

Question: You have always had your home in Jackson as a base?

Welty: Yes. I'm very grateful for that. I'm the first generation
Mississippian in my family.

Q: Did you notice that there were conflicts or misunderstandings
when you were growing up—with your mother, coming from West Virginia?

Welty: No, just the opposite, I think. In a way we were romantically
interested in where both our parents came from, my two brothers and
myself. We loved what they told us about them. We were part of it, of
course—we went up there every summer. It was a great treasure of
the year to get to go back to the two family homes in Ohio and West
Virginia. We loved it, and of course I feel extremely grateful that I
grew up knowing there was more than one side to everything, including the Civil War. They had parents on both sides. I mean, one was
from the North, and one was from the South. That was a good lesson
to learn.

Q: So that gave you a rather more objective view than perhaps
some other Mississippians or southerners had?

Welty: Well, I think so. I think that's what they hoped, too, my
parents, but they were very gentle about it.

Q: Do you think there is something about the Civil War that
captures the writer's imagination, especially in the South?

Welty: I don't know. It doesn't capture mine. I abominate the Civil

War and everything about it, and I don't feel anything but horror and infinite regret, even just despair sometimes that it happened. I mean, despair over the tremendous loss of life, which is the way people felt about the First World War in England. It just took the flower of the whole country, North and South.

Q: What do you think the defeat did to the southern imagination?

Welty: Oh, unquestionably it dealt it a great psychological blow that's never been recovered from. And it wasn't merely the defeat; it was the long seeds of reconstruction that were so punitive and went on for such a long time. You've seen Mississippi, seen how poor it is. Well, it's an awful lot better than it was for years and years when I was growing up.

Mississippi was a battle field. Every inch of it almost was torn up with war. All the houses were burned; the schools were burned; the churches were burned, and the crops were burned. There was nothing, nothing, nothing to start with.

Q: What about when you were growing up?

Welty: Things were better, but the poverty was so great that the state never really has quite recovered from those blows, besides the punitive blows, such as having to pay a penalty for being in the South, to ship goods anywhere.

If you had lived somewhere and they had burned your house down and taken an axe to your mahogany dining room table and cut your grandfather's portrait to pieces, you would hold it personally against the North.

Q: Yankees?

Welty: Yankees. The way in Ireland after Cromwell had burned everything—the same principle of destroying. Just what we did in Vietnam. After we got through with Vietnam it looked a good deal like a photograph of Jackson after the Civil War.

Q: You've written only one story about the Civil War, haven't you?

Welty: Yes, it wasn't any good. I can't imagine what made me write that story. I mean, it's a historical story, and all I understand comes from what I myself know first hand and see first hand and comprehend first hand, not from tales. I've never looked at it again since I wrote it—because I don't know enough.

Q: What is life like for you in Jackson these days?

Welty: It's very comfortable. I've always liked living here. I have ties in many generations and friends of long standing. At my age I've lost a lot of friends—which makes it all the more precious to have those that still remain.

Q: Did you enjoy going up to the Lamar Life Building yesterday?

Welty: Yes. In the days when my father had his office there, I'm sure he used to sit there in that bay window part of the building, with all the windows open, of course. When he was ready to come home in the afternoon, I'd drive down in the car to get him and would make a U-turn in the middle of Capitol street, which anyone could do, and pull up and give our signal on the car horn. You know, like "shave and a hair cut—two bits." My father would come to the window and say he would come down. So it was very cozy.

Q: What sort of influence did your father have on you in terms of your work?

Welty: Cautionary, probably, because he knew I was pretty venturesome. I think I probably shot off a good deal in writing things for the school paper and all, and he tried to curb this in me. I think it was right he should; however, I don't think he succeeded. He wanted me to be sure that I knew what I was talking about—a good, good rule.

Q: Serious?

Welty: He was serious, yes. When he did make a joke, my mother would say, "The sense of humor men have is beyond me. Men always laugh when somebody falls down and bumps his head." Which is true. We'd go to the movies and all the men would laugh at the Keystone Cops. She was much more ebullient and volatile.

Q: What did she teach you?

Welty: I think to have the courage of your imagination, and by that I don't mean fantasies. I mean using your imagination as well as your reasoning power. Both of them believed that what you went to school for was to learn. You know they really wanted us to learn. I value that more than anything in the world. That's why they had so many books in the house. And if they had had money, they would have sent us to all kinds of good schools. They did the very best they could, and it was pretty good.

Q: They didn't have a great deal of money?

Welty: Oh no. They didn't have anything but what my father made, you see. Of course, back before the 1920s there wasn't much money

anyway. We never knew whether we had money or didn't in our
family.

Q: Can you describe what your days were like when you were
growing up?

Welty: I lived in the family house on North Congress Street, right
across the street from the school. It was very friendly. We used to
play out at night all the time with little steam boats made out of shoe
boxes, with windows cut out in the shape of the sun, moon and stars,
and colored tissue paper on them, with a candle inside. We'd run up
and down the sidewalk pretending to be steamboats on the Mississippi
River. That was so romantic, you know, that first dark and lots of
homemade games. We had a sand pile and a tree to climb. Just very
simple. We took long rides all the time in the country. We had one of
the early automobiles.

My father was always for science and the advancement of science.
My mother did not want an automobile; she wanted a horse. But we
got the car.

Q: What kind of child were you? Were you a shy child?

Welty: I was shy, but I went all the time, and I loved school. We
also had lots of little girl playmates, you know, paper-doll age, and
we had lots of parties in those days. So it was a normal childhood,
I'm sure. I went to Sunday School every Sunday.

Q: What happened when you started growing up? Can you describe
that period when you moved away, and then why you came back?

Welty: I had agreed that I would go to college in Mississippi for two
years if possibly I could go away for the next two. I wanted to go a
piece away. So I'd been to the University of Wisconsin and graduated
there before I went to Columbia.

My father had taken me with him on business trips when he went
to New York and we would go to the theater. He was crazy about the
theater, just like me—or I was just like him. The year at Columbia
was the most marvelous year. For instance, I saw Noel Coward and
Gertrude Lawrence in *Private Lives*. It was a marvelous introduction
to New York City, although it soon ran into the Depression and
sadness everywhere.

Q: So what brought you back to Jackson?

Welty: I wanted to do some writing on the side and yet earn my
living, on the advice of my father—good advice. I wanted to get a job

in New York, and I did get one, but it didn't work out. There was some skullduggery in it—I won't go into that. It left me in the lurch, you know, with an apartment taken and theater tickets bought and everything.

Q: What was it?

Welty: It was an advertising job I got through Columbia. I worked in the office for two weeks and then they said that I would not do. They had promised the job, and so on the advice of a friend I reported it to Columbia. I knew I'd done the work well because they'd used it. Columbia investigated and found they'd been going for two years that way, getting people from the college to work a certain length of time and then telling them that they wouldn't be good enough. I was so disillusioned. I thought it was so easy to go up there and get a job, that I could just do it. Well, that set me back on the heel, and I was completely out of money.

Q: So that drove you home?

Welty: In a way. But my father was also ill and I came home. He died in 1931 at the age of fifty-two. I stayed here and got a job at the radio station, which was brand new—another thing my father had dreamed of having because he believed in communications. I'm glad I did because then I learned in the course of my work here something about where I'd come from, which I hadn't paid any attention to before.

Q: So if you hadn't been cheated by that advertising company Jackson might never have seen you again?

Welty: I don't think what I wanted to do would have worked out. I had a dream of working all day, going to the theater every night, seeing all my friends, going out dancing, and writing in my spare time. You can imagine, that would never have worked.

Q: You'd have had a lot of fun.

Welty: I would have had a lot of fun, but I couldn't have done what I really wanted to do. It was my secret, you see, that I wanted to write. And I knew it was something I had to teach myself.

Q: How did you go about teaching yourself?

Welty: I wrote stories and sent them off to magazines whose addresses I got out of the library. I submitted the stories all over the country, and I learned something from rejection slips or from letters that encouraged me, or from any communication from the outside world that showed someone had read it. They'd say, "Send us something else," and they'd get it by return mail—too much, I'm sure. It took me a long time, but that was a good way to learn because it was remote and yet like handing a paper to the teacher, you know, to get a grade on it.

I think it worked out well for me that I always knew I would need to earn my living and also found out quite plainly that I couldn't count on earning it by writing stories. I never expected to, but it made it really nice that things fitted into two different categories. I could earn my living here, and yet not damage anything I wanted to write, not interfere with it, even though I was using words in both cases with public relations [with the Works Progress Administration] or journalism or whatever job I got—book reviewing later on. That is, I could make enough to pay for some time and then I could write awhile. I still have done that by going to colleges and lecturing. That would buy time for a couple of months, or a month at least. I have never really been alarmed about being absolutely broke—have never been in danger of starving, unless I lived in New York.

Q: But now you're very successful.

Welty: I've had some good, good times. Of course, it comes and goes, so that there's no possible median. The *New Yorker* pays well, and they took a bunch of stories of mine after many years of not touching one. I owe a lot of that to William Maxwell, my editor at the *New Yorker,* who besides being a marvelous editor was a writer himself, one that I loved and a very good friend, one of my closest friends.

Q: Would you talk about some of the places you have written about? What about Rodney?

Welty: I'd read about it in some history of Mississippi in the days when it was a port on the Mississippi River, reached only by water, of course. It was bigger than Natchez at the time. They said ships from Liverpool used to dock there regularly. . . . Well, I went down to see what was there, and there was almost nothing because the river had moved three miles away from it. It was really fascinating to find the old graveyard was stuck on a sort of shelf above the town. Most of the people had moved down together so they wouldn't have to walk up the hill.

Q: And it has inspired two stories?

Welty: Well, it did *The Robber Bridegroom,* I know. And I did write some other stories, I think.

Q: "At the Landing."

Welty: Not a very good story. I haven't read it in a long time. I didn't feel too satisfied with what I was able to do with it, but anyway it was about that place.

Q: What about people, because those are really your subject?

Welty: They are my subject, and in a way I think in writing I use place as a necessary frame that I set around things and also a platform on which a dramatic experience can take place. It has its exit and entrance possibilities. I try to use place as a sort of embodiment of the emotion I am trying to convey, which I think it truly is. You know, Rodney would breed a certain kind of emotion down there, that's perfectly legitimate. I try to show it.

Q: What's your favorite kind of community to write about?

Welty: A small courthouse town would be my ideal because it's the center of activity of that particular place. The people who are there usually have some gumption, some work to do that gives them a life of their own. There are visible and describable human relationships in a courthouse town. There're a school teacher and a mayor and a newspaper editor; there are all the trials, the wonderful murder trials. We have good murders in Mississippi.

Q: Still?

Welty: Very notorious. Maybe any place does, but we have had some extremely romantic murders in Mississippi. A lot of people would write a book about them, but their descendants are still living, and you can't hurt people by telling about their murderous ancestor. . . . Southerners are supposed to be—and I think it's true—very passionate people, that is, they give vent to their emotions often without careful thought. I suppose a lot of other people do, too.

Q: You said that there are some very good murders in Mississippi?

Welty: One such happened a number of years ago. A lady was arrested and tried for the murder of her mother, part of whose body was found, but not all. She was convicted but sent to the asylum, to the state hospital in Jackson. While there she played bridge with some of the other people who were confined to the hospital, which speaks for the kind of social feeling that can be engendered anywhere, you know. One day, according to the story, one of the foursome suddenly threw down her hand and said, "Not another card will I play until you tell me what you did with the rest of your mother." There's just a relish of stories like that. I don't think that's too bad.

Q: There's a tradition that the South is very well known for its storytelling. Can you tell me about that?

Welty: I think it's true, and I think it comes of another thing that comes from the remoteness of the South and the family feeling of the South and how many families live with almost nobody living anywhere near them. They depend on the family for their entertainment and their well being and knowledge and so on.

My mother had five brothers and they used to tell all kind of tales about life in West Virginia, and when they'd come down here or up there they would sit around for ages telling stories. One of the features of it is that everybody already knows the stories, of course. They just want to hear them repeated the way you like to see an old Charlie Chaplin movie. The familiarity is part of the charm—and the presence of the family itself is part of its pride, you know.

Q: Is storytelling dying?

Welty: I don't know, and I'm not in a position to know. Really all I know is my own generation, though I do go around to colleges a lot. So many students say to me, "You talk about a sense of place and a sense of belonging. What do you do if you don't have a place and you don't have a sense of belonging?" And they're conscious of that. They've never lived in the same town, never stayed in the same school for more than a certain length of time. Never have the same friends from year to year. To me it sounds like some form of hell, but it's their real life, and they're rightly concerned about what the significance of it is to them, especially when they want to be writers.

Still, I think people always find a way to write and always have something to write about. It's human nature, and everybody is full of imagination and venturesomeness. I don't think you could kill out the novel and short story.

Q: What was life like in Jackson in the 1920s and 1930s when you were growing up, going out and about in the town?

Welty: It was still a small town but we had a very good time. There was so much to do, and we loved things coming to town—in the theater and so on. The Century Theater, then an old opera house, would bring many Broadway plays on their way from Memphis to

New Orleans. They had to spend the night somewhere so they stopped in Jackson and gave a performance.

There was a grand record store then on Berry Street which had what were then called race records, that is, records all-black artists made really for themselves. Of course, all the people that liked jazz used to haunt that little store down there, and that way we learned about what black artists were coming to Jackson to perform, such as Bessie Smith, who came to the Alamo movie house on Berry Street, the black movie house. We happened to know the owner of the theater and we—there were two couples—managed to get seats. They didn't mind our coming because, you know, we knew one another. It was intended for an all-black audience, but we went and it was simply glorious. I'll never forget when she came out on the stage, this absolutely all-embracing, big, happy-looking woman. She was a beautiful woman in an apricot satin dress, you know, just opening her arms to the world. She sang and sang and sang, never could get enough encores. It was just wonderful.

Q: Was she like that for a white audience as well?

Welty: Most black performers who came through here gave two shows, one for a white audience and one for a black, but I don't believe she gave a white performance. Surely I would have been there. I have no recollection of it.

Q: Where were you sitting at the performance?

Welty: In the peanut roost, that is, the balcony. Just where we made black people sit in those days when they came to our movie houses. We were glad to be allowed in; it was a real, real compliment.

Q: They didn't mind you going there?

Welty: No, we just explained that we loved her and wanted to hear her. We knew the man who owned the theater and he asked—they said it was all right.

Q: What was Farish Street like then?

Welty: It was always the black business street and had everything on it from churches to pawn shops to small retail stores. It also had the best ice cream store in town. We used to go down there and park outside some of the places where they were having wonderful dances just so we could hear the music. I don't think we would have been allowed in to dance, but we just sat in the car and could hear the band playing through upstairs open windows and see their silhouettes dancing up there. We were invited often to church services, not services exactly but special occasions, like a Bird Pageant, which I photographed. I don't ever remember anyone having a feeling of exploitation or condescension. Usually it was someone you knew who told you about it and said it would be fine if you'd like to come. You went in a perfectly ordinary way.

Q: What about later when the Civil Rights Movement started?

Welty: Well, later things got to be very self conscious on both sides. There are five colleges situated here, black ones and white ones—now integrated, of course. Some of the colleges were the first places that voluntarily integrated—Millsaps College, for instance, a white liberal arts college. I had often been invited to go and speak at the black colleges, and we all knew one another. I had friends on the faculty, and some of the students there, the dramatic students, were members of New Stage. There was a considerable give and take there, but these relationships got to be rather frozen, you know, just sort of stuck where they were. Everybody knew that sooner or later things would resume and warm up, but it was difficult, both for blacks and whites, and very, very complex.

It was a complex time and a very sensitive time; everybody's feelings were right under the skin. Now things have changed so completely that you never think of those days, and I don't think there's any kind of open sore anywhere that I can see, and I'm used to moving among black people the same as white, both in Jackson and in many of the colleges where I go all over the country.

Q: Although if you come to Mississippi not knowing Mississippi and look around the cities and the towns, you see that the black poverty is extraordinary.

Welty: And so is white poverty, in many parts. They're trying to do things about it, make recoveries as well as they can. We have a number of black public officials now, but we don't have any money. We are the poorest in the country and have the lowest educational record—they are tied together. Much work is being done, but it certainly is a slow process, and it shows.

Q: You have said you shouldn't crusade as a novelist, but presumably you have a sense of morality.

Welty: If I didn't have that, I wouldn't be a short story writer. I don't like to editorialize. I like to read what good people say who know what they're talking about, as I do when I read the *New York Times* for my favorite columnists, James Reston and Flora Lewis and Tom Wicker and Russell Baker. I thought many things written by novelists who did editoralize were poor work fictionally. A good cause and a good warm heart, but not very well written.

Q: What about religion?

Welty: What do you mean "what about it"? It's around.

Q: How were you brought up? Were you brought up in a religious household?

Welty: Not particularly, compared to most of my friends. I think everybody in my family feels as I do. I have a reverence toward, well, you can call it God or something over and above—but I don't like to be preached to any more than I like to be editorialized at. My parents were both brought up in very religious households. Maybe it's a reaction—both of them had preachers in the family. My mother was brought up in the Methodist church, and my father, too. His father led the choir in the Methodist church in Ohio in his little town. And I was brought up going to the Methodist Sunday School, for which I'm glad, and learned the Bible, which I love to read.

Q: When you were at Sunday School, you sang hymns?

Welty: Yes, we sang hymns all the time. I know them all.

Q: Like?

Welty: "Work for the Night is Coming," "Bringing in the Sheaves," "Throw Out the Lifeline, Someone Is Sinking Today"—these are all old Methodist hymns I think the Wesleys brought over from England. I've been told that many of them are based on good rollicking old English dance tunes from the Elizabethan days. That's why they're so jolly, although the words are pretty frightening.

Q: Religious temperament seems very deep in the South.

Welty: That's true, and, besides, a lot of them came here as dissenters and so on. Many of our early settlers were people who came over here for that reason. During the Civil War when all the schools were burned down, the churches were usually the ones that raised money to educate children. That's why so many schools and colleges in the South are church supported—because no one else could start building back an educational system when there was nothing on the ground to go to school to. Most of the good colleges are church supported, though in the best of them the church does not attempt to direct the teaching or control any of it.

Q: What about religion in the small towns in Mississippi? There are all these rival churches, aren't there?

Welty: Well, that's what I always think of them because you always see them on opposite sides of the road, as if they were crouched ready to jump down one another's throats. Usually, it's the Methodists and the Baptists. They're the most prolific. Presbyterians next. Now there's also a rising Roman Catholic population in the South.

Q: Earlier you were saying that in a courthouse town relationships are very visible and easy to describe. And people are very aware of their roles, aren't they? Can we go to Edna Earle Ponder, who seems to me to be very aware of her social position?

Welty: Well, she would be right at the top, you know, because their family was so well known and a lot of it, of course, is heredity. Everybody knew each other's families so nothing could really be hidden.

Q: Could you introduce this lady—who she is and where she lives?

Welty: Well, Miss Edna Earle Ponder is a spinster who runs a hotel called the Beulah Hotel in Clay, Mississippi, a small courthouse town. It's a hotel that's situated, as most of them were, right across the street from the courthouse. When the crowd comes to town to attend court, circuit court, everybody there has to eat dinner at the hotel. They all just get up in a body, including those on trial and the lawyers on both sides, and come over and eat at the hotel, and then move back. It's where all the drummers, the travelling salesmen, come, so really it is the center of life. She runs this, but what she mainly wants to do in life is to take care of her uncle, Uncle Daniel Ponder. He's difficult to describe, but he's an old gentleman—they come from an old family of landowners and so on—and is a simple sort of person. I guess in some places he would have been locked up because he didn't know how to get along in society. What he wants to do is give them everything. He wants to give away everything. She knows that he must be protected against himself.

So the story is about that situation. We see Uncle Daniel through her eyes, which would not be through the eyes of just everybody. Also, we see Edna Earle through our eyes because she's the narrator and what I wanted to do in the story was to show them both in this dramatic plot.

Q: How do you do that? You seem to have used the first person narrative several times.

Welty: I like to do that because it's a way to let a character tell a reader what they're like without their knowledge. I don't mean behind their backs but just hearing it in their own words. We see how they look at things.

It wasn't anything monumental, but it was a story of a human predicament, of good will operating without too much common sense.

Q: Which gives rise to both pain and humor?

A: And comedy. Edna Earle evidently has someone by the lapels who's come in to register at the hotel and can't get away, you know, like the wedding guest. She assumes you want to know everything about everybody in town, and starting on that basis, she pushes you right into the middle of it. I loved writing it.

The only way Uncle Daniel exists for me is through her, through her eyes. Really what I know about him is what she says, and I know what she would say about him. I never hesitated about what she would say—I knew exactly.

Q: I was thinking about that leap you make, actually getting into the skin.

Welty: You have to do that in any story, but you have to be experienced and knowledgeable to be on safe ground. I mean I couldn't leap into a Dutchman riding on a yak through Tibet because I don't know either one, either the yak or the Dutchman or Tibet, but I can do it where I know everybody, or the kind of person it is, or the kind of place. The place tells you a lot—everything.

Q: Thinking about the courthouse town where *The Ponder Heart* is set, I want to ask you about the Mendenhall Hotel.

Welty: The Mendenhall Hotel is just one we ran across in my family a good while ago. We went down the highway to go swimming in the Strong River, which is at D'lo, Mississippi. It's a strange little river that is cold and full of fast-moving water, not like any other river in Mississippi. When we went, we found the Mendenhall Hotel close by and went in and ate there. I believe it's been in the same family for quite a long time, and it's typical of a small hotel in a small courthouse town. It fills the function of being always there when court is in session for people to come down the hill or across the street and have dinner. And many people are frequent stoppers there on the way, and it's just fun to go to.

It's not what the Basic Eight used to go to [a group of male and female friends in Jackson during the 1930s and later]. That was an old mineral wells watering place north of here, which was in a giant kind of frame structure of a building, where you could go and spend a week or the night. You drank water from the wells for your health—that was going on all over America about the turn of the century. It had a huge dining room that was very festive, but it burned.

Q: But the Mendenhall Hotel?

Welty: It wasn't the same kind of hotel because this [Allison's Wells] was really like a small country resort where people went to stay—it was more social.

Q: What about the Mendenhall Hotel in connection with *The Ponder Heart?*

Welty: There really isn't any connection except that in *The Ponder Heart* there is an imaginary hotel in an imaginary courthouse town. The Mendenhall Hotel could be an example of such a thing, but it was not modelled on it. It was the sort of place that the Beulah Hotel probably would have been in *The Ponder Heart*.

Q: Would you talk about *Losing Battles?* You had a huge cast there.

Welty: I had a tremendous cast. I knew I'd been getting too deeply into introspective stories, people anguishing about things, and I was telling what they thought instead of what they did. So to give myself a refreshment I decided I'd try to write a story—little knowing it would be a novel—that was all action and dialogue, to see if I could convey everything outwardly the way a play does. Never once did I get inside a human being in that story, except for the little boy at the end. I couldn't help it because I was crazy about him, and he was all by himself, so I got inside his thoughts. Otherwise, it's all on the outside.

Everything about that novel was deliberate. I chose the poorest part of Mississippi, the poorest town, the Depression, and the poorest kind of family. I split everybody up, every possession, and all they had was one another. And then I brought all of them together for a family reunion and just let them go to tell stories, the way it is often done at family reunions. It was so much fun, but hard, too, to try to do so many things in one scene. I took a long time doing it, but I loved it.

Q: How did *Losing Battles* get so big?

Welty: I think because I worked on it over too long a time. There were complications in my life at that time, and I only had pieces of time to work in. Whereas I usually revise as I go and tear up the revised part, in this case I would revise by writing a new scene and throwing it in a box, not going back and comparing it. So I just accumulated a terrible amount of material. I could have written it in four or five different ways, you know, showing them doing this, talking about that, equally revealing. I was writing it by ear and I could hear only too much.

Q: Did you try the book out on friends as you were writing it?

Welty: No, I was afraid to. What I was really afraid of was that over the period time, which was eight or ten years, I guess, was that the spark had died in it so the light would have gone out. It didn't seem to me that it had, but I wasn't sure I could trust it. But I had time; I rewrote it all from the beginning, that is, I wrote it as a finished thing, throwing out and shortening. I just prayed like a good Methodist that it still had the spark of life, but I didn't know until I sent it to my agent and he said it did have a spark of life. And I sent it to William Maxwell, who helped me to get some of it typed with a typist from *The New Yorker.* Everybody was helping me and pulling for me, but that didn't mean it was going to be good, you know.

Q: But it was.

Welty: But it turned out that it was. It was all right; it did what I hoped it would do.

Q: What sense of Faulkner did you have when you were writing in the early days?

Welty: I was always aware of his enormous existence to the north of me. The hard part in my case is that when I was coming along and wanted to read him his books were all out of print. I had to go to New Orleans, to second-hand stores and different places and pick up copies of his books. None of them were in the library, of course, not in Mississippi. They didn't think much of him here. They thought he was putting a bad face on Mississippi, and he was in bad repute. I did get hold of his books and liked his work very much.

It never occurred to me I'd ever see him, but later I did get to meet him when I went to Oxford to visit some friends who were also his lifelong friends. At a dinner party for about six people he and his wife were guests. That was the ideal way to meet him, in a setting of his old friends and mine, some friends I've known forever, but in different places. He was very kind to me and invited me to come to see him. He took me sailing in his sail boat and couldn't have been nicer, but we never had any kind of talk about the literary world.

Q: Had he read your work?

Welty: He read one because he wrote me a letter once from Hollywood. He had read my little book *The Robber Bridegroom* a long time before, and he wrote me a letter and said he'd read this. He said, "Who are you? How old are you? Where do you live?" You know, he said he liked it and that if there were any way he could ever help me in Hollywood to let him know. I was just galvanized when I read the letter.

Q: Do you have authors that you are passionate about?

Welty: Oh, yes. The ones I return to again and again. Well—I love Chekhov, I think, above everyone in the world, and keep going back to read him.

Q: Why Chekhov?

Welty: I think he has all humanity in what he writes, and I like him because he is such a complete artist. He lets everything speak for itself and doesn't harangue anyone. He lets everybody—characters— reveal themselves in the most tender and truthful and succinct way. He's just a lesson to our writers, but I don't read him for that. I read him because I love him, his work. And Turgenev, too, almost the same reasons. And Elizabeth Bowen.

Q: Going back to *Losing Battles*—can you tell me who Miss Julia Mortimer is?

Welty: She was a schoolteacher, the one who attempted to educate all the people in a little one-room school house in this poor little hill community in Mississippi. She has already died in this story, and there is a funeral being held for her, which is a rival occasion to the reunion being held in the family. They begin to talk about Miss Julia and how she had tried to teach them. They were pretty proud of the fact that they could withstand her pretty well. Not too many people were going to tell them what to do, but yet they respected her deeply in their heart of hearts. What connects the two stories is that Miss

Julia's protege, who also wanted to be a schoolteacher, is the young bride of the son of the family of the reunion. She, too, is ambitious—I don't know whether that's a losing battle or not, but somehow I think things will work out all right.

The odd thing is that when I first began the story I thought it was just a story about the family. I hadn't invented Miss Julia Mortimer, but as I kept going she just moved in on the story. The family didn't have anything, and they thought they could manage without too much assistance from the outside; they were independent, like many people. And so I put Miss Julia's character in, which I wanted to gradually move in and then just sort of shadow over everything, not to obscure but really to illuminate the other people. She really is the heroine of the novel. If I had written it and sent it in right at the beginning, she might never have come on. Maybe it was the long gestation I had that produced her.

Q: Do people ever think that they recognize a character in your books?

Welty: They do if I've used a name. But in fact I can't write a story if I use a name that I associate with a person. Sometimes I do use a name that I think is just a fine name, and people that I don't even remember knowing come up and say, "What do you mean using my name in your story?"

Names are in public domain. I collect names a lot from reading the paper because it's so important in a story to get a name that conveys just the kind of family and stratum that you come from, the kind of people that name their children this, that, and the other. I learned this from reading William Faulkner. He can tell a world by somebody's name. You know just what part of the country they could come from, and although I don't expect the reader to know that, I know it.

When people don't have very much money at all or much to give their children, as in *Losing Battles,* they think they can at least give them a pretty name. Lots of very fancy names have been given to the people who don't have very much. I learned that when I went to Mississippi State College for Women—every possible part of Mississippi society was there, and every county was represented. And, of course, I have a fancy name, but I was named for my grandmother.

Q: What does Eudora mean?

Welty: It's "good gift" in Greek. "Eu" is good, and "Dora" is gift.

Theodora is gift of God. My mother told me this when I was a child, when I cried because nobody could understand my name and they laughed at me for having such a funny name. I always had to spell it everywhere I went. My mother said it's a beautiful name—"You're named after my mother." I think they named people things like that in Virginia more than they did in the [Deep] South. They often gave Greek names at a certain period.

Q: Your mother was a schoolteacher. There are a number of schoolteachers in your fiction.

Welty: There are, and some are based on things my mother told me. There was a line in *Losing Battles,* several lines from *Losing Battles* from that teacher, that came from my mother, who taught in a poor mountain community in the hills of West Virginia. When she took her first job at the age of about fifteen, when her father died and she needed to go out and help with the family, she got a job teaching in a one-room school house. Some people older than she were in the school, and it happened just like the first day of my heroine's teaching at school. All the children came and their fathers came with them to see what kind of teacher it was—and if she would stand up to them. My mother said that nobody would get away with different things there, and she said, "I see some of the fathers here." Oh yes, she said she would have to whip the children if they, you know, set the school on fire when they were building the stove or refused to go out for the water or such things. And she said, "I see some fathers here, and if they would care to contest this, I'd be glad to give them a whipping, too," says this fifteen-year old child. And they respected her then. They not only felt she was a pretty good teacher, but she could handle them, too.

Q: Your mother married, though. Did she ever feel that she'd sacrificed her independence?

Welty: She kept right on with her own children, I think, and she taught them. She gave books to the schools here. She wanted to be sure they had a good library to read in. Sometimes she gave my books to it, and I cried and she went back and got some of them back, some that she thought I'd outgrown.

Q: What about Miss Eckhart?

Welty: The music teacher. Well, I think she was a sort of frequent occurrence in the state in small towns when often foreign ladies, for reasons of their own, alone in the world, would settle almost for no reason in a small town and begin to teach something they knew, like music or elocution or drawing. In Jackson, when teachers came here to do things like that, they were rather mysteries in the town. They had no connection with anyone there, but they were artists. That's really what they were.

After World War I we had teachers who appeared here from France, and the stories used to be that they had been jilted by an American doughboy and had come to this country only to find not what they expected. I used to hear that all through my childhood of teachers in college. I don't know if any of those stories were true, but they came from somewhere for some reason. They weren't born here.

Q: You once said that in a sense Miss Eckhart could be you?

Welty: What I was trying to say was I identified in ways that had to do with the interior life, you know, and in that way I thought I could identify with Miss Eckhart, that I was trying to pursue art and communicate in that way. I meant nothing about her life.

Miss Eckhart was trying to communicate with Virgie, whom she thought had the potential for going on in the same way. In my own case, teachers have given me that sense from time to time, which made all the difference to me in my feeling for the language, literature, writing—not for music because I'm not talented in that. But in "June Recital" I had to have an art that could be described from the outside, I mean a performing art. You don't perform when you write; you just sit down.

Q: In *The Optimist's Daughter* you write a lot about your mother. Can you tell me about what you were doing there?

Welty: Well, Becky is not my mother; the whole story was different. My mother suffered from a long illness, which is not what Becky had. I mean none of that was true to my own case except that in the matter of the eye my mother always had problems with the eye. She never had a detached retina, but she did have eye operations and she did lose her sight in the end. What I gave the judge was really what my mother went through when she had a cataract operation. In those days you had to lie absolutely stone still for weeks and weeks, which is what the judge had to do. That is, I wasn't telling my mother's story but I gave Becky part of my mother's past. None of the story between Judge McKelva and Becky had anything to do with my parents. My

father was not at all Judge McKelva, who was an old man. My father
died when he was fifty-two and was not a lawyer or a southern
landowner or anything like that.

Q: Why did you put those elements in?

Welty: I used pieces and parts of different people. When I want to
show something, I use something I know, but that doesn't mean my
character is that person. There was a good deal more of Becky, or my
mother in Becky, than I normally use in any character. I gave her
many of the things in my mother's life, but her death was not Becky's
death, and she never distrusted my father. You know, none of that is
true. I wasn't writing it to be a story of my parents. I was writing a
story and used my parents—one of them, not the other one.

Q: Your mother had died recently? Were you in a sense resolving
something there?

Welty: I think I was. The feeling of the daughter who can't help,
you know, who wants to understand and help—it's removed in different stages and in different parts of the story. My emotions are in that
book, my true emotions. You can't make those up, don't want to
make them up. And I was writing about people who were just as
serious and passionate as my parents, but my parents were not
enacted in the story.

I've heard there's been a scholar, maybe more than one, who's
been going up to West Virginia looking in court records, trying to find
out about my mother and her father, who was a lawyer and left
records in the court. About how many days he was sick, and other
things, as if I have tried to cover up something in *The Optimist's
Daughter*. As if I were writing the story of my mother with cover-
ups, you know, which is really an insult to my mother and to the
story—to the principles of fiction. I get so that I hate to write anything
that people can associate with anything that's true because then they
think that what isn't true in it is something I'm concealing, whereas
it's omitted because it has nothing to do with the story, you know.

Q: With that work of art [*The Optimist's Daughter*], what are you
trying to express of what you know?

Welty: I'm trying to put almost everything in it that has to do with
real life as I see it, what I've been able to learn, and what experience
has taught me. Really the meaning of experience, not in a preachy
way, or an abstract way. I mention the difference between some of

the characters and others—Fay, for instance, who doesn't know the meaning of anything that's happened to her. She lives through something, but she doesn't know what it means. That's just like Purgatory, not to know, not to understand what's happened to you, or the real sense of the relationship between oneself and other people, the feeling of love, the act of memory. I try not to put things in abstract terms in the novel—but I suppose that's a way of saying what I tried to do in the novel. But I don't think in those terms when I'm writing; I think in fiction. Like, Laurel would do this, not "a person" would do so and so. That's the way I understand.

If people ask if your work is not exactly what happened to you or your parents, as if that's a clue for them, well, they've missed it. So, I'd like that to be clear.

Q: So by writing that fiction, you were aiming at a general truth, using things that you knew?

Welty: I was trying to reach it.

Q: Did it teach you in return?

Welty: It certainly did. Both the fact of it and the act of it taught me, and by being able to make it as eloquent as I could of its own self—nothing I imposed on it—it taught me a great deal. It was a very painful story to me. I had heard my mother tell it [the account of her accompanying her dying father to Baltimore], and I could never have told it to anyone else. It was a terrible story. But when I wrote it this way, I didn't even think about the pain in myself because it was serving its use in a piece of work that had a lot of what I felt in it and wanted to say. That wasn't why I did it, but that was a by-product. I did feel a little more peaceful about it, but I don't write things to get them out of my system.

Q: How do you start imagining a character?

Welty: It's hard to tell where imagining characters starts, whether it does come from something you have observed in real life ten years ago, or something you may have dreamed last night about a person, some little detail. You don't know where it begins, but all of a sudden what happens is a connection between that and something you are writing. There's a click where two pieces fit together, and that's when the electric charge happens. I don't think you can sit down and say, "I am going to write a certain story. Now, how can I use so and so?"

Q: When you were young, would you imagine things about people that you saw in the street? Would you sit and watch people?

Welty: I did watch people, and I put what I saw together, probably, with fairy tales or things I'd heard. I remember there was an old man that used to pass our house on Congress Street carrying a croaker sack—that's just a big, woven sack that everybody carried things around in—over his shoulder. I used to wonder what it was he was carrying. And we had a maid who worked for us who told us that if we were bad he came by to carry off children in that sack of his. How do I know where the imagination started? Or whether that detail came from the sack? Or what? It all goes together, doesn't matter where it came from.

Q: You wrote *Losing Battles* at the same time as *The Optimist's Daughter,* didn't you?

Welty: I started *Losing Battles* a good while before I wrote *The Optimist's Daughter.* In fact, it was my mother's long illness for which I stopped writing *Losing Battles,* but then I began thinking about *The Optimist's Daughter,* and I wrote it as a long story and finished it. It was published then in *The New Yorker,* but I knew I wanted to go over it again when I felt calmer about everything before I published it as a book. So I waited. I think *Losing Battles* was published first and then *The Optimist's Daughter;* it was sort of in tandem and yet overlapping two completely different kinds of novels. And written under stress. I knew that in order to think clearly I should give them time to sort of settle in my mind and then go back.

Q: In distress because of your mother's illness?

Welty: Things to do with it and so on.

Q: Did your brother die the same year as your mother?

Welty: The same week, actually. Neither one knew the other was so terribly ill. Both of my brothers had rheumatoid arthritis of a very virulent kind and died young. They were both healthy, athletes, and so on. My younger brother died first, which just about killed my mother. The youngest in the family. And then my older brother died. He was in a hospital here and she was in a hospital in Yazoo City, and I was going back and forth trying to keep each one from knowing the other was so terribly ill.

Q: That must have been a terrible strain.

Welty: Well, it was. Almost unreal, sort of mysterious the way things kind of converged at one time. I'm glad neither one knew the other was ill, that ill. We had been a very close family, and when my father died so young, that was so hard on our mother. I realize now she was a widow in her forties. Of course, I thought both my parents were old—my father was fifty-two. I don't know how much comfort I could have been to my mother with my lack of realization of what she must have felt. In addition to her grief, her married life was ending at such an early age. I don't know how she bore that. They were very close and devoted.

Q: Would you like to have been married?

Welty: Would I what?

Q: Would you like to have been married?

Welty: I think so. I like love and affection and friendship—it just never did work out that it'd happen. But I would have been very glad if it had.

Q: Do you think you would have written in the same way?

Welty: I don't know. Probably so. I have been told by different writers that I had it easy because I had no husband and child, as if that were a reason, you know. Maybe that's true, I can't tell. But I feel I've had a full life, not only with my work but with so many friendships, enduring ones, in my life. I've been very fortunate in my family and, well, in everything.

Q: What's it like being your age?

Welty: I keep forgetting it, that's the trouble. You really don't realize it. I went to the eye doctor this morning—he called me up and said I really was supposed to come over and get my eyes checked. He meant because of my age—to check for glaucoma and cataracts. I've always had fine vision, but he'd been checking it regularly just to be sure. He said I really ought to remember that I need the checkup, and I was suitably humiliated.

I forget I'm this old. I notice it in lots of ways, but the only bad part is the death of friends, people I've known fifty years and am used to seeing all the time. I have close friends that I've made in different places, and those things hurt. That's the worst.

Q: So how do you resolve that? In a sense, with reading *The Optimist's Daughter* I felt that you'd somehow come to terms with death.

Q: I suppose I had, but I was too young to come to terms when I wrote that. That was what I was trying to do, of course. You can come to terms, but you have to keep coming to terms because each loss is a new loss and a different kind of loss. I'm very grateful for having had all those friendships.

What happens is that when people return letters to me that I've written to them or [to a relative who had died], I can't bear to open the boxes or look at them. Of course, I've got all theirs, too, somewhere. I keep thinking, "What am I going to do with all these things?" There are people's lives in those letters. I don't know what one does. I don't want anybody reading my letters. I agree with W. H. Auden they should be torn up, but of course what happened to him is they didn't carry out his wishes and they did it anyway. Not that I've anything to conceal; it's just that privacy is the whole basis on which letters are written to and from anyone, and it just doesn't make sense to me.

[In the following segment Welty discusses her Pinehurst Street house in Jackson.]

Welty: Our family moved from North Congress Street to Pinehurst Street when this house was built in 1924-25. It went up the same year as the Lamar Life Building, and with the same architect.

Q: It's not your average southern house, is it?

Welty: True, I think at the time we built it, it was the only one in Jackson with a basement. My father was from the North, and people had basements and so on. And we had a furnace in the basement and central heating that wasn't all that common. We never had had it before. We had open fireplaces in every room on North Congress Street. We also have a double door, a vestibule, which nobody else that I know of had. Two doors that guard you against cold winds.

Q: Cold winds in Mississippi?

Welty: Well, we've got them in the winter time.

Q: What's it like living here?

Welty: Living here's very pleasant. I like being in the house where nobody else has ever lived but my own family, even though it's lonely being the only person left. But I never have felt lonely here—perhaps it should be lonely.

I live all over the house. It was built for a family—all the rooms open into something else, and you don't feel shut off. It's not nearly as quiet as it was when we moved out here, when we had Rural Free

Delivery with our mail and little wooden bridges crossing a creek down there that now has been concreted over. It was different, but I still like it. Jackson has grown up far beyond here, but we are a sort of little enclave where there hasn't been much change in this neighborhood.

Q: What kind of neighborhood is it?

Welty: Well, it's mostly people like ourselves, middle class families and nice houses, but not grand houses such as appeared when oil was discovered in Jackson and people built rather grand houses further out in the country. It just suited us, still suits me.

Q: Your Jitney Jungle [grocery store/supermarket] matches your house.

Welty: That's right, it was in old English. I don't suppose either one—the Jitney Jungle or we—ever thought about that. I think it was the first little shopping center that came up here.

Q: Can you tell me about what it's like living here, being so well known?

Welty: It's not too different because I've always lived here, so people have known my family and me all my life. Of course, I do know people that I hadn't known before, people connected with all the colleges and professional people who have moved here. I like meeting new people in addition to my old friends.

The arts have taken quite a hold on Jackson. We have all sorts of things here that we never had before, such as the International Ballet competitions every four years. The best ballet dancers from the whole globe come here and have their competitions over a period of several weeks, and the classes and practice rehearsals are made free to the public. You can go and watch the finest ballet dancers in the world going through their paces here. We've an international jury who comes—it's very exciting for a town like Jackson to have it.

Q: Can you tell me what connection you have with the New Stage theater?

Welty: New Stage Theater was organized as a breakaway theater—I was in on it from the beginning. It broke away from the Jackson Little Theater because there was a small group of younger people and people who wanted to try more inventive, imaginative, even experimental things in the theater. I was pleased to be invited in on it from the beginning. We set up a theater in a small Seventh Day Adventist

Church house that was to have been abandoned—at the other end of
town—and made it into a theater and stayed there until, literally, the
roof just about fell in. We kept it going as long as possible, and then
we moved to a bigger and rather more solid theater.

Q: They've performed some of your novels and stories?

Welty: New Stage has done adaptations of a number of my stories,
and they've re-written plays that have been produced on Broadway.
It's been fun to deal with them both on New Stage and for Mississippi
Educational Television. It has been very helpful to me, by the way,
although I had nothing to do with the rewriting. I leave it to those who
know, but it's been helpful to see what happened. They've been most
generous and sympathetic and understanding toward my work, and
it's meant a lot to me all through the years. Jane [Reid-Petty] was
Edna Earle in *The Ponder Heart* and Charlotte [Capers] earlier was
Edna Earle in *The Ponder Heart* when the Little Theater put it on,
many years before.

Q: Can you tell me about your family now?

Welty: In Jackson, I have some family, although both my parents
and both my brothers are gone. One of my brothers left his wife, and
two nieces of mine, and their children. I have another sister-in-law
who does not have children—I don't see her as often as I see Mittie.
My sister-in-law Mittie [Creekmore Welty] lives very close to me,
about three blocks away. I see them always on important days of the
year, birthdays and holidays and things like that. It's often in the
cleaners where we can manage to get together, with busy children
going to soccer games and trips and dances.

I feel very close to my family, and they to me, I think. I also have
some kin in Virginia and West Virginia that I see when I can, a great
many first cousins. Two of them came to Jackson for the library
christening [Eudora Welty Municipal Library]. So I feel close to
my family.

Eudora Welty

Hermione Lee / 1988

From *Writing Lives: Conversations Between Women Writers,*
ed. Mary Chamberlain (London: Virago, 1988), 249–59. Reprinted by permission of Hermione Lee.

E.W. I never in my wildest dreams thought I would write anything
autobiographical. Of course, many things in my life were used in the
stories, but they were very much transformed. I never expected to
write about my mother, or anything like that. The unhappy fact is that
usually by the time you're ready to think about your parents they're
gone, and can't tell you anything. That happened with both my
parents. But I'm awfully glad I did do this book [*One Writer's
Beginnings*], because it made me explicitly know what I owed things
to.

H.L. Was it a difficult book to write?

E.W. It was difficult mostly because it was a matter of choice. So
many things crowded in—maybe to make the same point, and I was
trying to use the one detail that would convey it in the most direct
way. I think in terms of fiction, and it's awfully hard for me to think
in terms of non-fiction, the explanatory. I tried to be selective, just to
tell the things that I thought contributed to my being a writer. That's
what I'd been asked to do. I threw away lots more stuff than is in
there, other things that I thought best left out.

H.L. But there are certain things that obviously keep coming back
to haunt you, like your grandmother coming in with her hands cold
because she's been out breaking the ice . . .

E.W. Oh—my mother told me that again and again. She would put
her own hands in front of her and say "Her hands, she had such
beautiful white hands, they were all bleeding from the ice on the well!"

H.L. You say in *One Writer's Beginnings* that you had a sheltered
life, and that your mother and father were equally supportive of your
wanting to become a writer, but in very different ways.

E.W. Very different ways. For a while I thought my father couldn't
be supporting me because—oh, he was against fiction, because he

146

thought it wasn't true. He said, it's not the truth about life. And he thought I might be wasting my time, because he thought I was going to write the sort of things that came out in the *Saturday Evening Post,* and if I *didn't* write those things I couldn't earn a living. We never really talked about the kind of things I did want to write. I couldn't have done that, with either one of my parents, with anybody. And how did I know what I *could* do? But he did support me. All he wanted to do was to make sure that I could survive, make my living. And that was good advice. I was rather scornful at the time—"Live for art," you know.

H.L. He never said, "Don't do it"?

E.W. No, he never did. But when I was growing up there wasn't much a woman could do to make a living, except teach, or else go into a business office as a stenographer or something low down the scale. I knew I couldn't teach, so I decided to go into business, and he was all for that. He sent me to a business graduate school in Columbia, and that was wonderful, it gave me a year in New York. I went to the theatre every night. Almost no work, it was so easy. Anybody could do it.

H.L. Later on, did you show your mother things that you were writing?

E.W. Yes, but I never could show them to anyone until after I had sent them away, because I was too fearful of having them treated as a school paper—"I think that's awfully good, dear," you know. I wanted a professional, objective answer, so I would send them to magazines, and that way I could learn what professional editors thought. If they sent it back I took that as a proper judgment, as indeed it was. If they praised me I was elated, and only after that would I show them to my mother, or friends.

H.L. And did you feel that she understood what you were doing?

E.W. I think she did. I know she tried with all her generous imagination. She was very proud of my work, because she was a *reader.* She loved the written word.

H.L. Many of your stories and novels have very powerful women in them, strong matriarchs.

E.W. Yes, they do. But my mother wasn't really like that, except she was a very powerful schoolteacher. I'm a first-generation Missis-sippian and though my mother was Southern in her origins and birth—Virginia and West Virginia—she didn't come out of plantation life. Those were the real matriarchies, which sprang out of the South during and after the Civil War years. I don't know that first hand, but I've read it and seen the results down the generations, where the sexes seem to me really divided, with the men galloping around outside and the women running everything.

H.L. You say your mother was a powerful schoolteacher, and you've written about the importance of these women schoolteachers in the South. They come into your fiction a lot.

E.W. Oh, they played such a large part. Because of the poverty in the South, the teachers were dedicated people. They never made any money, they were people who gave their lives to it, like the new women who went into colleges in the Middle West. After the Civil War, when all the schools had been burned and the land was levelled and everything had to start over and there was no money, the churches had to try to raise the money for schools. That's why there are so many church-supported, small private colleges in the South still. It was the immediate need for education, and they were doing it the best way they could. Where my mother came from, in the mountains of West Virginia, there wasn't any money at all in teaching. I remember she told me she was paid "thirty silver dollars" in salary for the first month she taught there, and she never was paid again. And just like in *Losing Battles,* she had to go across the river to teach. I told the real facts of that in this book [*One Writer's Beginnings*], how she went riding horseback over the mountain, with a little brother on the back to take the horse home, and would row herself across the river, and come back in the evening. And the little brother would meet her and ride home again. If you stayed the night you had to sleep with the family, with two or three children in the bed. They really were marvellous women . . . Of course the men were doing other things, they left the teaching to the women. But people who went to school with them almost never forgot them. We had, if you can comprehend this, the fiftieth anniversary of my high school class—Jackson, Miss., Class of '25—and we all still remembered this Miss Duling who taught us in grade school. And some of our teachers were still alive. They remembered everything about us, and they would say, "Well, I never thought *you'd* amount to anything."

H.L. Do you think you had a good education?

E.W. Yes, I had a good basic education, because reading was respected, and writing too. We really had to learn those fundamental things.

H.L. You read a lot at home, from early on?

E.W. Yes, I did. Of course, you learn to read early when you want to. I went to school when I was five and I could read by then. I think that was common in those days.

H.L. Are there people that you read between the ages of say, twelve and sixteen, who still matter to you?

E.W. Oh yes, people like Mark Twain . . . Ring Lardner . . . the Brontës. Books I found in the house, and in the library. I didn't read, you know, Homer and all that lot, like people are supposed to. I always liked fiction. I'm not terribly well-read, I'm sure, I just always read for pleasure. Now, that counts Homer!

H.L. Was it difficult to move away from home? Did you feel a pull between wanting your independence and feeling guilty about the people who loved you?

E.W. Oh yes, I still feel it. It haunts me. I think about how I could have managed it better. And I realized later that both my parents must have felt exactly the same thing when they left home. My mother was especially torn. And distances were so far then. Communications were hard in those days unless you were rich. But daily letters travelled back and forth, and we always knew how each other was.

H.L. Did you know that in the end you were bound to come back to Jackson?

E.W. No, I didn't feel that. I wanted to, and I still do, regard it as a base, which helps me in writing. I feel it's some sort of touchstone. It's what I check up by, in the sense that I know it so well I don't have to wonder about whether I have got it right. Either I have to know everything about a place, so that I don't have to think, or else I must never have seen it before, so that I'm wide awake to everything as a stranger, and can write one thing out of what I see and feel, as I did once with a story about Ireland ["The Bride of the Innisfallen"]. I didn't know Ireland and I didn't mean to write a story about it, but it left an indelible impression on my mind.

H.L. Do you think it's especially true that Southern writers in America have to use the place they know as a base?

E.W. I feel that what is maybe kin to the Southerner is the New

Englander, who has a sense of place. In urban life, that really isn't possible, in the way that I feel it, as a knowledge of seasons or changes or stability. Of course, the South now is full of people in motion, just like the rest of the country. But when I grew up it was so changeless that it was like a base you could touch and be sure you were accurate about something. But I think New Englanders and Southerners are alike in this, and it's odd how each had their flowering time in literature, New England first, and then the South in Faulkner's day.

H.L. Do you think you get your sense of narrative from the South?

E.W. I do feel that. Because of the pleasure that is taken in it in the South.

H.L. Is that a particularly female thing, do you think?

E.W. No. I think it's really more male. Women are supposed to be waiting on the men and bringing them food while they tell stories. That's the way it was in *Losing Battles!* And my mother's brothers in West Virginia were like that. They would gather and tell stories, and the women just kept bringing food so they'd keep talking and going on, and sometimes the women would scoff and say, 'Oh now, don't tell it that way!' But mother loved it all.

H.L. But it's very often the women who tell the stories in your books.

E.W. Well, maybe what's according to my story wasn't quite true to life . . . I know when I was in William Faulkner's house a couple of times, I heard him and his cronies telling stories, and they were all men. But those would be the stories they would tell at hunting camp or out sailing. Or stories about crazy people in Oxford, Mississippi. Men know more stories, at least they did in those days, because they get out and live in the world more, and their stories are more adventurous and full of action. More to tell.

H.L. But it's women who make up the fabric of gossip, who know what's going on?

E.W. That's true—the gossip, the domestic kind . . . I think women tell their kind of story to women and men tell theirs to men. But when there's a reunion, and everybody comes together for an occasion, then the stories are mingled. Everyone's in one company, they tell them together. It's like a set of voices joining one after the other, sometimes. I made this seem like a chorus in *Losing Battles,* to give the crowd effect.

Story-telling is *part* of life in the South, it's a social activity, always arising in family gatherings. Stories are told not to teach or learn from—everybody knows them already—but to participate in, to enjoy all over again. Their character is the thing. "Wasn't that exactly like Aunt Maggie?"

H.L. Do any of your stories come out of the photographs you took in the Depression years in Mississippi?

E.W. I am an observer, and I would notice the same thing, I would look for the same kind of thing, whether I was carrying a camera or just watching. But I didn't make up stories from my pictures. The odd thing is that some of the photographs turned out almost to illustrate stories that I wrote later on.

H.L. Did you ever find that it was a disadvantage to be a woman journalist in those days, travelling around Mississippi?

E.W. The only thing that annoyed me was that I was called junior publicity agent, and I was working with somebody called senior publicity agent, who was a man. We did exactly the same work, and of course he got a lot more money. I sort of wondered about that. But I was so happy to get a job that it didn't bother me any then. Otherwise, I never had difficulties. I would go into the poorest parts of the State, in the depths of the Depression, and I would say to people, a lot of them black people, "Do you mind if I take a picture?" and some of them would say, "Never had a picture taken in my life." And I'd say, "Just stay the way you are." They'd be in some wonderful pose, a woman on a porch, leaning forward from the hips, like this, her elbows on here and her hands crossed, with this wonderful curve of buttocks and legs, bare-footed on the porch. Beautiful woman. I would say, "Do you mind if I take your picture like that?" "No," she'd say, "if that's what you want to do, I don't care!" . . . It taught me so much, about coming upon people I didn't know and taking this minute of their lives. But I had to go on to fiction from photographing. That's the only way you can really part the veil between people, not in images but in what comes from inside, in both subject and writer.

H.L. When you started publishing your stories, I believe Katherine Anne Porter was very important to you?

E.W. She was indeed. I suppose Katherine Anne was the first living writer I'd ever seen. I published almost my first story in the *Southern Review,* which was published by Louisiana State University and edited by Robert Penn Warren and Cleanth Brooks. Katherine Anne was living in Baton Rouge, and she was married to Albert Erskine, who was also on the *Southern Review.* She wrote me a letter and said that she thought my work was good, and would I like to come and see her. That petrified me. I thought, how *can* I go! It was a long time before I did it. I was really scared to go. But I did, and she was so supportive, as she was to many young writers. If it had not been for *her* work, we couldn't ever have published, because she had such a hard time winning her place as a writer. Indeed it took *me* six years to be published in a national magazine, and that would be about average.

H.L. Do you think that was partly because you were a woman?

E.W. I don't know. I never did think of that. I don't think it was that, I think it was the short story form.

H.L. Do you think the short story, as practiced by Katherine Anne Porter, and Flannery O'Connor, and Elizabeth Bowen, and yourself—with a very vivid sense of place, and a lot of close detail, and a strong narrative voice—is a particularly female art form?

E.W. I just don't know. I suppose Mary Lavin would be another example of that kind of writing? But then there's Frank O'Connor and Sean O'Faolain, and they're not female. No, I can't express an opinion about that. But it sounds rather interesting.

H.L. Do you think of yourself as an objective writer?

E.W. That's what I try to be, but I know I'm not. In my work I try to be objective, and I can't really feel a story is finished until I can stand off from it and see it objectively. But in fact I'm sure I'm an absolutely exposed and naked writer. I mean in the way I feel and think about the world. I feel very exposed to it, and I've probably learned from that. But your work has to be objective.

H.L. But are you moved by your own writing?

E.W. I'm afraid I am! That is, there has to be some criterion of whether or not you brought it off. It has to meet that emotional test. You feel that only you yourself can judge it. Something tells me when I have not been objective enough, and I've got a story now that I won't let go for that reason. I know that it's not controlled enough.

H.L. Is there a moment when you know, when you can say to yourself, "I've got it"?

E.W. Yes. Or so I say.

H.L. And then you're completely confident?

E.W. Well—as near as you can be. I have a friend who's a writer—I won't tell you his name because he might not want me to, I mean it's his story, not mine. He kept all the versions of a story he'd written in a drawer, till he'd written about thirteen versions, and then he opened the drawer much later, and found that number seven was it. I think that's a wonderful lesson.

H.L. Do you revise a great deal?

E.W. Yes, I do.

H.L. And do you work quite slowly?

E.W. I revise very slowly, and I like to revise. I like to write the first draft quickly, to do it in one sitting if it were only possible, and I would like to write the last version all in one sitting. That's hard to do! But revision, I don't care how long it takes. I love it.

H.L. Do you think a writer's life is a lonely life?

E.W. No. I feel in touch. I like doing things, you know, privately. But I like to write with a window that looks out on to the street. I don't feel that I'm in a cell. Some people like that feeling—to be a monk or a nun or something. But I like to be part of my world. No, writing is solitary. But I don't feel lonely.

A Conversation between Eudora Welty and Cleanth Brooks

Humanities / 1988

From *Humanities,* 9 (September/October 1988), 10–11. Reprinted by permission of the National Endowment for the Humanities.

It rained in Oxford, Mississippi, the morning of June 30, 1988, but further south, Jackson baked under a relentless sun. The hot topic for most conversation was possible crop damage and barges stuck on the Mississippi, which had reached its lowest level in years. The subject for Eudora Welty and Cleanth Brooks was the state of narrative in contemporary American literature. The following conversation for *Humanities* took place in the airconditioned comfort of the Mississippi Department of Archives and History in Jackson.

Humanities: What are your thoughts about the state of narrative in contemporary literature?

Welty: I'm not truly a student of things as they happen. I read for pleasure, and I mostly like to read for narrative content. I don't see how narrative can ever be truly lost because it is inherent in any story, no matter how distantly something may be based on it. It's a sort of spine connecting what happens with what happens next and why it happened, and all the questions that go with it—human character, what made people do things, what happened to people as a result of something.

Brooks: Surely it is true that the narrative element is always there, even if muted, even if implied. But if you push past it, you're really getting into things that lyric poetry and meditative poetry can do better. It seems to me that some of our fiction writers, trying to depend so much on subtlety and nuance and change of atmosphere, are really giving us a kind of tepid, prose poetry that doesn't take advantage of the formal elements of poetry and loses some of the values of narrative poetry.

Welty: I couldn't agree with you more. I don't see the value of trying to make a change for the sake of change. If something drives you to do it, something that is a very strong conviction, then you should follow it and see where it goes, but it's still a matter of communication.

Brooks: Have you ever taken a creative writing class?

Welty: No, I haven't. It wasn't that I spurned them; I never heard of them. But nothing good was ever written out of anything but the individual, personal self with a great passionate desire and conviction behind it. I think you can pick up and learn the trimmings with the intelligent help that comes through a writing class. If you've got what it takes to begin with, you can be helped by criticism of method, etc., that steers you accurately toward what you were going toward, but it's no substitute for talent.

Brooks: The editor, if he's really a good editor, can help the writer, and I suppose the person in the so-called creative writing class can perform the same function.

Welty: What you need is an objective, intelligent point of view—someone who is sympathetic to what you're trying to do. What you need is the time and the opportunity and the space around you to work something out for yourself. You can get plenty of help from creative writing classes, the right kind of editors, and, heaven knows, from reading. That tells you more than anything in the world.

Brooks: Walker Percy in a recent essay ("How To Be An American Novelist in Spite of Being Southern and Catholic") warned the young southern writer not to try to imitate the great figures of the southern past who have done their job and came out of a certain context and won their victory. We're all proud of them, but they had a different situation to face. He is asking in this article that the young southern writers face up to a world that has a great deal of disorder—"an amalgam of economic prosperity and spiritual dislocation," he puts it. In effect, he's suggesting that they face up to a different situation. It seems to me, Eudora, that in *The Optimist's Daughter,* you were doing exactly that, long before Walker Percy made any of these comments. You were facing the fact of the young southern girl, who's got a job in Chicago, who sees the old world change in many respects, who's going back to a job in Chicago, who's got to find out her past, relate herself to it, accept certain things in another way. Would you agree that this is exactly what the young woman in the novel is doing?

Welty: Yes, it applies. Of course, I did it all through personal application because that's the only way I write. I think all of writing should reflect the real world, which is always changing. Life is fluid and on the move, and a story has got to catch it at a certain point to show what's going on.

Brooks: That wonderful passage toward the end when Laurel is getting ready to go back to Chicago and back to her job, leaving the bridesmaids, leaving the father buried, is a beautiful account of a young woman who is not putting her past behind her at all. She's accepting it. On the other hand, she has no intention of living in that past; she's going to live, do her job somewhere else, but she doesn't have to choose.

Welty: She doesn't have to choose. They can coexist.

Brooks: I can't answer for Walker Percy, but I would think that this would illustrate very well his suggestion that the young southern writer coming along should look around, face the facts, look at the urgent issues, shape that into his story.

Welty: You've got to do that. I keep forgetting how old I am, but I had some students ask me, "Miss Welty, you always write stories about *olden* times!" I replied, "Well, the stories you are talking about I wrote back in the forties or something. I was writing when those things were happening; I wasn't writing about the mysterious, hidden past." It is important to understand reality but not to obliterate what's gone before in the interest of saying that nothing is real but the present.

Brooks: So much of our society is trying to forget the past or obliterate the past. Students are not being taught about the past.

Welty: They really do not know it. When this museum mounted the first ever exhibition on the civil rights movement in Jackson, it had marvelous posters, photographs, everything. School children—black and white—were invited to come. None of them had ever heard of civil rights. They didn't know there had ever been a time when there weren't any. They never heard of Medgar Evers. It was amazing. They passed through this as if it were a glass wall. It's part of not knowing what's happened or caring.

Brooks: So it's really a false dichotomy, if any of us allow ourselves to accept it, the false opinion that holds that a writer has to disown the past in order to accept the present, or accept the past and live in it and disown the present.

Welty: One of the problems in modern short stories that I read is the inability to get out of the present tense, out of the first person. To me, that is a symptom of what we've been talking about.

Brooks: The whole pressure of modern literature is toward the lyric, the I, the subjective person. The epic dealt with the national hero. In the drama, the characters speak for themselves in a situation. But if you're very obsessed with yourself, it's all lyric. It's what *I* feel, it's what *I* want to confess, it's what *I* think. Obviously there is great lyric poetry, but if you try to turn drama, epic, realism, everything into the lyric—not what reality is but what *I* make of reality—that get's awfully boring.

Welty: It sure does, and it's a trap. If you can't get out of yourself, how will you ever learn about life? How can you accept the fact that other people are seeing the same thing and that they may have a few ideas too and that you might relate to one another? It would be a trap never to get out of your own self, your own body, your own preconceptions.

Brooks: Would you say, Eudora, that one of the things we're likely to get, particularly in southern fiction, will be brilliant accounts of social manners—the way people behave, the way they talk—which can reflect the quality of the whole society? If the whole of the South were just blotted out—bang!—and I were commissioned to reconstruct the society in the way it behaved and acted, I could do so—or somebody better qualifed—for the lower South from the novels of Walker Percy and Eudora Welty, and for the upper South from the stories of Peter Taylor. It's all there, and I think that's a valuable service and very much fun to read.

Welty: Thank you, sir. That's what we've had to depend on in all past literature—to reflect life as it was and to stand as a record of the society that existed.

Some Talk about Autobiography:
An Interview with Eudora Welty
Sally Wolff / 1988

From the *Southern Review,* 26 (Winter 1990), 81–88. Reprinted by permission of Sally Wolff.

The inspiration for this interview came partly as a result of a conference on southern autobiography at Arkansas State in the spring of 1988. In July of that year I visited Eudora Welty at her home in Jackson, Mississippi, where we discussed correspondences between *One Writer's Beginnings* and her highly autobiographical novel, *The Optimist's Daughter.* Miss Welty also relates memories and details which reveal more of her personal involvement in this novel.

Wolff: One of the issues at the recent conference on southern autobiography is whether there is a distinct body of work that might be thought of as southern autobiography. Do you think certain aspects of southern life and culture might predispose writers to autobiography?

Welty: Yes, I think probably so, don't you? It occurs to me that southerners take certain things for granted—such as certain classes, certain strictures, different backgrounds—people immediately make certain assumptions. Southerners want to place everybody. This was especially true in former times, when someone might say "Oh, so-and-so, his father was so-and-so." It used to be so simple—you might be born on the wrong side of the track. I remember as a child being taught not to make this count. I was warned against it. But it's a way southerners have of locating themselves.

Wolff: What else in southerners might encourage them to write about themselves?

Welty: It's entertaining when it's done well. It helps you get a narrative sense of continuity when there are so many stories through the generations—something that connects people together. I missed that when I lived in other parts of the country. People were friends but had no sense of their ancestors. No one was interested. I did have a good friend—David Daiches—who invited me to visit his family in Edinburgh. The family I met there was so warm and welcoming. His three aunts met me at the door with arms extended. I felt at home with them. In the South we combine a feeling of family and of place. They are twin strands, the sense of family and place. I didn't grow up with this sense of the whole family. As you know from *One Writer's Beginnings,* much of the family was away.

Wolff: In West Virginia?

Welty: Yes.

Wolff: The feeling of being somewhat isolated from the extended family also comes through in *The Optimist's Daughter* in Becky and Laurel's memories about West Virginia.

Welty: Yes, I used it in the work in general. I used the point of view of the child coming to something new. I did the same thing in *Delta Wedding* where the child's perspective is a narrative device to lead the reader into something new. In lots of stories it's the stranger to the family that provides this perspective. Maybe that is my point of view.

Wolff: The rejection of *Flags in the Dust* seems to have turned Faulkner inward, down into himself, after which he began writing *The Sound and the Fury.* I'm thinking about that introduction to the book in which he says, "One day I seemed to shut a door between me and all publishers' addresses and booklists . . . and set out to make myself a beautiful and tragic little girl." That book seems autobiographical to me, so much a reminiscence of and a lament for lost childhood. Can you say that some set of events or some factor led you to turn to autobiography?

Welty: Well, in *One Writer's Beginnings* a particular event did. I was asked, as you know, to give the series of lectures at Harvard, and I thought, "I can't possibly say anything they don't already know." But Dan Aaron, my good friend, came to see me and said, "Yes, there is something you know that they do not—what books were in your grandfather's library." I thought, "That's intriguing to think about it that way." If it hadn't been for Dan the book wouldn't have happened. I wrote a great deal more material than I used. I threw away four times what I kept. I may not have chosen well, but I had to choose. One memory calls up another. Like Thomas Mann says, memory is like a well: the deeper you go, the more you recover. It's probably a good thing the book had to be compressed or I might have gone on forever. I'm not used to writing anything but fiction. I didn't make up anything in *One Writer's Beginnings*. I couldn't help but use my experience in knowing, for instance, what makes a scene—the dramatic sense. I think of things in scenes—trips in the car, being on the ferry boat, my mother and father arguing about their different attitudes about drowning—it was better than making a simple statement. I remember things that way—in scenes, as little wholes.

Wolff: Would you say, then, that the autobiographer uses the same tools in writing autobiography that the fiction writer does?

Welty: My own bent is to use those tools. I would want certain things to be brought out in act, in deed, and in what can be observed. It's natural for me to do it that way. A poet would do it differently, I suppose, as would a railroad engineer.

Wolff: Could you say that any other factors in particular led you to write autobiographically, especially in *The Optimist's Daughter?*

Welty: I did use things about my mother, as I have said. In *The Optimist's Daughter* I was trying to understand certain things, some of which are reflected in the character of my mother. All that was true. But my mother did not marry a southerner the way Becky does. So much of what I wrote about was not my mother. And that is true for the other characters.

Wolff: I could not imagine that there was a "Fay" anywhere in your family.

Welty: There is no Fay in any of my life, except as she exists in the world.

Wolff: Fay has always seemed highly symbolic to me.

Welty: Yes, I think she is.

Wolff: What other aspects of the novel might you say were particularly autobiographical?

Welty: There are things I never realized growing up that I began to realize. I used certain things that I had been familiar with. You do this when you write any character. My mother had eye trouble, but she didn't have a detached retina. I did know someone who had a detached retina, though. I nursed my mother through cataract surgery, and some of the details I used for the judge. She had sandbags, for instance, and she couldn't move her head. It's not literal, though. If it were it would be a damn difficult task to write the literal truth. It was hard to do in *One Writer's Beginnings,* to give an account of family illness. I don't think I could have done that in a novel.

Wolff: Would you say, then, that writing autobiography is more difficult than writing fiction?

Welty: When I was writing *The Optimist's Daughter,* I never gave a thought to myself—my self did not enter into the novel. It's much easier for me to write fiction. I try to put myself into the characters and see how they felt. Any nonfiction is so different from fiction. A book review, for instance, is completely different from using your imagination in a story.

Wolff: In an earlier interview, you said that in *One Writer's Beginnings* you wrote for the first time about yourself and that the experience was enlightening. Could you elaborate about what this writing experience taught you?

Welty: Well, I'd like to think about that for awhile. I will say that it came about without my realizing it at the time. Writing about anything teaches you—it teaches you the recognition of things in your life that you remember, but you might not have recognized their portent. It's like you have an electric shock—and you can say that's when I recognized so-and-so. Writing is a way to come to terms with whatever you've done or not done—what your life has meant to you—good or bad. One thing leads to another subjectively, and you could probably go on forever.

Wolff: Do you have that same experience writing fiction?

Welty: Yes. That same feeling comes from writing fiction. In the course of writing a scene of interplay between two characters, you build to a confrontation that needs to take place—and you realize that's why you were diddling with it and fooling with it in the first place—there was something in there. It's like a belated understanding. I seem to come to understanding belatedly.

Wolff: Lately I read a statement by Sarah Orne Jewett that all the materials you need to be an artist you know by the time you are ten years old. Would you agree?

Welty: How could you ever prove it, though? But yes, I think I know what she means, don't you? Your capacity for realizing the other people in the world, your physical world, even if you can't define them, you know what they are.

Wolff: And memories of childhood are an important source for the artist.

Welty: Yes, they are a fund.

Wolff: I'm interested in the remark you made earlier that when you were writing *The Optimist's Daughter* you did not envision yourself in the novel. Laurel has characteristics which are both similar to and unlike yours, doesn't she?

Welty: Yes. In a wider sense, I would say it was my own inquiring mind that corresponds to the girl's in the novel, to the effort to understand your roots and the decision in the end that you can't be held back by the past. I used things that would be useful in the novel. The war was very important, for instance. My friend in World War II married into—well, when someone was lost—like Phil is—I knew what that feeling was like. How could I not have? That was a war people believed in. We still had the belief in World War II that war could be ended by licking the Nazis. The difference in attitude toward war now is striking. Some of my friends put on a production at the New Stage of the songs of Irving Berlin. The young girls were giggling at songs like "Over There!" and the director stopped them and said, "When those songs were written, they *meant* that." It was a bad war. The boys we knew were involved and we were with them. These young people in the theater couldn't conceive of fighting for a cause. This applies to Phil. The part in the novel about the kamikaze happened to my brother Walter. He was in the Navy at Okinawa, and later he was asked, "How close have you come to a kamikaze?" and he said, "Close enough to shake hands with." So I put that in the story. Who could ever make up a thing like that?

Wolff: No one could. Was Phil made up?

Welty: Phil is an amalgamation of a lot of boys I knew. My other brother, the middle child, has some of his characteristics—those double-jointed thumbs, and he was an architect. Phil has not got his character, though. Although he did make a breadboard. But no one ever acted badly about it.

Wolff: No one ever acted the way Fay does?

Welty: Not in my family: but I've seen a-many, a-many. And anyone who's ever had anyone in the hospital will recognize the people who sit in the waiting rooms and eat and drink and talk. I wouldn't want anyone to think that I was using their *sick* in the novel, but these things come back to me, like air, and I use them.

Everybody told me I was absolutely right with the hospital scenes. I heard people say some of those things, like "I'm not gonna let him die wanting water." It's the inadequacy of their comprehension, or maybe they can't express it. They say, "What is *yours* doing? *Mine* is doing OK."

Wolff: Mr. Dalzell's line, "Don't let the fire go out, son!" is tragic and funny at the same time.

Welty: I love Mr. Dalzell. The fire, of course, is life too. He talks in terms of the things he knows—country things. He and the judge were so different, but I thought it would be good to have them in the same room together. They each had a sense of honor and would have respected each other. He was a gentleman—like Fay's old grandfather—these are affinities among characters that don't have anything to do with their circumstances.

Wolff: Let me go back to Laurel for a moment. I was surprised to read in one of your interviews that you identify most with your character Miss Eckhart rather than with Laurel.

Welty: It's not that I shared any of my life with Miss Eckhart. She was devoted to her art. I could identify with Laurel in wanting to know about family and relationships, in living through World War II when my friends and brothers were fighting, and also in my sense that Laurel had left home and had a life elsewhere that had something to do with the arts. I wouldn't have thought of making her a writer. The fact that she was in the arts allied her with Phil, who is also a maker, and in the end she goes back to that life, but without leaving anything behind. She knows the future is to be valued. I sympathize with all these attitudes. I am not Laurel. But I have the feeling of the close-knit family—do you remember the scene where they're holding each other's hands? I've gone through that feeling a lot though my own father died when I was just out of college.

Wolff: Miss Eckhart and Laurel are alike, then, in their dedication to their art?

Welty: Miss Eckhart is a teacher, though—I've never seen myself as a teacher. Both Miss Eckhart and Laurel had belief in the individual—in what an artist does. In her own way—you know, I really hadn't thought of it until now—Laurel was as isolated in the town as

Miss Eckhart was. Laurel was protected and pampered by the town, but when it came down to it no one could share in her deepest feelings about life and responsibility. We don't ordinarily talk about things like that in the South, or maybe anywhere.

Wolff: Laurel's privacy and isolation are reflected in the narration, too. We do not see into Laurel's thoughts until the very end of the book.

Welty: She is subservient to what she endures going on around her, and then she is activated by this. She has a muted position. It's not her place to yell and scream. She's kept a lot of things inside her. In the part about New Orleans, when she and Fay are in those cheap rooms where you can hear through the walls—I wanted that to be foreboding.

Wolff: It is, especially when Fay sees the bride and groom skeletons at the carnival.

Welty: I took that part from real life. I took a picture one time at Mardi Gras in New Orleans of a man and woman dressed as skeletons, and she was holding a bouquet of white lilies. And I saw the man with the Spanish moss; he was dressed entirely in Spanish moss. It was all over his hair, like he had a permanent of long curls, and he was dressed in a whole suit of Spanish moss.

Wolff: In one of the early versions of *The Optimist's Daughter* you wrote out some scenes depicting Phil and Laurel courting, and in one scene Phil's mother asks Laurel how far apart their children will be spaced. Why did you decide to delete this material?

Welty: That's a good middlewestern touch in the kitchen, isn't it? I remember writing the courtship scene, but maybe I left it out because it didn't fit my purpose as well. I wanted the relationship of Phil and Laurel to be taken for granted for my purposes in the novel. It gave it a more proper depth and allowed me to concentrate on the scene in which Phil says, "I wanted it! I wanted it!" It's really a short novel, and I still think of it as a long short story. You have to get the proportions right. You have to keep in mind the good of the whole story. That is true for writing short stories, too; you have to get the balance right. Dozens of possible scenes show the same point, and I have to choose as in *One Writer's Beginnings*. I just have to feel my way to it.

Wolff: Did you save the material for *One Writer's Beginnings* that you did not use?

Welty: I saved the notebooks I wrote it from. I did write those as lectures, and I did have the deadline of timing—length was one thing I had to go by because they were lectures. I probably threw away some of it that didn't show an event as well. I can remember things in stories—the choice I made for stories—more than in that book.

Wolff: You said earlier that in the end of *The Optimist's Daughter,* Laurel learns to move to the future. She packs up the family home, and she leaves for the North. Would you say that autobiographical writing allows you to imagine your own life choices in another way? Is this a freeing experience?

Welty: It can be. The end of the novel embodied Laurel's whole experience. It had to be settled and then done with as far as her practical life is concerned. She would never forget any of the past, though. Miss Adele was very sensitive to what was going on with Laurel. I like my character Miss Adele. Laurel could not be the only one who felt things, who was aware. That just worked out as I was writing it. I'm glad it happened.

Wolff: Do you recall any other changes that emerged from the experience of writing *The Optimist's Daughter?*

Welty: The publisher might have wanted to go ahead and print the novel as it was published in the *New Yorker.* But I wanted a waiting period to let things settle to see how I felt about it. I wanted to let a little time pass. I always change things. I don't know exactly what changes I made in the different versions; it all seems the one thing to me now.

Wolff: There are some provocative changes; one is the change from the *New Yorker* title—"An Only Child." Would you comment on that change?

Welty: I wanted to have something about the eyes. I first wanted to call it "Poor Eyes," but that was voted down. Bill Maxwell and Diarmuid Russell didn't like it. Bill did like *The Optimist's Daughter.* He said it gave a nice "chill of apprehension." But I've never been very good at titles. After the book came out I had letters that had the title wrong: "I so much enjoyed *The Optimistic Daughter.*" Another one said *The Optometrist's Daughter.* That's a good one, don't you think? The Optometrist's Daughter? Because of the eyes?

Wolff: Yes, that's good. Is there a sense in which "An Only Child" is an autobiographical title, even though you are not an only child?

Welty: Yes, I dramatized the sense of being an only child. If Laurel had had brothers, like I had, she wouldn't have had the trouble she did. I was not an only child but the only girl—that is difference enough to understand the feeling that you are by yourself.

Wolff: By yourself in confronting the deaths of so many family members?

Welty: Yes.

Wolff: That reminds me of Mrs. Chisom's summation of Laurel's predicament: "So you ain't got father, mother, brother, sister, husband, chick nor child." I like that: "chick nor child."

Welty: Isn't Chisom a good name for them? And I like the sound of Wanda Fay. I love that.

Eudora Welty

Dannye Romine Powell / 1988

From Dannye Romine Powell, *Parting the Curtains: Interviews with Southern Women Writers* (Winston-Salem, NC: John F. Blair, 1994), 327–342. Interview conducted on 29 August 1988. Reprinted by permission of the publisher.

Eudora Welty has opened wide her bank of living-room windows to welcome any stray late-summer breeze. On the hearth are two small electric fans, ready to be plugged in should the afternoon grow too hot or too muggy.

Welty's parents, Chestina and Christian Welty, built this two-story Tudor house on Pinehurst Street in Jackson, Mississippi, in 1925, when Eudora was sixteen, brother Edward thirteen, and brother Walter ten. Only five minutes from town, it was considered country property. Today, tree-shaded Belhaven College across the street still provides a cool curtain of green. But even in midafternoon, Pinehurst Street rumbles with traffic. Since her mother's death in 1966, Welty, who never married, has lived alone in the house.

Until arthritis struck, she made her office in her upstairs bedroom. It was to that room she returned—with a Bachelor of Arts degree from the University of Wisconsin and a degree from the Columbia University Graduate School of Business—to write the short stories that have become classics: "Death of a Traveling Salesman," "A Worn Path," "A Piece of News."

In fact, all her short stories and novels have been evoked in this house and in this town where she was born.

The most autobiographical of her novels, *The Optimist's Daughter,* was written after her mother's death and published first in the *New Yorker* in 1969. After it was published in book form in 1972, it won the Pulitzer Prize. Most of her work is set in Mississippi and concerns the strange and mysterious workings of the human heart.

In 1983, Harvard University Press published Welty's *One Writer's Beginnings*. That autobiography—to her surprise, and to Harvard's—became a longstanding bestseller.

Welty has moved her office downstairs, to a room opposite the living room. To her frustration, she says, every flat surface in that room is stacked with mail she must answer and manuscripts she must read. But as she settles on the couch—making certain her guest is comfortable and at right angles to her good ear—she leans happily into her subject: The writing life and the imagination.

Interviewer: It seems so many people who grew up to be writers—you, Walker Percy, Anne Tyler—spent some time in bed as children or youths with an illness. As a child, you spent time in bed with a "fast-beating heart." Do you think that that leisure enriched your already fertile imagination?

Welty: It did give me a glorious opportunity to do what I loved to do: Read. 'Cause I lay on the bed with books all around me, like Robert Louis Stevenson's [poem] "In the Land of Counterpane." So that really was a feeling of being perfectly free to read to my heart's content. Or look out the window to my heart's content. I suppose anything that leads to, or even panders to, the habit of uninterrupted meditation, uninterrupted enjoyment of your imagination. I can't say I've meditated, but I've imagined.

Another thing: I used to—I think at the same time—enact plays I'd made with dolls, which you could do in bed. You could make a stage and a landscape. That may have played into my dramatic instinct, which storytelling is.

Interviewer: I'd like to talk about your parents. You were fortunate your own mother passed along her passion for reading to you. Do you believe there's something magically contagious about passion? Do you think it's the best way to teach?

Welty: Maybe it's the inevitable way to teach. And it certainly is the effective, it's the *critical,* thing in learning. It's sort of the essence. But it has to be real. I don't think it would come through if it were not true.

Interviewer: Your mother couldn't help herself. But what would you advise parents who aren't themselves passionate, but still want to nurture their children's creativity?

Welty: Even if you didn't have that, and you instigated a love of reading in the children, then it could follow. What worries me so much about now is that people grow up without having read anything. *Anything!* And the sense of the language is getting so muddied and imprecise. The poetry of the language is being lost. I can tell that also from letters I get. I think that's the most important thing in the world in education: The written word.

It can't come in cassettes—not all of it. That helps. But if you don't have a base knowledge of the word and of the existence of the word, the indelibility of the word, which you don't get from hearing. I don't mean not to hear anything. But that the other should be primary.

Interviewer: With your father, it wasn't so much a passion that I sense in him. But it was his unselfishness. His ability to put his children ahead of himself.

Welty: Absolutely. They both had that. I suppose a lot of it, at least to some extent, was because both of them came from families without much money. You know, everything had to be earned. They were educated, as it turned out, through their own efforts. And it had meant so much to them that they were determined that their children . . . Of course, that's the great story of America. Never, never did we get the idea that our family was sacrificing for our education, although I'm sure they were.

It wasn't this burden like, "I'm paying for this year at college, and you ought to study." That never happened. I guess we really studied anyway. But they didn't make us feel that they were suffering deprivation for us to be educated. They weren't, actually. But they would have. In some ways, I know they did give up things. But we were always comfortable in our family. We were small-town comfortable. They did everything they could for us.

Interviewer: You just fell into the right hands, didn't you?

Welty: I'll say I did. I realize it more all the time.

Interviewer: You've taught writing from time to time, and I understand you taught Ellen Gilchrist in your workshop at Millsaps College.

Welty: I never was a teacher, I'll tell you that. I needed to earn some money, and I couldn't leave home. My usual way was to go to colleges, when invited. But I needed to get some money because of illness in the house, and I couldn't leave. So I thought maybe I could do something at Millsaps College. What we really had was a workshop. And I told them right in the beginning that I didn't believe I could teach writing. We could have a workshop and have a back-and-forth among ourselves and see what came of it. We worked it out as we went. And I would say I learned more than any of the students, by the things we did.

Interviewer: What did you do?

Welty: Well, the method I set out was to have each student read when and if they felt like it. Whatever was natural to them. Every day, or once a month, or whatever, to bring their story to class and for them themselves to read the story aloud and see how it sounded objectively. And then the class would ask questions, comment as a whole.

And I did that, too. I'd read before. But it was only when I read my work aloud that I saw for the first time all its weaknesses, and I could objectively judge it. In writing, that had never happened to me. But in reading it out loud, I learned so much.

Interviewer: But you've also said you don't believe in teaching writing. That it's something people have to learn for themselves.

Welty: I've felt that way. But I know that there are things that you can learn that you wouldn't have to learn by yourself. You can learn pitfalls and how to avoid them. You can be guided and learn something about form and things like that, just from the practice of it. And I will say that the stories I've read in different colleges and universities in the country—where I go there to visit and I read a bunch of manuscripts—they are all very accomplished. And I know I could never have written like that in college myself. They are very competent.

Interviewer: How do you account for that?

Welty: They are very accomplished in that they don't do anything wrong. But that isn't to say that they will go on even being writers, because that has to come from inside. You have to really *want* to do it and want to do nothing else.

It couldn't hurt anyone to learn to write in an accomplished way. You learn the language, and so on. But after they went out of college and decided they wanted to do something that would earn a living better—and God knows, most anything would do it better—then they might not ever come back to writing.

It's just like people who are good at dancing, painting, music when they are young. But it isn't sustained. And I do think that depends on what you were born with, which you can't help, and you can't get it. You've got to have that if you're really going to go on with it. You've got to have a talent for it, a gift, whatever, and be willing to work hard to develop that. That is, it can't all come from outside.

Interviewer: Do you ever come across people you feel have the inside thing but don't yet have the appropriate skills?

Welty: Sure. That's exactly the way I must have been for most of my young life. Because I think I had some kind of gift—I know I must have, or I wouldn't have kept on to be this old and still doing it—but

I did teach myself. And it probably took longer. I don't do anything very well in a group.

Interviewer: You've always said your writing talent was a visual writing talent. I've never heard you mention your excellent ear, which I'm wondering if you think you might have inherited from your very musical West Virginia uncles. I'm wondering if that ear for dialogue has anything to do with that musical ear.

Welty: I don't know. I had a brother who was very musical. I was interested in dialogue after I started writing, I think. That got me interested, and then I started listening. I love dialogue, and when I read something or write something, I can hear it. So that's a good test for it. It also helps you remember, something you hear. But I think it's apart from the visual sense. Some stories are all one thing, and some are all the other.

Interviewer: Talk about the visual, too. When you read a letter, for instance, part of the experience for you must be visualizing what you read.

Welty: I see anything I read. The longer you live, the more you have seen things, so you can call up the image that is literally familiar to you. That you literally have seen. It's been on your retina. But also as a child, reading fairy tales and happenings—Ali Baba and all those *Arabian Nights* and King Arthur.

Interviewer: In all the interviews I've read with you, you were getting letters from people who took it upon themselves to analyze the symbols in your stories. Does that amuse you?

Welty: By now, it kind of baffles and tires me, because I think, "What can I do about this?" There are some things now I don't even try to answer. Every room in my house has got stacks. The room across the hall—every flat surface has unanswered mail. Sometimes, I just feel like giving up the ghost. It's nice to know that people think they can connect with you. And I'm very moved by that fact. But what can I physically do about it? I just don't know. I just don't know what to say. They don't understand. I'm sure it hasn't occurred to them that someone else might be doing the same thing. I'm sure it doesn't occur to them.

Interviewer: I hope you keep your own writing room free of those stacks.

Welty: That's my trouble. I've had to move downstairs. My own

room is directly above this one—my workroom where I have files and
drawers and my desk and my typewriter. But I have arthritis in my
knee, which means that going up and down stairs is not good. So I
just moved downstairs a little at a time. Trying to switch books and
things. So every room has got stacks. It's just awful to look at. I'm
nowhere, really. I've been doing some work right in here, right in the
living room. That's so inhospitable.

Interviewer: I'd like you to describe—in as much detail as you
will—your ideal daily writing routine.

Welty: Oh, boy!

Interviewer: I say ideal, because on an ideal day, you would've had
all your mail answered yesterday.

Welty: Oh, boy. Nobody's ever given me this chance before. Okay.
Wake up early. I'm one of the people who think best in the morning.
I like to wake up ready to go, and to know that during that whole day
the phone wouldn't ring, the doorbell wouldn't ring—even with good
news—and that nobody would drop in. This all sounds so rude. But
you know, things that just make a normally nice day are not what I
want. I don't care what the weather is. I don't care what the temperature is. I don't care where I am or what room I'm in. I'd just get up
and get my coffee and an ordinary breakfast and get to work. And just
have that whole day! And at the end of the day, about five or six
o'clock, I'd stop for good that day. And I'd have a drink, a bourbon
and water, watch the evening news—"MacNeil-Lehrer News
Hour"—and then I could do anything I wanted to.

I would like to see a friend for dinner or something, or go out. You
know, completely cut off, and have the river start going the other way
again. And then part of the perfect day would be to have the next day
to follow also perfect. Not to think, "I'd better make the best of it,
because tomorrow . . ." I'd like to think, "I can do it tomorrow,
too." And I'd also like to think, "Yesterday was a pretty good day."
I'd like to have it work at both ends, toward the past and toward
the future.

It used to be easy to do that, strange to say. When my family was
living here, I would just go upstairs and shut the door, and I could do
that work. And I was doing jobs at this time, too. Like book reviews
or going to colleges. But I could shut it on and off better than I can
now. And also, it didn't occur to me that there might be a time when

I couldn't find that freedom to write. Part of it now is the experience of knowing that you really can't get that situation. It's just not to be had.

Life is different now. Pinehurst Street is different. Big traffic thing. Lots of noise. Also, everybody thinks it's okay to send all the mail by Express Mail, which means you have to go to the door and sign for it. All of those things life is just full of. It's just made with intrusions now. It's nobody's fault. It's just the way it is.

Sometimes, I think that maybe this partial deafness I have is brought about by my wishing I didn't have to hear so much. I hope not. But it could be.

Interviewer: During your ideal day, wouldn't you stop to eat lunch?

Welty: Oh, yeah. Yeah, I'd stop and eat. Yeah. But I would pick a good minute to do it, and I would fix something I could just slap together—a sandwich and a Coke. I wouldn't stop and cook something and all that.

And I wouldn't have any set time for it that I'd have to look forward to. Because it wouldn't matter. That would be wonderful. I feel as if I've had a day like that.

Even if I found out the next day that what I had done was really not very good, I would know it was important, because it was a bridge to something. I would know where to go from there.

I don't think any writing is ever really lost, because it all teaches you something. Even the bad teaches you something that you wouldn't have known otherwise. So I would like to be working on something sustained, to be writing a short story which is sustained and all of a piece.

I wouldn't be writing at all without the idea of what I wanted to do. I wouldn't just sit down and type. That would never do. It would be toward an end. That's a lovely question. Nobody ever asked me that before.

Interviewer: I know the act of writing, and even revising, makes you very happy. Please talk about how you feel or the state you're in when you're hard at work on a story or a novel.

Welty: I think you're unconscious of the state you're in, because you're not thinking about yourself. You're thinking about the piece of work. Totally absorbing. I guess if you stopped to think about yourself, it would stop you in your tracks. What am I doing here?

[Laughter.] It's the act of being totally absorbed, I think, which seems to give you direction. The work teaches you about the work ahead, and that teaches you what's ahead, and so on. That's the reason you don't want to drop the thread of it. It is a lovely way to be.

And there was a time when I drove my car every other day—I was going to see my mother, who was away at that time—and on the trip, I wouldn't try to be thinking of my work, but it's sort of hypnotic to be behind the wheel of a car and take a well-known road you've done many times. Everything would start flowing into my head about the story [*Losing Battles*], and I would think, "This is the word I was trying to think about yesterday!" And so I'd write it down. I had a shorthand notebook with a hard back, you know, so I could write with one hand without taking my eyes off the road. Of course, I'd have to transcribe it pretty quickly when I got home, or I couldn't make sense of it. But all these things, it was just like your mind was saying, "All right. I've got you now, and I'm going to fill in these things that you missed yesterday."

It wasn't a note of direction. It was a piece of work. Sometimes it was the wrong idea.

Interviewer: That's just amazing.

Welty: What your mind does is so peculiar.

Interviewer: Especially when your mind is on automatic.

Welty: That's right. It was on automatic drive.

Interviewer: Aren't you glad you were a broken left-hander, so you could write with your right hand?

Welty: I certainly was. I would've had to get an English drive.

Interviewer: You had started *Losing Battles,* and it was under way, and your mind was just supplying.

Welty: I'd been working on it a long time, but never in a sustained way. I can't remember now—I have so many different versions of things.

Interviewer: Do you save them all?

Welty: I had saved them all. Then when I wrote the novel, I went back and put all these things together, looked at them all together, and selected what I could use. They were all in the shape of scenes. The scene was to tell you something about the character or the action. But I might have thought of another way to do it and have another scene. You didn't want both of them. So you would say, "Which one did it best?"

Interviewer: If was as if, at some level in you, the whole thing was there, and pieces were just floating up, but not in any order.

Welty: It was really weird. The mind is very strange. And I suppose everybody's mind has its own whatever it is—strangeness or method.

Interviewer: Or its own way of focus or order.

Welty: Focus. That's right. Because not in that novel, but in other stories I've written, which I've done in pieces of things, I've suddenly realized while doing something else—like riding on a train or washing the dishes—that the focus had been wrong in something. It was like I had the wrong spotlight on it. And instead, it should've been from this character or this year. But the story was there all the time, and I had seen it in the wrong light.

Isn't that strange? I guess I must be very slow-witted in lots of ways to be so belatedly aware of things.

Interviewer: I think you trust your unconscious more. You don't feel the need to rush.

Welty: I think so, too. I know what to trust. When I get an idea like that, I know it's right. You don't get a wrong idea like that. At least, I don't think so. It's a correction when you get a better idea. Just like, "Correction, please," in a Japanese accent: "Collec-shun, preeze."

Interviewer: Let's go back to revision a minute. You've said your ideal way to write a short story is to write the whole draft through in one sitting, then to revise, then rewrite the final draft in one sitting. Talk about your method of revision. It's with scissors and pins, isn't it?

Welty: That's right.

Interviewer: Your mind predates computers, because we have a way to "block-save" on our computers. You can take this piece of material and "block-save" it and put it down here.

Welty: Oh, you save the block.

Interviewer: That's right. That's exactly what you're doing with pins and scissors, right? You're doing what the computer has finally learned to do.

Welty: Except that with a computer, I don't know whether it stays in view.

Interviewer: Well, that's the trick. You have to scroll it up. Your method has the advantage.

Welty: I think it's an advantage, too, because then if you don't like what you've done, you can put it back. All you have to do is unpin it. You can try things. But you can with a computer, I suppose.

Interviewer: Well, you still don't have it all in view at once.

Welty: I have to have things in view. That's one of my troubles. Someone showed me a darling little typewriter. They said it was so lightweight, and it was wonderful. I said, "Oh, let me try it!" I went over there, and I saw that you did not see—it was not visible—the line you were typing. I said, "I couldn't even write a sentence that way."

Interviewer: Let's get real specific about your pins-and-scissors method.

Welty: Did you ever cut out and make dresses from patterns? Well, I guess it's that that made me think of it. Anyway, I think probably also it goes back to newspaper days. When you write copy, as you know, you're in a room with a lot of people. But there's a space bar on your typewriter, and if you don't like something, you rip it off. And so you have this long roll of paper. I think in a way it was to use that lesson. If it's not good, throw it away. Then write it again and use that.

Except I was too prudent, I guess, to really throw it away. I would save it in case I might need it after all. So I had these strips. But you do that in a newspaper office.

Interviewer: We used to.

Welty: Now you use computers. I could never work on it.

Interviewer: I think you could. But your way sounds better.

Welty: I have to have something under my hand to write on. I know at the *New York Times Book Review,* you never touch anything. Ever. There are no galleys. I'd be incapable . . .

Interviewer: You wouldn't.

Welty: Yes, I would. Maybe touch is part of it, along with seeing and hearing. All of this about one draft, of course, means it's a very short story—the kind I used to write. I couldn't do that now. I couldn't possibly do it all in one day. But that is my ideal way of writing a short story. Really.

Interviewer: Can you say why?

Welty: Because you then see it as a whole. You conceive it as a whole. And it's easy to follow its plan of action in a straight line that way. You know, well, it is a straight line. It's a tense line. It has tension in it. You can't relax it. It goes together with writing in one spurt. But of course it's been years since I wrote anything I could do like that, because I write so much more lengthily—too lengthily. It's a different kind of story now.

I do know this much: Everybody has a different way. And you have to figure out that way.

Interviewer: You've said you must know exactly what's in a character's heart and mind before he ever sets visible foot on stage. You've also said a story grows like a thorn under your skin, festering, until it's ready to be plucked, or written. This means you've already done a lot of work before you start writing.

Welty: Oh, yeah. I didn't know I'd ever said that about the thorn. Heavens! It sounds so painful. I don't really feel pain in this. Anyway, I think maybe my perception of the character would be something else than the kind of thing we put in words or outlines. I think of the character as a whole. But really, the only way I know how to express the character is in the story. So that I couldn't make an outline and say, "Enter, so-and-so."

I think of them in the whole from the start, but as to how it's to work out, that does come in the writing. Or if I change my mind of what I thought was a good way and see if there's a better way.

Interviewer: But the knowing of the character, what does that feel like? Does that come upon you silently? Do you even consider it work? You've also said that the story smolders until you're ready to light it. But that process that goes on inside you at some level—maybe you're not even conscious of it. Maybe you only know it when it festers.

Welty: I think now, on looking back, that since I'm interested in human relationships, I think of the character as within a relationship also from the beginning. So it's more than just a single, lone creature there. It's the pattern of relationships, all affecting each other and causing things in each other and creating a development, making its own pattern.

But I don't know. Because it's not very self-conscious. I'm trying to be honest, but it may be different in different stories. I could not

begin a story if I did not have the whole clear intention as a single
thing in my mind to what this story should exist as. Sometimes, I can
find a better way to work it out than I had thought of in the beginning.
But it's what I wanted to do in the beginning.

Interviewer: But that part before you start writing is, as far as you
know, effortless?

Welty: I don't know. I don't feel strain about it. I can't be sure. It's
not very conscious of itself. If it were, I probably couldn't do it at all.
It is a mysterious thing. As I say, I'm sure it's different in different
people, which makes it even more mysterious.

Interviewer: You talked about memory in *One Writer's Beginnings*
as a source and a force. I find the force really intriguing.

Welty: I've forgotten how I used it.

Interviewer: That by getting in there and getting those memories
going, a person could do something very positive. Maybe even revital-
ize ourselves.

Welty: Yeah. I think so, too. It's very illuminating. I think it's a
great corrective force.

Interviewer: What do you mean?

Welty: Well, it sets you straight. You know, "I think that must be
so-and-so." Then, "No . . ." And you start thinking about it. And it
sets you straight. You can remember things wrongly. You assume
something through the years, and then you realize you probably tinted
that up a little bit.

Interviewer: In your essay "Words into Fiction," you talk about a
writer choosing his subject and a subject choosing a writer. You say,
"He has taken the fatal step when he puts himself into the subject's
hands." That line makes me think of the writer standing at the edge
of a cliff.

Welty: That was very dramatic of me, wasn't it, to put it that way?
That's true with me, always. I mean, that's my true thought: That
once you have committed yourself to a story, if you're embarked on
it or if you're jumping on it, you can't go back on it. There's no way
to unimagine something once you've imagined it. I don't mean it's
going to be a success, but the act of imagining has its own velocity,
its own power, its own . . . it calls up what it needs as it goes on. I
know I'm sounding too fancy. But you can't unthink something, just
as you can't disremember something. Or you can't snatch back a

dream you've had. It has its own arrow. Like time. That does sound too fancy. If you're really committed—if it's a strong idea you're committed to—I think you'll carry it on. Whether it succeeds or not is another matter. It doesn't guarantee anything.

You can't halfway start something. You can't put one foot over. You've got to jump. I don't know why I think of everything as diving and jumping. I'm a very unathletic person.

Interviewer: And what about subjects choosing a writer?

Welty: Certainly, when I wrote *One Writer's Beginnings,* it got hold of me. It was suggested to me as a subject, but no one could've done it but myself. And I really was in its grip when I was writing that very book. I thought about it night and day. And each thing would suggest something else and something else, and everything linked up. Connections appeared everywhere that I hadn't realized before. But if that isn't choosing you, I don't know what is.

Interviewer: Did *One Writer's Beginnings* surprise you when it became a bestseller?

Welty: Oh, of course. It surprised Harvard University off their nuts. They couldn't imagine it. A university press!

Interviewer: Are you writing short stories again?

Welty: I haven't found that beautiful consecutive time yet. The uninterrupted time. That's what I'm waiting for. I had some stories on the way and stopped to write *One Writer's Beginnings,* and I haven't gone back to see if they're alive. To see if their vitality is still there. I'm kind of scared to. I don't want to pick it up and immediately have to drop it again. So I want to wait until I have clear time again, which may be forever away. I want to very much. It's the only kind of writing that I really, really love to do.

Interviewer: There's a story I've heard about how you came to Duke University to lecture, and Reynolds Price, who was an undergraduate at the time, met you at the train station in a white suit. Didn't you discover him as a writer even before he had published *A Long and Happy Life?*

Welty: I wouldn't say I discovered him. No, I couldn't. He was in Mr. [William] Blackburn's class, and he was the editor of the magazine at that point. I think [novelist] Elizabeth Bowen had read his stuff. A lot of people had. Anybody who read him knew that here it was, the real thing. All I did that maybe the others wouldn't have had any way to do was to introduce him to my literary agent, Diarmuid Russell, who was such an unusual and sensitive man and just really an extraordinary agent that I thought good would come of that, and I think it did. But that would have happened, too.

Interviewer: But you and Reynolds had an immediate affinity for each other, didn't you?

Welty: We became friends right from the beginning. And he has meant a great deal to me.

Interviewer: And how did he look in that white suit? I've heard Josephine Humphreys say that she went to Duke because she'd been so impressed with Reynolds Price in his blue seersucker suit during her interview there.

Welty: Oh, he's a marvelous dresser. A wonderful dresser. Well, when I saw him, it was in just the glimmer of whatever early hours of the morning it was. Just one light at the station. Of course, I wasn't expecting to see anybody. He was very slender and youthful. Very dark. Of course, his hair's gray now. But then it was very dark. He was very romantic-looking. But I couldn't see anything that night except a savior dressed in white.

Interviewer: You were doing a workshop at Duke?

Welty: I think I did some readings. I was there a week, I believe.

Interviewer: Your uncle—or your relative—is Walter Hines Page, for whom Duke's Page Auditorium is named.

Welty: My grandfather's mother and Walter Hines Page's mother were sisters. He was a first cousin of my grandmother's. I've had some letters from some of the people that connected us—by the name of Robbiteau, a French Huguenot name. I was at Randolph-Macon [College] earlier this year for something, and I was given a book to sign—to Page Robbiteau somebody—and I wrote on the book, ''Whoever you are, man or woman''—I didn't know who it was—''you're bound to be kin to me.'' And it is a woman. She wrote to me after I got home, and she said she'd been too shy to appear in person, but she knew we were kin.

Interviewer: I read a *Paris Review* interview with you in which you told about the first time you met William Faulkner in Oxford, Mississippi. You said you were at a dinner party where there was a lot of hymn singing.

Welty: There was some hymn singing.

Interviewer: And ballad singing. And then you said, "He invited me to go sailing the next day." Did you go?

Welty: Yeah. Faulkner and a bunch of his cronies had spent a long time making this sailboat. And he would go sailing on Sardis Lake. I think it was still new to him then. There was a man from home who was up there with me, and he invited us both. We went down to where the lake was, and the lake was so new that there were all these stobs- or what we called stobs. Stumps and stobs. It was like a cypress swamp standing there in the lake, and it was just mud. And the boat came up sort of far out. And Faulkner said, "Well, come on!" So we had to wade out.

Interviewer: What did you have on?

Welty: I guess I had on a cotton dress and probably my white pumps. I don't know what I had on. I had on clothes. I didn't have on pants, I know. So we walked out there and got into the boat, climbed in. I was so petrified, sailing. I don't think anybody said a word the whole time. Faulkner just placidly drove—steered, sailed—the boat. I sat behind, and John [the friend from Jackson] sat behind. It just felt like a dream going all around. And then he brought us back, and we went to his house and talked a little while. He was as kind as he could be. He didn't have to invite me to go sailing.

Interviewer: What did you think of Faulkner when you met him the night before?

Welty: I just thought he was fine. Of course, I was scared to meet him. I was surprised he was small—or compared to me—because I think of him as a giant. He was very quiet and small. He always spoke in a low voice. He did his part in the conversation. But I have seen him in company when he didn't say anything. Not that night. I was thrilled.

Interviewer: Whose idea was the hymn singing?

Welty: Oh, it was a bunch of cronies. That's who I ate dinner with. I was a friend of Miss Ella Somerville, who was one of the grand ladies of Oxford. She'd invited me to stay with her. So the Faulkners and two other couples were old friends that met all the time. I was meeting the Faulkners for the first time. I knew some of the others already. So it was the best way. Just a small dinner party—the two Faulkners and Bob Farley, who was dean of the law school, and I

can't remember who else. I think they often did this way. I don't
know whose idea this was.

Interviewer: You'll be eighty in April. I remember Winston Churchill
said when he turned eighty that it got there much faster than he
thought it would. Do you feel that way?

Welty: I don't know. It seems impossible. Ask me after the fact. If
I'm still here, ask me after the fact.

It's always a shock to think of your age in any way. I'd like to just
be in England and doing something I enjoyed. In Jackson, since I've
lived here all my life, everybody just loves to celebrate things with
me. They're very sweet about it. But I don't know if I could stand to
have that celebrated. It's too much. The other day, I said I thought I
was going to be in France or England. It struck me with a blow. They
just can't do anything. They've done it all. There's nothing left. Too
much. Too much.

Interviewer: You've said you write from a feeling of praise and
celebration for life, and that your wish would be not to point a finger
in judgment, but to part the curtain.

Welty: I think a writer of short stories writes to let their characters
reveal human nature. That's what I mean by parting curtains. In
writing a story, it's not *I* as a writer who wants to appear to be doing
this, but the people of the story. The way you feel when you read a
wonderful story by Chekhov or somebody: You feel you've been
present at something.

An Interview with Eudora Welty

Wayne Pond / 1988

From *National Humanities Center Newsletter,* 10 (Fall 1988), 1–5. Reprinted by permission of Wayne Pond, Director of Public Programs, National Humanities Center.

When the renowned writer, Eudora Welty, took part recently in a conference sponsored by the Department of English at the University of North Carolina at Chapel Hill, she was invited to the National Humanities Center for a radio interview on "Soundings," distributed to over 250 stations in the United States. At his studio off a corridor on the ground floor of the Center, Wayne Pond, Public Programs Officer, talked to the author of such highly-regarded books as *One Writer's Beginnings,* published in paperback in 1985, about her work. The following is a slightly edited version of the interview aired on the "Soundings" series during the week of March 5, 1989.

WP: Eudora Welty, welcome to the National Humanities Center and to "Soundings." Let's talk about *One Writer's Beginnings.* I remember your quoting a friend, I believe an editor, who said to you, "Be sure to get your moon in the right part of the sky." What does that mean to you?

EW: Well, it means to know absolutely your fundamentals and have your feet on solid ground when you venture anything. That was a marvelous piece of advice to give me, because I was prone to be rather free-handed with things I would say. You know, if I wanted a sunset, I'd have it even though it might be two o'clock in the afternoon in the wrong direction.

WP: Did you ever get the moon out of the sky, and what happened when you did?

EW: Why, I don't know. I nearly always had moons in the thing. You know, a romantic turn of mind. This was Herschel Brickell, a good critic. That was sound advice. I would give it to anybody. To get your facts right. I don't want to be confined when I write a story, because I want to get at the human truth and human relationships.

WP: Well, you say that you always move from the particular to the general, that you'd never begin with generalities. What kinds of particularities are on your mind now?

EW: Well, suppose I were writing a story now. I would take this location and who you were, and why you were here, and what kind of day this was, and your gesture, like punching your cheek with your fountain pen. And then whoever was sitting here, the same way. And then what kind of relationship was struck up just by our conversation, I would start from scratch, you know.

WP: You write, for instance, about seeing, and acquiring a voice, and listening. Do you hear what the critics have said about your work? Has it in any way shaped your expressive voice?

EW: I'm not sure that I have kept up with a great percent of it. It just doesn't come my way. It's not that I'm disparaging it; I'm interested, of course. For instance, Louis Rubin. The things he's written about my work I find very valuable. I don't try to keep up with things in general that way. I mostly am a fiction reader, just as I'm a fiction writer. And the theory part has never been very conscious with me. I've tried to act conscientiously and consciously in the critical things, and I've done my share of essay writing and book reviewing, but while you're writing fiction, it's like being downstream on a river. And writing criticism is upstream. Your mind is not working the same way in both directions.

WP: Speaking of streams, again in *One Writer's Beginnings* you point out that the streams that feed your imagination have been both dark and bright.

EW: That's true.

WP: That instantly made me remember a line from a wonderful story by Nathaniel Hawthorne, "Blessed are all the emotions, be they dark or bright." It's the intermixture of the two that you have to look out for.

EW: Of course it is!

WP: Tell me about that in your writing.

EW: Oh, I hadn't thought about looking out for it. I hadn't thought of any conclusion to draw from that. I just thought they both exist. Well, it's just because what you try to do, I think, in fiction is to reflect life the way it is.

WP: Let's put a loaded word like "guilt" on the table. You pointed out that that is an element in your writing. Can you comment on that for me?

EW: I don't know. Again, it's thinking of work in a way that a writer doesn't think of it. You know, if it comes into play in the course of a situation or a character you're using in fiction, all right, but I don't look around and say, "Let's see, I better bring some guilt into this." I don't do that.

WP: Two cupfuls.

EW: Yes, two cupfuls. Certainly it's part of our life. I mean we all feel it from time to time, and it's very potent.

WP: What did you mean when you said that the emotions do not grow old? They haven't stayed static, I take it?

EW: No, they're alive! No, I think they always stay susceptible and aware and analytical, perhaps, I mean. Whatever is your personal nature where your feelings are concerned, you keep on handling them that way.

WP: I remember reading in an essay a line from the American biologist, Louis Agassiz, who says to his students, "Look at your fish." How did you acquire that ability, that talent for seeing?

EW: I don't know. Most people are born looking about them, I guess. And I have a visual mind, the most common form, I'm sure. I visualize everything, and I'm a pretty good observer and I'm sure I've trained myself to be a better one in the course of my life. And I draw ideas and conclusions from what I see often, but never by idea.

WP: Who is it that you read today?

EW: Everybody. I mean I read for pleasure. I'm reading the new editions of Chekhov that Echo Press has just brought out in thirteen volumes, and V. S. Pritchett has just published his new biography of Chekhov, which I got the day I left home.

WP: Is there a young Eudora Welty on the literary scene today? Do you think of yourself as having some sort of a mantle that you want to pass on, in literary terms?

EW: No, I don't hand out or pass out any kind of advice. There are a lot of people writing now that I'm thrilled to read. Your writers here, Anne Tyler, Elizabeth Spencer, and Clyde Edgerton, and . . .

WP: Writers in and around Chapel Hill.

EW: Writers, yes, all these around Chapel Hill are fascinating to me and I have been reading them all along. I haven't just found them. I've been reading them.

WP: Let me look at you wide-eyed and ask you a question: What good is literature?

EW: Heavens! That does leave *me* wide-eyed! It's all the good!

WP: Let me be just a little impertinent. Isn't it a little old-fashioned and kind of stuffy to talk about literature in those terms?

EW: I hope not. I don't think it matters whether it's old-fashioned or not. It's here to stay. No, I mean, I can't imagine life without a recourse to a treasure like that. It'd be like saying, let's throw all the paintings that have ever been painted in the Atlantic Ocean, you know. Bring on Michelangelo, everybody. It would be the same way, or worse, if we lost our literature.

WP: A footnote to our conversation: As you look back on the fiction that you have written, do you have a favorite story or character that has stayed with you more so than others?

EW: I don't know. They've all been favorites for different reasons when I've written them, and some of them that I really like wouldn't be remembered by other people, perhaps. It's hard to think back. It's like saying, "What member of your family do you think really stands out?"

WP: Well, let me give you an example. What about R. W. Bowman, a character in the first story that you published? Is he still present in your mind? This is "Death of a Traveling Salesman."

EW: I guess so. Yes, I respect him, and so on, but I don't go back and think about my stories that way.

WP: Do the characters still talk amongst themselves, and talk to you?

EW: I don't know. I guess they're too close to do that. They're too close to me. They're being invented by me; I don't have to call them up, you know. I like Edna Earl Ponder a good deal in *The Ponder Heart*. I like some of my more frivolous characters, whose lines would come to me—like I'd hear somebody say something on a bus. It would bring up a character to me that had no relation to what I heard on the bus. I remember those people. I can hear their lines. I forget who said it in my story, but I love her, because she said, "She can spend all day trying to figure out how the little tail of the 'C' gets through the 'l' in the the Coca Cola sign.'' I just love her. That's not a rational reason. I just love people for various little tags.

WP: You're certainly entitled to it. Another very quick footnote to our conversation: Is the South, in your opinion, still as important in American literary culture, still distinctive as a region, and important to us?

EW: I think we have just as many writers, if not more, now. But I think perhaps they've all come to the same conclusion I have, that we don't want to be identified by being called Southern. I think that's a great limitation to set yourself behind. I'm proud that I'm Southern and it's taught me a lot, but to identify me by that one word is to subtract something of what I'm trying to do, and this goes for all of us I'm sure. There was recently, at Millsaps College, a little bunch of Southern writers talking about Southern writing. And that can get to be pretty cozy, you know. I'm proud of it and like it. This is not to deny it. It's just to say, "O.K. That's where we stand. Now, let's look around.'' And I think everybody feels that.

Eudora Welty and Photography: An Interview

Hunter Cole and Seetha Srinivasan / 1989

From "Introduction" to Eudora Welty, *Photographs* (Jackson: Univ. Press of Mississippi, 1989), xiii–xxviii. The interview was conducted at Eudora Welty's home in Jackson in January 1989. Reprinted by permission of University Press of Mississippi.

You call the published pictures in One Time, One Place *snapshots and called it a snapshot album. Why do you consider them snapshots and not photographs?*

Well, they were snapshots. It refers to the way they were taken, which gave meaning to the book. They were taken spontaneously—to catch something as I came upon it, something that spoke of the life going on around me. A snapshot's now or never.

What camera did you use?

I started with a small Eastman Kodak with a bellows, that used Number 116 film. It wasn't expensive, but it had a good lens, and a shutter which I remember allowed for 1/25th and 1/50th and 1/100th of a second exposure and time exposure. I could really see the 116 negatives before I printed them or made enlargements—I could learn from the mistakes I'd made.

And you used other cameras?

As time went by. One was a mistake. I bought a Recomar which used a film pack. Another Eastman Kodak, it was large and expensive and for me it proved unhandy. One time in New York I took it and sold it back to the same place I bought it. Then later I was able to buy a Rolleiflex, which in these times, of course, would be unaffordable.

And you preferred it above the others, of course?

It was above all. Mainly for the wonderful ground glass viewfinder, which was the exact size and shape of the picture I was going to take. So that I got a sense of composing a precise picture, and the negatives were lovely to work with. All this time I was printing my own, after I had the film developed at Standard Photo. My brother Edward made me a contact exposure thing like a little box frame. Then I got an old castoff enlarger from the Mississippi Highway Department. I set up a darkroom in my kitchen at night with a red light to work by, and the enlarger clamped on the kitchen table. It had only one shutter opening—wide open—and the only way you could control or graduate the exposure was by timing it, which you could learn by doing.

Once when I was in New York, I went into a camera shop, Lugene's on Madison Avenue, to buy some supplies and saw the owner had an exhibition around the room of an amateur's photographs, prints that were made there. So I wondered what he would think of mine. And he looked at my pictures and decided to show them. He supplied me with a lot of stuff that I never knew about—better paper, chemicals, and things like that. He was helpful, too—he marked on each one what was wrong, like not enough contrast, too much, and so on. And so I printed up a collection of the best ones for him, and he did exhibit them, as you probably know, and a little program too. I read here the reason he showed them was that they had been printed in Mississippi under "primitive conditions." And I realized that all this time I had been a "primitive."

How were those pictures received in the North?
I doubt if anybody knew the difference. They wouldn't have been reviewed. It wasn't a gallery, it was a shop, and even if reviewers had seen the show, they would have found it enough to say that here are primitive pictures by an unknown from Mississippi.

Was it your father and his love of mechanical instruments that interested you in photography?
I suppose indirectly. The pictures he was taking were mostly of us, but we were hardly conscious of that. I do remember being allowed to handle his camera. He had a nice Eastman camera with a bellows that pulled out a good long way. He made the exposure by pressing a little bulb, as I remember. It took postcard-sized pictures. I learned much later on that he'd had other cameras that produced different-sized photos—I found the negatives he had made. He and my mother used to develop them and print the pictures at night, before we children were born, my mother told me. Domestic scenes, early in their marriage—Mother putting up her hair, Daddy reading. They charm me.

Didn't he encourage some entrepreneur to develop a camera store or a photography shop in Jackson?

He did—when the Schleuters came to Jackson. My father's insurance company, the Lamar Life, was then a little Greek edifice, if you remember, with columns, on Capitol Street, near Mrs. Black's grocery store and the Pythian Castle. On its other side was a vacant lot. The Schleuters came in and asked my father about it and he was interested because he liked photography and because they were two brothers, young and starting out in a strange place. He did encourage them, I don't know in what way. And they started Standard Photo Company, built on the vacant lot, and made a success. They did my pictures all through the years, and advised me and were good friends.

When your pictures were printed, did they give a surprise? A good one or a bad one? You know that various camera lenses have personalities? Did you detect that when you were printing your pictures?

Well, I had only a single lens in those days, you know. I just thought: that was the lens. After I got the Rolleiflex, the only other lens I bought was a portrait attachment, which I didn't use too much because I like showing background, a long perspective, in the kind of portraits I attempt. I wanted to set people in their context. And I think I had a cloud filter; but that's all. I never used lights. I'm not in any sense of the word a professional. I just wanted to get the subject and play with it afterwards; cutting and enlarging and so on, I find my composition. Let it show what was inherent in it.

When you were traveling and taking photographs, you really began to see the state in which you lived. Would you say that your experience with photographs heightened your sense of place?

I think it did. I think the same thing that made me take the pictures made me understand the pictures after I saw them, the same curiosity, interest. I've always been a visual-minded person. Most of us are. I could see a picture composing itself without too much trouble when I started taking landscapes and groups and catching people in action. Practice did make me see what to bring out and define what I was after, I think.

As you reflect on your pictures, what do you see in them now after all these many years?

I see a record. The life in those times. And that's really why I thought *One Time, One Place,* in 1970, would make a book. It stands as a record of a time and place.

You have said that a camera is a shy person's protection and that you came from a sheltered life, but you've had the spirit of daring required of an artist. Would you comment on how a shy person such as you took some of these daring photographs?

Well, the daring I meant was referring to my writing instead of photography, but also I think my particular time and place contributed to the frankness, openness of the way the pictures came about. This refers to both the photographer and the subjects of the photographs. I was never questioned, or avoided. There was no self-consciousness on either side. I just spoke to persons on the street and said, "Do you mind if I take this picture?" And they didn't care. There was no sense of violation of anything on either side. I don't think it existed; I know it didn't in my attitude, or in theirs. All of that unself-consciousness is gone now. There is no such relationship between a photographer and a subject possible any longer.

Why is that?

Everybody is just so media-conscious. Maybe it's television. Everybody thinks of pictures as publicity or—I don't know. I wouldn't be interested in doing such a book today, even if it were possible. Because it would assume a different motive and produce a different effect.

What did the pictures teach you about writing fiction? Did they teach you anything?

Nothing consciously, I guess, or specifically. I was writing all this time, but I think perhaps a kindred impulse made me attempt two unrelated things—an inquiring nature, and a wish to respond to what I saw, and to what I felt about things, by something I produced or did.

Did they teach you anything about perception or anything about technique?

I'm sure they taught me about the practice of perception and about technique, but the lessons were not in the abstract. Some perception of the world and some habit of observation shaded into the other, just because in both cases, writing and photography, you were trying to portray what you saw, and truthfully. Portray life, living people, as you saw them. And a camera could catch that fleeting moment, which is what a short story, in all its depth, tries to do. If it's sensitive enough, it catches the transient moment.

You studied studio art, you painted, you sketched. In these, do you suppose, as perhaps with photography, that you were searching for a way to reach your calling as a writer of fiction?

I don't think so. My way to learn writing was through writing, from the start, and I did write in strict concentration. It may have occurred without my knowing it that the two interests cooperated in their own way, but I wasn't thinking about either writing or photography except through the doing. Technique springs out of the doing; there's something in the heart of a given story that tells me how to do it and do that only. It's *after* the fact of writing a story that I realize what it has taught me.

It was during one of your WPA trips that you discovered you were truly a writer. In Tishomingo County, Mississippi.

Well, I assigned it there because that is the furthest in Mississippi I ever went. I didn't have a blinding moment of revelation. But just when I was working on *Losing Battles,* a novel set in that part of the world, so much came back to me of what I had absorbed. It was so remote from anything I knew in Jackson or had seen in the Delta or on the Coast or in the Black Prairie country, or any of the other parts of Mississippi where I've been. It appealed to me as a stage to put *Losing Battles* on because life there had been so whittled down to the bare bones of existence. No history but the struggle to keep alive. What was life but family? I was trying to describe what the characters' lives were like without benefit of any editorial comment at all, or any interior description. I wanted things shown by speech, by action, and by setting, location. And characters to reveal themselves and each other by conversation—action and conversation. I confined it all within a big family reunion, to a time length of two days and the night between. Plus the essential flashback.

That technique is very much like in photography?

Except that what is shown is selective. Chosen, specific, pertinent, and thus revelatory.

There is no interpretation in a photograph. It's the viewer who interprets it, and what you've described as your technique in Losing Battles *seems very much like a photograph.*

There's a profound difference. The writer interprets before it can begin. Writing fiction, I am interpreting every minute, but always by way of the characters' own words and acts. My usual method of narration is more introspective; I am in the characters' minds all the time. So I was trying to see if I could do without any of it. It proved to be the most difficult novel I think I ever wrote.

As in a story, your photographs have a trace of mystery. In your essay on Chekhov you said that "the very greatest mystery is in unsheathed reality itself." Is this "unsheathed reality" what your photographs were exposing?

That's too abstract for me. No technique was set forth in my mind. I just wanted to capture a moment and use the right light and take advantage of what I saw.

The young girl in your story "A Memory" composes the intractable world by looking at life through a frame she makes with her fingers. In your essay "Place in Fiction" you say, "Place to the writer at work is seen in a frame . . ."

It is.

". . . not an empty one, a brimming one." Do you recognize the close alliance of photography and fiction writing in your use of a frame?

A frame is fundamental to both, for me. I was conscious of that when I was getting my pictures, at least when I was printing the results. I knew I needed a frame. Well, when I took art from Mrs. Hull [Marie Hull, Jackson painter and teacher], she taught us that device: framing with your fingers. Studying drawing and painting made me aware in writing a story of framing your *vision,* as a way toward capturing it.

When taking a picture, what was your own personal technique in framing an image? Do you recall any?

Using the viewfinder. That's why I liked the Rolleiflex. You see exactly what you are taking, and in the same size.

Have your ever relied upon any of your photographs for a scene or an element in a story you've written?
No. The memory is far better. Personal experience casts its essential light upon it.

I'm thinking of the suspension bridge in Losing Battles, *or . . .*
It was the bridge itself that made me think of it in fiction. It was having been on it. It also made me want to photograph it and show the dramatic quality of it.

Do you think that maybe some scenes, the Mardi Gras scene in The Optimist's Daughter, *for instance, are subconsciously a reflection of one of your Mardi Gras photographs?*
Not as a reflection; I've seen it directly in life. But I went back and looked up my photographs after I had written this to get some exact costume that I could give a person. You can't *make up* something fantastic. So I used, in the way I might refer to notes, certain snapshots of costumes, but it was the Mardi Gras itself, the living experience, working in my imagination, that made me put it in the story in the first place. My fiction's source is living life.

You said of the pictures in One Time, One Place, *"I did not take these pictures to prove anything." But the photographs do prove something, don't they?*
I think I meant "prove" editorially. *Let Us Now Praise Famous Men,* for instance, was entirely different in motivation from my own photography. I was taking photographs of human beings because they were real life and they were there in front of me and that was the reality. I was the recorder of it. I wasn't trying to exhort the public. When I was in New York during the Depression, it was the same Depression we were feeling here in Mississippi but evident in such another way in the city: lines of people waiting for food and people selling apples and sitting there in Union Square, all reading the daily paper's want ads. It was a different homelessness too from what we see today in New York. These people of the Great Depression kept alive on the determination to get back to work and to make a living again. I photographed them in Union Square and in subways and sleeping in subway stations and huddling together to keep warm, and I felt, then, sort of placed in the editorial position as I took their

pictures. Recording the mass of them did constitute a plea on their behalf to the public, their existing plight being so evident in the mass.

Do you think someone, an outsider, for instance, who sees the collection of your black photographs together makes editorial comments?

They might. They might or might not know that poverty in Mississippi, white and black, really didn't have too much to do with the Depression. It was ongoing. Mississippi was long since poor, long devastated. I took the pictures of our poverty because that was reality, and I was recording it. The photographs speak for themselves. The same thing is true of my stories; I didn't announce my view editorially. I tried to *show* it.

"Unsheathed reality."

It was unsheathed. And when it was published, *One Time, One Place* constituted a statement of that reality. It wasn't needed for me to say, "Look what a bad thing." Or, "Look how these people are facing it, facing up to it, meeting it, hoping as well as enduring it."

Will you tell of a proposed book called Black Saturday?

It was essentially the same as what later became *One Time, One Place,* plus a number of my short stories. I was trying to interest a publisher in my stories through the combination. I got a composition ring book and pasted little contact prints in what I fitted up as a sequence to make a kind of story in itself. I used the subject of Saturday because it allowed the most variety possible to show a day among black and white people, what they would be doing, the work and the visit to town and the home and so on. I submitted along with the pictures a set of stories I had written, unrelated specifically to the photos, except that all were the South, and tried to interest book publishers in the combination.

And what was the reaction?

Rejection. It was an amateurish idea.

Did they give a reason?

Well, there were obvious ones to such a combination as I was offering. They said they were sorry. (Most of the letters are in the Archives [Mississippi Department of Archives and History].) They were understanding and kind, but it was a fact that such a book was unpublishable. They were sympathetic to the stories, but weren't much interested in the photographs—they were not that kind of editors, that was not their department.

Were any of the stories later published?
They were all published. First in magazines, then in *A Curtain of Green* and *The Wide Net,* five or six years later.

And most of the photographs were later published in One Time, One Place.
Yes. I'd like to point out that when a publisher *did* bring out the book of photographs, thirty years later, it was a literary editor who did it, and saw it through: Albert Erskine, of Random House. He was editor of my last two novels at Random House.

And you didn't publish a story until 1936?
1936 is right. That was the first story I submitted to a magazine, "Death of a Traveling Salesman." A so-called "little magazine" accepted it, called *Manuscript,* published in Athens, Ohio.

It seemed that your taking photographs stopped or seemed considerably slowed down as you began publishing stories. The collection of photographs in the Archives indicates that by about the mid-1940s you had set aside your camera. What happened?
I guess I was still taking pictures. They were for my own pleasure, of my family and friends. The new jobs I had all had to do with journalism, not pictures. And fiction writing was my real work all along. That never let up.

I think the latest photos were in the 1950s.
That's when I lost my camera.

Will you tell about that?
I was on my first trip to Europe, and I carried my Rolleiflex and took pictures all the way through. As I was getting ready to go home, it was May Day and I was in Paris, and I had friends there and had spent the day with them in Meudon, near Versailles I think that is. It was the home of the Mians. He was a sculptor, Aristide Mian. His wife was the American writer Mary Mian. They had three growing daughters. All were on hand, and all kinds of people they knew. So I

took pictures of everybody and everything. A record of happiness. Then I left on the train, got off at Gare Montparnasse to take the Metro to my hotel off Boulevard St. Germaine. They'd given me a bunch of lilacs, party food, presents, everything, saying goodbye, and I sat down on the bench in the station holding it all, with my camera beside me. And got up without the camera. I missed it as soon as I got on the subway and took the first train back. Of course it was gone. I never saw it again. Of course what I grieved for most was that that roll of film was still in it, the pictures that I had taken. If I could have just got that back, the May Day party, I would have almost given them the camera.

And those people would never be assembled that way again.
Never assembled. Never again.

So that slowed you down in your picture-taking?
I punished myself. I didn't deserve a camera after that. I was so crushed, and by then cameras were much more expensive and of course now they are out of sight.

When the team of Farm Security Administration photographers came on their individual trips through Mississippi, you too were working for a federal agency, the WPA. Did you chance to see Walker Evans or any of them or their work?
Oh, no. What I should have said a while ago is that the difference between my pictures and Walker Evans', among other differences— those people were professionals—is I never posed anybody—that was on principle—and his are all deliberately composed pictures. I let my subjects go on with what they were doing and, by framing or cutting and by selection, found what composition rose from that. So, I think that's a quality that makes them different from those of professionals who were purposefully photographing for an agency, or a cause.

Some of your pictures show people at a sideshow at a carnival. What drew you to photographing oddities like carnival people?
Oh, I love crowds to take pictures in. I photographed everybody. I always did love the fair and circuses. Once or twice to photograph them, I got up early before daylight and went down to see them arrive, watch them set up the tents and the rides down at the fairgrounds.

And I remember once happening to eat breakfast with some of the carnival people in the bus station. *That* was getting close to life!

Some of the people are freaks. Are you familiar with the photographs of Diane Arbus?
Yes, somewhat.

How do you react to photographs of freaks, the kind in her work?
I think that it totally violates human privacy, and by intention. My taking the freak *posters*—not the human beings—was because they were a whole school of naive folk art. And, of course, totally unrelated to what you saw inside the tent. The posters show bystanders being suddenly horrified at a man who could twist himself like a snake. They are all looking with hands drawn back and shrieking, and *they* were all perfectly dressed, probably wearing evening clothes.

Did your story about Little Lee Roy, "Keela, the Outcast Indian Maiden," rise out of your experiences in viewing carnival people?
Actually, it grew out of my job with the WPA. In the publicity department, one of the chores we did was set up a booth for the WPA in county fairs. While I was doing the job, I didn't ever see the midways or shows. Someone told me about something like "Keela, the Outcast Indian Maiden," which I'd never heard of. Of course, I know now it's a geek, and an act that's very prevalent. Nothing in this world would have induced me to go and look at the show. It's a psychological story I wrote in "Keela." I was interested in what sort of points of view people could have toward such an atrocious thing, including that of the victim himself. He, I guessed, like people in many a kind of experience, might have rather enjoyed it years later in his looking back on the days of excitement. You know, things, awful as well as not, get to be kind of interesting in a different way after you've lived through them and they are embedded in your past. Lee Roy had eventually forgotten all the humiliation and the horror.

But all of his children are there.
All of his children are there, and *they* don't want to hear about it. They just say, "Hush, Pappy!"

Could we speak of some of the notable photographers who have taken pictures of writers? You have been in photographs by Jill

Krementz, Kay Bell, Thomas Victor, Jerry Bauer, Rollie McKenna,
William Eggleston, and others. Do you mind being photographed?
Yes, it's not my nature to be on the other side of the camera. It
came about through the circumstance of my being a writer. Many of
my stories were in *Harper's Bazaar* and it was through the editors'
wish that I was a subject for Cecil Beaton and Louise Dahl-Wolfe,
and Irving Penn.

Will you tell about being photographed by Cecil Beaton?
He's the one I was most scared of because I was the most familiar
with his work, over the years of seeing it in *Vanity Fair*. I had to go to
his apartment in one of the hotels up Fifth Avenue. I didn't know
what to wear. I thought I wore the safest thing, "a little black dress."
And went up in the elevator and he met me at the door. It seemed to
me he was the most shy and reticent and kind person I'd ever seen.
And he held a Rolleiflex. It looked just like the one I had lost. And it
was hand-held, and he had no lights anywhere. And it was in the
winter time, a grey cold day, but he had a great flowering mimosa in
the window. Not *our* mimosa trees, but the South-of-France kind,
with little powdery yellow flowers all over it, so it looked very tropical
in the window. It was fragrant. My black dress of course *was* wrong.
But he gave me a wicker armchair to stand behind. It looked very
"Cecil Beatonish." Everything was very decorative and summery.
And I don't remember anything he said except just kindnesses. He
offered me some tea or something, and everything was very muted
and peaceful. He took the pictures, and we parted. It was like a social
visit in a way, but there was not much conversation back and forth.

He stood you over by the window, didn't he?
I've got one of the prints. He sent me one and had autographed it,
which I thought was extremely sweet of him.

Will you tell about the photographic session with Louise Dahl-
Wolfe, who was a Harper's Bazaar *photographer? A fashion photog-*
rapher.
She was interesting. I enjoyed it.

In the photographs of you, it looks as though you are against a
rock on the beach.
It's in Central Park. I was to lie back on a rock in Central Park. I

had on a tweed suit and a sweater. The session was brisk and very
lively, and she was an interesting woman. It was Irving Penn who
took me to Central Park too, and we made some funny photographs
along with the ones he used.

What kind of funny photographs did he take?
In one of them I was kneeling on the ground by a sign that read "To
restrooms and bear den." And one of them was sitting up in a tree,
sort of like the one Frank Lyell and I concocted with myself perched
in a tree at Annandale while wearing a Spanish shawl, and Frank
serenading me from below.

*You as a photographer yourself observed how these photographers
worked. What specifically did you note about their attitudes and
techniques? Anything?*
I doubt that I was able. I think I observed rightly that Irving Penn
was at an early part of his career. He was venturesome. Whereas,
Louise Dahl-Wolfe and Cecil Beaton were majestic figures, whose
work everybody knew. What I noticed about all of them was how
none of them gave you any directions, laid down any rules. I don't
know whether because I was hopeless or whether they just didn't ever
do it; they didn't say, "Stand here," and "Put your hand here." They
never said, "Smile, please!"

*In "Why I Live at the P.O." the narrator tells that the only
"eligible" man ever to appear in the town was a photographer who
was taking "pose-yourself photos." Could you tell what a "pose-
yourself photo" is?*
A man that came through little towns and set up a make-shift studio
in somebody's parlor and let it be known that he would be taking
pictures all day in this place, and a stream of people came. He had
backdrops—sepia trees and a stool—then let them pose themselves.
That was an itinerant livelihood during the Depression. Itinerants
were welcome, bringing excitement like that, when towns were remote
and nobody ever went anywhere.

*Some of those funny photographs that you and Frank Lyell took
are set up like the "tableaux vivants" Julia Margaret Cameron
photographed, costume pieces. Hers were a kind of "pose-yourself"
photography.*

Oh, they were high-minded. I think they belonged to the Rossetti period, taking themselves seriously as art.

You and your friends created some "tableaux vivants." Will you tell about those?
Well, as I say, during the Depression we made our own entertainment and one of our entertainments was to take funny pictures. We dressed up a lot, something to do at night. Even when we had little dinner parties for each other with four or six people, we wore long dresses. And everybody came, you know, we came *as* somebody, like parties in *Vanity Fair,* people like Lady Abdy, and the Lunts, all the people that Cecil Beaton photographed doing things at parties. We were doing our version of that. We didn't take ourselves seriously. We played charades, word games.

There is one photo of you satirizing Elizabeth Arden and Helena Rubinstein, "Helena Arden," showing you draped in a sheet and applying some very strange cosmetics.
That's right, out of the kitchen. Bon Ami.

Was the photography here a parody of "smartness" in the Mencken sense?
No, we were satirizing the advertising game. In the thirties you could laugh at advertising. It was all fun. A lot of it came out of our admiration of the smart world, our longing for the artistic scene we were keeping up with: the theatre, art, and music. We'd all been to New York! The year before, at Columbia.

Didn't you yourself do some freelance fashion photography?
I tried to earn a little money doing that. I took one picture every Sunday for a shop called Oppenheimer's. And the Emporium later. I got my friends and my brother's girlfriends to pose.

In their fashions?
The shops' selections. I would pose them in different places the way they did in *Vanity Fair*—in front of the New Capitol, around the town like that. They were not very good.

And there are some time exposures in which you and a friend are set up as women of fashion.
Right. Helen Lotterhos, Margaret Harmon, and Anne Long. With

jars of pampas grass, and rising cigarette smoke. Subtle lighting. These were all fun, you see. And nothing cost anything. We had jobs, most of us, by day, and thought up our own entertainments in the evening. We'd just come out of college. We were young. We had a good time in the Depression.

What do you recall about photographing Katherine Anne Porter?
I did it every minute. A summer at Yaddo. I went to Yaddo, I'm sure, at her instigation, which you know is in Saratoga Springs, New York. A retreat for artists. She had been there a number of times as a resident. I was reading proofs of my first book. Katherine Anne was supposed to be writing the preface to my book. And my editor used to write me and say jokingly, you're supposed to make her do it. Which, of course, I never mentioned! She was busy writing what was then called *No Safe Harbor*. It was eventually *Ship of Fools*. She had also bought an old run-down clapboard farmhouse, perfectly beautiful, sitting in a meadow outside Saratoga Springs. It was heavenly, in the real country, and she was restoring it. We went out there every day. She bought a car, a Buick, first time she had ever had one, and had just learned to drive. I helped her drive some of the time, if I remember. I would rather help her drive. Anyway, we went forth. So, of course, I took pictures of all the progress of the house and of the daily life of Katherine Anne. All the good pictures I took of her in my life were out there. She found in the walls of this house honey bees' nests that must have been there since it was empty, and she found a whole lot of tiny ladies' slippers and men's shoes from, she thought, Colonial times. And some hoops to be worn with hoop skirts. I was at Yaddo for six weeks or something like that. Katherine Anne and I were already friends, but we became very good friends then. Katherine Anne was a cook. She made French onion soup, an all-day process. I was the grocery girl. I couldn't work in Yaddo. Everybody had a sign on their door saying, "Silence, writer at work." I read my proofs, but I couldn't write in there. Everything was so tense, even exalted. So I walked into Saratoga, and to the races, and took pictures in Saratoga. And I would bring home groceries for Katherine Anne to cook with, and so we had a good time.

Will you comment upon this wonderful photograph of Katherine Anne Porter?

Yes, I was pleased with it because I thought it showed something of
her inner spirit, which she didn't usually show in her photographs as
a beauty or a performing artist, reading for the public on stage. Of
course, those are all radiantly beautiful. But this quiet, unposed one
was the inside story; the awareness of the writer I think came through.
Its regard is introspective, deeply serious. And I think it's more
beautiful. I don't know what she thought of this. I don't know what
she thought of any of them. But this one has held up for me, all these
years, as a sobering glimpse of this artist's inner life.

*Henry Miller was not a friend of yours, but he showed up in Jackson
and you and some of your friends took him to see the ruins of
Windsor. Is that right? And you took some photographs?*
It's a long, stupid story, I think.

Please tell the long and stupid story.
He was not a friend or an acquaintance. He had just come back to
America from being an expatriate all these years. And Doubleday, his
publisher, thought it would be a wonderful idea for Henry Miller to
go all over the country, which he had not seen in, lo, these many
years and write his impressions of America. They were going to buy
him a glass automobile, so that he could see everything and, in turn,
be seen everywhere. He was to write a book to be called *The Air-
Conditioned Nightmare*. So, John Woodburn, my beloved editor, who
was a big tease, thought, "O.K., I'm going to route Henry Miller by
Mississippi to see Eudora." With a big laugh. Well, my mother said,
"Indeed, he won't enter my house." He was the only person in her
life she ever said that about. She was quite firm. But he was going to
be here three days. I didn't know exactly what we had that he wanted
to see. I did my best, and showed him everything.

I got Hubert Creekmore and Nash Burger, and from time to time a
third friend, also a male, to be with us as we drove about in the family
car. I took him all around. He was infinitely bored with everything.
Nash, who knew a lot about the local history, tried to tell him
something about the country we were passing through. He didn't even
look out. He wore his hat all day. Hubert knew all of Henry Miller's
works, but Henry Miller didn't want to start on that. Windsor was
one of the places we took him to, and Natchez, and the Mississippi
River, and the lost town of Rodney—and Vicksburg. And every night

we took him to the Rotisserie to eat. If you couldn't have people to dinner at home, as was our case, there was only this one good restaurant to take people to. Sometimes we went to the drive-in part, sometimes to the steak part, sometimes upstairs to the dance part with the band—it was ramshackle. And finally, Henry Miller said, "How does a town like Jackson, Mississippi, rate three good restaurants!"

Well, you had a good story for John Woodburn, didn't you!

Oh, John was crazy about Henry's visit. And, of course we were safe—Henry Miller didn't mention the existence of Jackson in *The Air-Conditioned Nightmare*. And as for the glass automobile—not a sign of that. We had to ride him in the Welty Chevrolet or he couldn't have budged at all.

So much of your writing is set in Mississippi, and you have said that it is from place that much of your fiction arises. Do you see that the photographs you took outside your native state of Mississippi—in Ireland, Wales, Nice, Mexico—show the imprint of place also?

I suppose that what made me take the pictures was some irresistible notion that I might capture some essence of the place I'd just arrived at, new to me and my eyes and my camera. Yes, I was smitten by the *identity* of the place wherever I was, from Mississippi on—I still am. Incidentally, the reason I was in England at the time of the Monk's House picture was to give a paper to a meeting of British teachers of American subjects, and I took for my title "Place in Fiction."

You were a guest of Elizabeth Bowen at Bowen's Court in Ireland. Will you tell about that and about photographs you took there?

Elizabeth Bowen, V. S. Pritchett, Mary Lavin, Katherine Anne Porter—all of them became in time my good friends, and what first drew us together in every case, I believe, was the affinity—the particular affinity—that exists between writers of the short story. Elizabeth Bowen and I had known each other's work for a long time, and we met when I went to Ireland and she invited me to Bowen's Court in County Cork. These pictures came of my first visit to her in the early spring of 1950 and from a summer visit a year or so later. I'll add that Elizabeth Bowen responded to place herself with the greatest sensitivity, and did so when she came in turn to visit me in Mississippi.

How did you happen to take a picture of Virginia Woolf's house?
English friends who knew of my veneration for the work of Virginia
Woolf drove me to Rodmell to see Monk's House. We stood there,
our backs to the River Ouse, and before us the flower-covered house,
the windows of the room in which she had written during the last
years of her life.

*Among your photographs are some remarkable portraits. Will you
recall the occasions when you photographed the composer and con-
ductor Lehman Engel?*
In a little woods behind our back garden, my two younger brothers
Edward and Walter put up what they called "the Hut"—scrap lumber,
with hammer and saw. It was a little boys' neighborhood club, with
passwords and all. I wasn't allowed in, but after they outgrew it, I
turned it into what my friends and I called "the Pent-House." It was
the Hut with its walls pasted over with photos out of *Vanity Fair*—our
favorite performers in the New York theatre—Noel Coward, the
Lunts, the Astaires. We had our parties there. It was where I took
photographs of my friends. Lehman Engel visited home from New
York every summer.

*And you met several artists at Yaddo in 1940. The sculptor José de
Creeft, the etcher Karnig Nalbandian, and the composer Colin Mc-
Phee. You took photographs of them.*
Yaddo was full of artists, and the summer was long enough to get to
know one another. Karnig Nalbandian and Colin McPhee were in-
stalled in the same farmhouse where Katherine Anne Porter and I
were, so we had a little neighborhood of our own. In our respective
backgrounds were—well! Karnig's family is Armenian, Colin's music
had originated in Bali, Katherine Anne was writing her novel then,
and she allowed me to read its beginning—in Mexico. I was on the
receiving end of it all. De Creeft was the great Spanish sculptor. I
came to know him and his work that summer and our friendship lasted
from then on. He allowed me once to write a requested article about
his work—I was the only writer he knew, so he named me! I did
my best.

*One of the most recent photos you took shows V. S. Pritchett
in Savannah.*

Victor and Dorothy Pritchett and I are friends who seize the day, the time and the place, where we can next meet again and continue our conversation. We've arranged it in New York, in London, in Nashville, and this time in Savannah. None of us had ever visited Savannah before, and we spent a weekend in a cottage with a garden, a delightful place to talk, with that wonderful city to walk in. This time, the camera was along to commemorate the reunion.

Black-and-white and color photography. Which do you prefer?
Well, black-and-white is the only kind I know anything about, but I really do prefer it anyway. I haven't anything against color photography, but I love black-and-white. Just like black-and-white movies. I hate the idea of tinting the old ones.

William Eggleston is a photographer whose work is in color. What do you find most significant about it?
You mean about the color of it?

About his work. Not necessarily the color, but what do you find especially important?
The photographs that make up his book *The Democratic Forest* are presented as a record of the world we have made, of what our present civilization is. And he uses his color very effectively, purposefully. The urban world is such a raucous thing, the color is used to express that. And in contrast he uses color very tenderly in showing the frailty, the vulnerability of what has survived the onrush of urbanization. I don't know what Bill Eggleston would say to that. That's what I see.

You have an interest in signs and billboards, especially the unintentionally ludicrous ones.
Oh, yes, I love those.

And sometimes photographed these. Do you have any recollections of some special ones?
There's the Tiger Rag Gas Station. The Old Miss. Slaughter Pen. There's one sign I saw just recently on the way to Ole Miss, in a town as we passed through, Kosciusko. There was a vacant lot grown up in weeds and a wooden sign on it, very low to the ground saying "Jesus Christ is Lord in Kosciusko." Apparently it's the site of a church

that's yet to rise there on the vacant lot. Behind it already is a motel, no connection, I guess, saying "Economy Motel." All signs reveal us.

When you photographed some of the poor people during the Depression, did you feel any responsibility in taking their photographs?

It didn't seem to me I was doing anyone any harm. I wanted to show the life in front of me. I wouldn't have taken a mocking picture; I wasn't taking it to exploit them. I was taking it to reveal them, the situation in which I found them. Some of the people I took said they had never had a picture of themselves in their lives and they wanted me to take it and in that case I tried to get one to them.

When you snapped the shutter, what was the right instant?

You didn't know it until you did it. Or I didn't. And of course, all around every right instant, I've taken others that weren't. I don't mean I took twenty-five shots of one thing like people do with cameras now. I usually just took a few. You shouldn't surround people, you shouldn't dance around people, I think. I didn't put them through any of that.

Retrace your steps when you were traveling as a publicity agent for the WPA. Where did you go and where did you stay and were you traveling alone? What was one of the trips like? Where did you eat?

There was more variety than pattern. It depended on where I was to be sent that day. In Jackson we had an office up in the Tower Building of five people. I worked directly under another publicity agent who knew a lot more than I did. He was a professional newsman, named Louis Johnson. He's dead now. He was senior publicity agent. I was junior publicity agent—which also indicated I was a *girl*. We sometimes traveled together, and he did the news work and I did feature stories, interviews, and took some pictures.

What you would do depended on the project. If it were a juvenile court being set up, you would interview the judge on it. We visited a project for the blind of teaching people braille. We'd visit the construction of a farm-to-market road. Mississippi had so few roads then and very little was paved. There were a lot of people who couldn't get to town, farmers who were mired down in bad weather. The WPA went about putting in roads—they'd be tarred sometimes or graveled. We interviewed people living along the road, and the road workers, about

the difference it made in their lives. If there was a new air field
opening where planes could take off and land, just created out of a
farmer's field, we would go and see that. They weren't *airports*. They
were just landing fields. I think Meridian and Jackson were the only
places that had better than that. I was sent to Meridian with my
camera to interview the Key brothers. They had a national reputation
of staying up for very long periods of time, testing planes. I'd never
been up in an airplane, and I was terrified that I was going to have to
do it with the Key brothers. At that time you just leaned out of an
airplane and took pictures of the ground below. You sat behind the
pilot, with the wind blowing. There was just one passenger seat. But
I escaped without being invited. When the tornado devastated Tupelo,
the WPA tried to help, and I went up there and photographed Tupelo
the day after it'd been struck and nearly demolished. You could
expect anything in the way of work.

Did you travel by bus or car?
I mostly went by bus. If it was just going and coming on the same
day, I used the family car. I couldn't use it always, since I had
brothers in school and my mother needed it.

Did you stay in hotels?
Stayed in hotels. The hotel in my story "The Hitchhiker" was a
perfect portrait of some of the hotels I stayed in. Not particular ones,
sort of an amalgamation. The good ones had electric fans in summer.
That was the only way you could cool off, before air conditioning. No
telephone in the room. You had to go to a landing or downstairs to the
desk. Very nice people ran them, and kind people.

*When you were taking photographs were there ever any angry reac-
tions?*
No, I don't remember any. I don't know why there would have
been. I remember in Utica photographing the black bootlegger who
said, "I'm gone kill you," which was her joke.

With an ice pick.
She had an ice pick. She didn't mean it. She was teasing, like "I'm
gonna get you."

*You were a young, white, southern woman in black neighborhoods.
How were you received when you went to the black districts?*

Politely. And I was polite. It was before self-consciousness had
come into the relationship or suspicion. That's why I say it couldn't
be repeated today, anywhere.

Were they curious about you and why you were there?
Perhaps casually. There was usually something to talk about that
we both knew, about either what they were doing or about the place.
I would say, "I grew up near where you are living now" or ask a
question. There were connections.

*How did you entice them sometimes to let you take their photo-
graph?*
I didn't "entice." My pictures were made in sympathy, not exploitation. If I had felt that way, I would not have taken the pictures. If
you are interested in what viewers of these pictures do say about
them, I can give you some idea in what they say to me. There's an
exhibition of my photographs (mostly black subjects) that the Mississippi Department of Archives and History has been sending for a
number of years around the country on requests from galleries and
schools. From the letters viewers write to me, I think the photographs
are seen as honest and recognizably sympathetic. I have never heard
from a hostile viewer, of either race, of North or South. When I was
invited to be present at a showing of my photographs at the Museum
of Modern Art in New York, and to give a commentary on each one
as it was shown at a slide lecture, I found the audience receptive and
openly interested. I recall among those who came up to speak to me
afterward a number of blacks, from the North and the South both,
who wanted me to know they regarded my photographs as truthful
and understanding. I get many letters from people who say they are
touched very much by *One Time, One Place.*

*Have you any idea of what ever happened to some of the anony-
mous people whose photographs you took?*
I hear from people who recognize themselves or family members.
Some of them write and tell me. I don't think of them, of any people,
as "anonymous."
In the case of the black people who had the Pageant of Birds down
on Farish Street—we got to be further acquainted because of Maude
Thompson, who invited me to take the pictures. This came about

when walking along Farish Street in Jackson I saw these girls with big
paper wings, carrying them over their arms along the street. I asked
about them, and they said they were going to have a bird pageant at
their church, Farish Street Baptist, and would be glad for me to
attend. And when I did, of course I wouldn't have taken a camera
into the place. I wouldn't have misused my invitation by disrupting
the program by taking a picture. Even so, they made us sit on the
front row, which already called attention to us. It was a marvelous
pageant, original and dramatic. Then Maude Thompson asked me if I
would come back and take some pictures of it. She got the birds to
come back, and she posed them. She posed herself, and told me how
she wrote and directed the pageant, and so we got to be friends. I
think I said in *One Time, One Place* I used to run into her in railroad
stations. She was a big church worker, and she would go to funerals
out of town and maybe do other churchly things, and we always
greeted each other and had conversation about the continuing bird
pageant.

How did you discover Ida M'Toy as a subject for photographing?

Taking her picture was an afterthought. She was a secondhand
clothes dealer who had a store in her house in the Depression. White
customers would bring her their last year's clothes that she wanted to
sell to her black customers, taking her commission out of the sale.
She was a Jackson institution. She considered that she did a good
deed to both white and black, and not for the first time: she had had
an earlier career as a midwife. The combination is why I thought she
was so fascinating. One of the pictures you have is "Born in This
Hand." At the name of any well-known citizen she'd make this
gesture, and intone: "Born in this hand." Children were all born at
home in those days, and she served white and black, of course. She
was a young nurse, too, in the days of yellow fever. She said she
remembered when there was a rope stretched across Jackson, and if
you had yellow fever, you couldn't cross that rope and go into the
other part. And she said, "I nursed them six at a blow." She was part
of the history of the town.

What ever happened to Ida M'Toy?

Until she died, in the sixties, I went to call on her time after time.
We were old friends. Her granddaughter, now 44 years old and a

nurse, is coming to see me soon at her request—she's one of my readers. She has said she is proud of my pictures and the essay I wrote about her grandmother. Now we can talk about her together.

Wonder what ever happened to "Mr. John Paul's Boy" in Rodney.
He was there as long as I was going there. He showed me the church, and where the post office was, and he told me he asked every day but he'd never got a letter in his life. So I used to send him cards sometimes. Never fear, the whole of Rodney looked after him.

One of your most poignant photographs is "Woman of the 'Thirties." What ever happened to her?
I don't know. I think she lived on the road between here and Utica, where I used to go quite a bit, and where I took a lot of pictures. And I think I did see her a time or two after that. She has a very sensitive face, as you can see; she was well aware of her predicament in poverty, and had good reasons for hopelessness. Well, she *wasn't* hopeless. That was the point. She was courageous. She thought it was a hopeless situation, but she was tackling it.

Some of the persons that Dorothea Lange photographed and those that Walker Evans photographed in Alabama were found not too long ago and shown as they are today. Have you seen any reports of things like that?
No. It would seem to me that that was exploiting them. For a second time.

Some of the children whom Walker Evans photographed are resentful.
I don't blame them. I would be too. I'd find that a cause for resentment.

As you said, a lot of the people whose photographs you took had never been in a photograph.
They had so little, and a photograph meant something. And they really were delighted. It didn't matter that it showed them in their patched, torn clothes. They wanted the picture. They were delighted at the evidence of themselves here—a picture was something they could hold. I've had people write to me through the years and say, "I saw my grandfather in your picture of such and such, and could I have a copy of the picture?" When possible I have tried to do that.

Of all a writer's attributes, you have said in "Place in Fiction,"
place is one of the lesser angels—that feeling wears the crown. These
photographs we've talked about convey great feeling. Was this deep
feeling the feeling that made you take the pictures?
Why, I'm sure it was. Human feeling for human beings was a
response to what I saw.

I think we're talking about passion in the real definition of the word.
I think we are too.

And the passion was there before you snapped the shutter, and you
certainly can see it in the photograph.
Well, thank you. That is the finest thing that could be said in
their retrospect.

Some believe that it is an artist's works that best express his or her
biography. How do you think these pictures you've taken pertain
to yours?
Not in any way, I hope, except indirectly. I wasn't trying to say
anything about myself in the pictures of people. I was trying to say
everything about *them,* and my taking them was the medium. The
photographs are saying what I saw. I was just the instrument, whatever you want to call it.

They're a record not only of what you saw, but they're a record of
your feelings.
Yes, but I didn't take them for that. If they do that, it's because I
took them with the right feeling, I think, to show what was there and
what it meant. I would have thought it was intruding for me to have
included myself in what I was doing. Any more than I would in a
story. The story has to stand alone.

Here's a hard question.
They're all hard. What?

This will be the last question. You've had a long career. All your
work is of great intensity and has from the very first been regarded as
superlative. Looking back over the entire body of your artistic work—
stories, novels, essays, and photographs—one is astonished by and is
in great admiration of your range, your talent, your passion, and your
compassion. But rising above all of these is your vision. What do you,

that artist, discern as the vision Eudora Welty has expressed in
this work?

Well, I think it lies only in the work. It's not for me to say. I think
it's what the work shows, comprises altogether. That was a very
beautiful question, by the way, which I thank you for, for the form of
it. But as in everything, I want the work to exist as the thing that
answers every question about its doing. Not me saying what's in the
work. In fact, I couldn't. Sometime, if I have the time left to me I
would like to do more, but of course you could never make it full
enough. You know, of what is out there and in here.

That's a good answer, too.
Well, it's the truth. I tried to tell the truth.

At Home with Eudora Welty

Elizabeth Bennett / 1991

From *The Houston Post,* 1 December 1991, Sec. E, 1, 7.
Reprinted by permission of Elizabeth Bennett.

Jackson, Miss.—Mention "Eudora Welty" to almost anyone in this bustling Southern city and the name is instantly recognized. The first lady of American letters has lived here all her life—the public library is even named after her—but it's not clear to everyone precisely what she *does.*

"They say (at the Eudora Welty Library) that I get lots of calls," observed the 82-year-old author in a recent interview. "People think I *live* there. They leave messages for me there."

While visiting a friend at a local hotel recently, adds Welty, who clearly relishes a good story, "the porter parking the cars said, 'Oh, I know you. You're the lady that lives at the *Liberry.*' I didn't say anything, but when he got my car he said, 'Well, I know you got to get *back* to that *Liberry.*' "

"I thought that was rather sweet," she says quickly, not wishing to leave the impression she is belittling the porter. "I didn't tell him I *didn't* work there. It would have hurt him, you know."

Welty is sitting in the living room of the brick, Tudor-style house her parents built in the 1920s—the same house she has lived in since she was a teen-ager. It's in a residential area filled with towering trees and spacious yards; immediately across the street is Belhaven College, a small liberal arts school whose grounds were once the rural hills of Jackson (when the Weltys first settled here).

She speaks in a cultured Southern accent, the kind where the "r's" aren't pronounced so that porter, for instance, comes out "PO-ta" and parking, "PAHK-in." She is surrounded by books, including a new one that particularly pleases her: the golden anniversary edition of her first collection of short stories, *A Curtain of Green and Other Stories.*

"It's beautiful, don't you think?" she says, pointing to the small volume on the table with its green and black dust jacket. Her publisher, Harcourt Brace Jovanovich, reissued the book in hardcover and paperback last month, along with seven other Welty titles in paperback. By happy coincidence, she was also awarded in November the $10,000 National Book Foundation Medal for Distinguished Contribution to American Letters.

And this latest honor is only one of many for the gracious, soft-spoken Mississippian who is also the recipient of the Pulitzer Prize in fiction in 1973 (for *The Optimist's Daughter*), the National Institute of Arts and Letters Gold Medal in 1972, a Guggenheim fellowship, and some half a dozen O. Henry (short story) awards.

Welty lives alone—she has never married—and continues to write and travel and do most of the other things she has enjoyed in a rich, full life. But a recent back injury has slowed her down temporarily—a result of osteoporosis, she says. She fractured her back in an airport earlier this year when the elevators weren't working and she had to climb a steep staircase. She spent a month in the hospital in early fall; it was the first time she had ever been hospitalized.

The table next to the chair where she's seated in the living room is piled with books—many of them new books mailed to her by the publisher. More new arrivals are stacked haphazardly on two sofas in the room. Still more are scattered around the room in piles here and there, and Welty apologizes profusely for the clutter.

"The family had to move me downstairs when I fractured my back," she explains with a trace of frustration. "I haven't been able to work on things and put things up so every room is like this. I hated to receive you in it, but what else could I do?"

Welty's "family" consists of two nieces living in Jackson, both of them married with "a whole stock of great-nieces and nephews," she says. Her parents are both dead, as are both her younger brothers.

The back injury caused her to cancel some dates for October, including the second annual Eudora Welty Writers Symposium at Mississippi University for Women (MUW). The conference attracted Welty scholars from across the country, as well as writers Clyde Edgerton, Larry Brown and Kaye Gibbons.

"I get a lot of invitations to colleges in connection with the English department," she says. "They have regular programs of inviting people and you go and stay a couple of days and give a public reading and meet with two classes, usually."

(She once remarked that colleges kept inviting her back because she's so well behaved: "I'm always on time and I don't get drunk or hole up in a motel with my lover.")

A "Do Not Disturb" sign is posted on Welty's front door. Her relatives put up the notice while she was in the hospital, she says, and she has scrawled in tiny letters underneath a brief explanation that she has been ill and is unable to greet visitors.

The personal touch is typical.

"I appreciate their interest," says Welty, referring to fans who often appear at her door uninvited to get books autographed. "But they sometimes bring 30 and 40 books. I don't mean to be complaining about it," she hastens to add. "I'm glad to have my books liked, but . . ." her voice trails off.

She also gets lots of interview requests. So many stories have been done on her, in fact, more than two dozen written between 1942–1982 were collected in a book called *Conversations with Eudora Welty* published in the early 1980s. And as she gets older, she gets more requests and turns more down, trying to save her energy for her work.

A very private person, she discourages questions about her personal life. Neither does she like to be photographed, although she reluctantly agreed to some candid photos if they didn't show the inside of her house in its current state. And when the photographer arrived, she once again apologized for the clutter.

Her "REAL SUBJECT" as a writer is human relationships, Welty noted in *One Writer's Beginnings,* published in 1984, and many of her stories probe such dilemmas as man's search for separateness and need for love. The *New Yorker* termed her first collection of stories, for which Katherine Anne Porter wrote the introduction, "deceptively simple and concerned with ordinary people. But what happens to them and the manner of the telling are far from ordinary."

Her work is set in Mississippi, often in the Delta. *The Optimist's Daughter* takes place in a Delta town where the old civilities—and snobbishness and privilege—collide with the vulgarities and materialistic values of outside forces.

Her work is often humorous and filled with the small-town Southern speech she couldn't get enough of as a child.

Welty writes about those early years in *One Writer's Beginnings*. Her father was a successful insurance executive and her mother a literate, witty housewife. Welty and her brothers grew up in comfort and a loving household and were exposed to books at an early age—and to lots of good talk.

Here's one of the tales she relates in *One Writer's Beginnings:*

When we at length bought our first automobile, one of our neighbors was often invited to go with us on the family Sunday afternoon ride. In Jackson it was counted an affront to the neighbors to start with an empty seat in the car. My mother sat in the back with her friend, and I'm told that as a small child I would ask to sit in the middle and say as we started off, "Now talk."

Welty started college at Mississippi State College for Women (now MUW, which holds the annual Eudora Welty symposium), where she helped to start a literary magazine; later she transferred to the University of Wisconsin from which she graduated in 1929. In the next few years, while writing short stories on the side, she worked at a variety of jobs, including one as a society columnist for the Memphis *Commercial Appeal.*

She held that job "until somebody took it away from me," she recalls with a chuckle. "Somebody went to the *Commercial Appeal* and said, 'That Eudora Welty, she doesn't need the money. She's a *rich* girl.' "

She swears the story, told her years later by the editor of the *Commercial Appeal,* is true. But it wasn't true that she was rich, she says. Her father had died of leukemia at age 52, about six years after moving into the house she now occupies, and while he had provided well for the family, she still needed to work.

"I needed everything I could get," she says. "Certainly the magazines that took my work didn't pay anything."

Those magazines were university quarterlies like the *Southern Review* "which were good to me," she adds. "But you know that's very different from being published where it's read . . . Mercifully, I was so ignorant of everything that I didn't even worry about this. I mean, of course I was dying to get published but I thought, 'Well, this is the way it is.' (Pause.) Not necessarily!

"So I just kept writing merrily along," Welty adds, "and I was just *blessed* with people and things that happened for me."

One of those blessings came in the form of Diarmuid Russell, a man who had just started a literary agency in New York and was looking for young talent. He wrote Welty a letter—a model of grace, candor and wit—asking to be her agent.

"I was so taken with his letter and his handwriting—and when he said he was the son of A. E. (a distinguished literary figure) I wrote back by return mail and said, 'Be my agent!' " says Welty. "And he wrote back, 'Wait! You don't know a thing about me. I may be a crook!'

"Well, anyway, that was a wonderful beginning, and he worked for years—slaved at it—without any luck at all (getting her stories published). Many would have given me up. So I owe a great deal to him and this book (her first) is dedicated to him, as you see. He didn't want me to do it; he said I should have dedicated it to my family. Well, my family *knew* that I loved them, but if it hadn't been for him there wouldn't have *been* this book."

(A recent book, called *Author and Agent,* also came out of that extraordinary relationship, which ended with Russell's death in 1973. It contains letters exchanged between Russell and Welty during their 33-year association; critic Jonathan Yardley called it a valuable book because "it affords us the chance to read some wonderful prose written by two singularly civilized human beings.")

The two got together when Welty was 31. It was another 10 years before her first book came out, and almost that long before her stories began appearing in major magazines. But she still wasn't making much money and continued to have jobs on the side.

One was with the Works Progress Administration (WPA) as a publicity agent, traveling all over Mississippi and shooting hundreds of photographs of mostly black people; they were published several years ago in yet another book—a handsome coffee-table volume called *One Time, One Place.*

She also worked for a time as a staff writer on the *New York Times Book Review,* but she didn't feel all that comfortable in the job.

"I didn't want to give a book a bad review" she says. "No matter what it is it's a year out of somebody's life and they did the best they could."

One of the things Welty has been criticized for as a writer is failing to comment on social issues, including Mississippi's racial problems. In an article in *Atlantic Monthly* (October 1965), she tried to answer that criticism by distinguishing the purpose and methods of a novelist from those of a crusader.

"Passion is the chief ingredient of good fiction," she wrote. ". . . But to distort a work of passion for the sake of a cause is to cheat, and the end, far from justifying the means, is fairly sure to be lost with it . . ." About the time the article appeared, Welty also began getting "a whole lot of phone calls in the dead of night," she says. The callers, often from the East Coast area, were insulting, she recalls: "What are you doing sitting back there on your ass? Why don't you get out there and do something about it? *You're* a writer."

Her number was in the telephone book then, "but that was about the time I quit having it listed," says Welty. "My mother was at home sick and these calls would come at 2 or 3 o'clock in the morning. She would get so upset. She'd say, 'Oh, I think my brother must be sick,' you know. And I just couldn't take that."

Welty also got "very indignant" with the kind of remarks often made to her during the '60s when she was visiting Manhattan.

"One day I was just coming down the elevator and I said something to whoever I was with, and a passenger on the elevator said, 'Oh, I know where you're from. *You* came from down there where they lynch black people.' This was just a gratuitous remark . . . but that was considered the right thing to do sometimes in New York.

"And then what would be worse are these people who say, *'We're on the same side,'* " she adds, speaking slowing and enunciating each word. "That was very tiresome."

Does she feel any embarrassment about her home state's former racial problems and its reputation nationally?

"No," she retorts. "Why should I apologize? I think it deserves credit for a lot of things. Of course I'm *mad* about a lot of things we've done here, but heavens no, I don't feel (she doesn't finish the sentence) . . ."

Unlike many Mississippi writers who couldn't wait to get out, Welty apparently felt comfortable staying in her home state. She has also lived and written in her parents' home most of her life; she had a loving, supportive family and never moved away for long.

But while Mississippi isn't exactly the literary hub of the world ("It doesn't claim to be," she retorts), Welty has mixed and mingled with many of the other major writers of the 20th century. Many, including

Katherine Anne Porter, Robert Penn Warren and Walker Percy, were good friends. Others, like Henry Miller, simply passed through Jackson and looked her up. And therein lies a story she has told many times over the years and still repeats with great relish.

Miller had written her ahead of time, recalls Welty, offering to put her in touch with "an unfailing pornographic market" that she could write for if she needed the money. (As the author of *The Tropic of Capricorn* and other sexually explicit novels, Miller was considered a pornographic writer in many circles.) And she had made the mistake of showing the letter to her mother.

"Why I showed it to her I don't know," says Welty, who wrote Miller back declining his offer. "Anyway, she was so mad she wouldn't let him cross the threshold (of her house) when he came here."

Welty and several male friends (she was afraid to be alone with the author) took Miller to dinner at the only good restaurant in town—not once but all three nights he was in Jackson. It was a large place with different areas of dining, she said, "but he was so unobservant he thought he was going to three different places!"

They also showed Miller all over town "because we thought he wanted to see the place. He just sat in the back seat, he didn't look at anything, he didn't ask any questions. It was so frustrating. We thought, 'What *would* he like?' He was *so* boring."

Welty's experiences with other contemporaries were far more pleasant. Several, including Warren and Porter, were instrumental in her career. Warren had been a co-editor of the *Southern Review* and published many of her early stories; Porter, the only woman writer from Texas to win a Pulitzer, was—like Welty—primarily a short story writer and offered the younger woman much encouragement and solid help over the years.

The two became close, lifelong friends, as Welty wrote in a long piece she penned last year for *The Georgia Review*. In that piece she writes about the two spending the summer together in 1941 at Yaddo, the writers' colony near Saratoga, N.Y., and "puffing on our cigarettes." She learned, during that summer, that Porter's whole writing life "was one of interruptions" and that writers "do generally live that way."

But she learned something from Porter that summer that was even more important. She learned that writing was, indeed, very hard work that would only get harder with experience, but "that writing well was for the writer worth whatever it took . . . Katherine Anne was helping me to recognize living with difficulty as a form of passion."

Welty also knew Faulkner slightly. They met at a dinner party given by mutual friends in Oxford, Miss., the Nobel laureate's hometown, she says, "but I didn't know him *well*."

They had actually been in touch many years earlier—she can't remember when—and he wrote her "a wonderful letter" offering to help her. He had discovered one of her short stories, though she can't recall which one or where he saw it, she says.

"He said (in the letter): 'I don't know who you are. Would you tell me? How old are you?' And he said, 'Is there anything I can do for you? I will be in Hollywood at this address.' "

"Wasn't that sweet?" Welty asks. "And then he added (in the letter), 'You're doing *all right*.' "

Eudora Welty was doing all right then and still is. She seems to be busier than ever these days, even with serious back problems. She is constantly working on one writing project or another, often as a favor to one of many people she knows in the publishing business. Just before her interview with the *Post,* she was on deadline to finish the preface for a friend's book on—of all things—a mule trader in Mississippi. ("I love mules," she says.)

She also has another book out this fall, *The Norton Book of Friendship,* that she put together with Ronald Sharp for Norton. It's a collection of writings on a subject that interests her very much. "The hard part was selecting," she says. "There was so much."

The subject of aging, on the other hand, is not something she seems all that interested in discussing. When asked if getting older has affected her writing in any way, she says, simply, "I don't know. I guess your whole life does . . . I think that you write when you have some idea you want to write about and your own circumstances are just incidental . . . Just go on and do it the best you can."

That seems to be what Eudora Welty has been doing all her life.

Eudora Welty at Home

Clarence Brown / 1992

From *Bostonia*, Fall 1992, 22-24. The interview was conducted at Eudora Welty's home in Jackson in March 1992. Reprinted by permission of Clarence Brown.

I.

I've long had the habit of shutting my eyes and taking a book down at random from my far too cluttered shelves, just to force myself to look at something that no amount of deliberate intention would bring to my notice. Inevitably, what I happen upon seems to be fatidic. Fate seems to be trying to tug at my sleeve.

Using this aleatory technique a moment ago, I took from the shelf the letters of Pliny the Younger. I have these in the little red Loeb Classics edition with Pliny's Latin on the left-hand page and, on the right, the English translation by William Melmoth, first published in 1745. I doubt whether I have glanced at them in thirty years.

Melmoth's translation has the independent status of a minor classic of English prose. It has all the charm and fluency of an eighteenth-century gentleman whose attitude toward letter-writing was hardly distinguishable from that of his first-century model. As a translation, however, it would not pass muster in Latin 101. With even my sadly decayed knowledge of the Roman tongue, I can tell that the right hand often knoweth not what the left hand doeth.

Pure fate: you see, I have just finished translating a Russian novel of 1920, Zamyatin's *We,* and am about to undertake the introduction. In this I will not be able to avoid defending my translation, which is in some respects as "free" as Melmoth's version of Pliny. Melmoth gives me certain courage. Fate clearly thought me in need of a psychological boost.

Melmoth was writing for the readers of his own day, not for his Latin master. His goal was not to find an English word for each of Pliny's Latin words, but to turn a provincial gentleman from a distinguished family of the Como district into an unbuttoned letter-writer from Suffolk. He did not want to interpret Pliny. He wanted to *be* Pliny—only in English. That exceeds my ambition, but I draw courage from his boldness.

More fate. Writing to his friend Titinius Capito, Pliny observed (p. 104): "Oratory and Poetry meet small favor unless carried to the highest point of eloquence; but History, however executed, always pleases, for mankind are naturally inquisitive, and information, however badly presented, has its charm for beings who adore even small talk and anecdote."

Ye gods! The man was speaking directly to me. After I spent an afternoon in Jackson, Mississippi, with Eudora Welty last March (I was there to speak to a group of alumni from Princeton, where I teach), I went back to my room and jotted down some of my impressions. Next day I remembered a few additional details. When I'd finished what was actually no more than a long entry in the journal that I have kept for years, it filled some ten single-spaced pages and looked like a "piece." Yet we had merely been chatting. Certainly I had not presented myself to her as a journalist in search of a formal interview.

Had I been intent on this, I should certainly not have spent so much time responding to *her* questions about *me*, or in talking about mutual friends.

But now an editor has asked for it, and his request leaves me embarrassed. It will look like an "interview," no matter how many disclaimers precede it, and as an interviewer I will look like a self-infatuated ninny. I will look like some neophyte who was so unaware of being in the presence of the greatest living American writer that he blithely babbled on about trifles, including the greatest trifle of all, himself!

Pliny (or Fate) to the rescue! Those who think it Oratory or Poetry (i.e., some traditional form, like the Interview) have only themselves to blame if they are disappointed. Most readers will take it for what it is, mere History, just an account of something that really happened in a natural and unplanned way. What a relief! *Di faciant ut talia tibi saepius nuntiem! Vale.*

II.

On the telephone she'd said, "Tell the driver it's the Belhaven neighborhood—he'll know where that is." Her house is across the street from Belhaven College, in northeast Jackson. She comes out onto the front step when the cab pulls into the yard of 1119 Pinehurst Street and smiles at the automobile.

There is some delay while the young cabby fumbles for change and the mechanism that will unlock my door. "Do you know who that is?" I ask, to fill the time. He says no, that he thinks he might have seen her, but the name does not ring a bell. He probably does not hang out at the Eudora Welty Library, as Jackson's Public Library is called.

At eighty-three, she looks all of her years, and more—closer to the ninety-three that the *New York Times* will erroneously report as her age in a few weeks from now in some story about her getting an award. Her face is haggard even when lit by a welcoming smile. She calls my attention to the bright new brass numerals 1119 that have been affixed to the old exterior. "They made me put up something people could see."

She leads me into the house. "I'd have come to get you, but I don't drive anymore," she says. "I don't do anything anymore." I have a sharp recollection of my mother, two years her senior, who might have said exactly those words in the identical tone of lamentation.

Nondescript interior. Entrance hallway. Stair. Living room with fireplace. An antique television on a rickety stand, with rabbit ears for antenna, in the middle of the large parlor. The sofa, covered in white fabric, is completely inundated with books. There is a low coffee table in front of her chair, which is one of those that raise up to help frail old people onto their feet. Letters in and partly out of envelopes. Many of the books are new. At my elbow is Anatoly Nayman's *Remembering Akhmatova,* with an introduction by Joseph Brodsky.

Seduced by this, and forgetting whose reminiscences have any value at the moment, I tell her something of my experiences with Akhmatova and Brodsky. Miss Eudora has the exquisite courtesy to appear interested.

We talk of Guy Davenport, my friend from childhood and college, one of the links between us. "I dote on his work," she says. She was in Lexington, invited by Guy to visit *him* and speak to *his* class (not to the University). She is greatly impressed and delighted with this eccentric daring as a way to get round the usual ennui of an official academic visit. She was in his studio and saw his "drawings" (she did not mention paintings). "He must be the most talented man there is," she said.

Near the Akhmatova is a new book in French about Eudora Welty's work. There is an inscription to her in English. She says that she cannot read French.

I ask whether people still write to ask about the grandson of Phoenix Jackson, whether he was dead or alive, in the story "A Worn Path." I recalled her having written somewhere that this tops all other questions in frequency. She nods yes and wearily rolls her eyes. School teachers dismay her, she says, putting their classes up to all sorts of stunts, such as writing better endings for the story. She tells me of one that amused her: Old Phoenix gets home with the toy windmill, gives it to her grandson, he puffs at it once, and falls over dead! "Can't you just see it?" she says, wincing.

She gets many letters from young students. By no means all of them are adulatory or even friendly. Some are hostile and somehow, to her astonishment, resentful: she mimics the tone of one: "What's the point of writing that dull old story about a stupid old black woman?" She said: "The teachers actually send me these letters. I can't imagine what they are thinking of."

She is wearing a black knit of some kind, an ordinary sweatshirt, I think, that has a band of writing in white across the bosom. I do not risk staring hard enough to make out what the words say. Authors' names, I think. She has a worn white sweater over her shoulders, the drape of it distorted by the hump it covers on her back.

She was recently in the hospital—for what, I don't know and do not ask. Except for us, the big old house sounds quite empty on this quiet afternoon. Azaleas bloom outside in the corners of a well-kept lawn. But there seems to be no one around to look after her. When I inquire in a gingerly way about her situation, she assures me that a nurse looks in on her. She used to have a woman who helped with the correspondence, not exactly a secretary, a friend. "Wrote it, actually. I could never dictate anything." But now she is sick, too.

It turns out that she has little use for Hemingway. The subject comes up when she asks what I am talking to the alumni groups about. I speak of the ending of "The Short Happy Life of Francis Macomber" and ask her opinion of my idea that Margot actually tried to save Francis, seeing a better future with him, now that he has been reborn as a man, at least as a Hemingway man. She'd never thought of it that way, and seems to find it unsatisfactory as an ending, though plausible. "But isn't that like him, though?" she said. "To leave it that way for us? He left a lot of things vague. He knew it would make trouble for people."

I see the name "Powerhouse" in the French book. Her face lights up as we discuss this favorite story, and her taped reading of it. I mention that when I was in the Army there was a mythical figure in GI barracks talk whose name was "Jody"—a figure in many ways like her Uranus Knockwood. Jody was back home, wearing your clothes, going out with your girl. This delights her. She'd never heard of Jody. She adores Fats Waller, on whom "Powerhouse" was modeled. She has a treasure of his music on old 78s in the attic—"If the heat hasn't melted 'em all."

I speak of the difficulty of getting today's students to believe that much of Southern writing is about the South of this century. They think that Faulkner's story of Nancy, "That Evening Sun," took place in the 1850s, and this in spite of Quentin's opening paragraph about street lighting, and so on. She agrees. She says that young people also think that her work depicts a much earlier period.

Someone sent her a dramatization of "Why I Live at the P.O." She said, "I told them it can't be dramatized. They had all these parts for actors to play people that were only in Sister's mind."

She is reminded of Bessie Smith, whom she saw once in Jackson. Somehow, she and her date managed to get in with another white couple to a concert by Bessie Smith attended only by blacks. It was at a theater called the Alamo. She and her friends sat in the balcony. She demonstrated how she almost physically restrained her date, who wanted to call out a request for a song. "It would have spoiled everything if they knew some white people were there." Her eyes rolled with pleasure as she described Bessie Smith's entrance upon the stage "in an apricot gown." Her arms make something like the gesture of a ballet dancer to convey the grace of that entrance.

I have brought along a copy of my translation of Madelstam's prose, *The Noise of Time,* which I inscribe to her. I find that my briefcase also contains a few xeroxes of *Ink Soup,* my newspaper column. I show her the one about my grandson, remarking that she'd been a

newspaperwoman once, writing the society column for the Memphis
Commercial Appeal. She asks if she might keep it. I show her the one
about the spotted owl, and she immediately notices my signature on
the drawing. As we talk, she keeps stealing glances at the columns,
but finally says, "I just hate it when somebody reads something of
mine in front of me."

I ask whether I might take her picture. She shrugs a polite yes,
which is hardly a surprise, coming from someone who has after all
published a book of her own photographs. The little Olympus that
Jeff and Kitty gave me interests her. As I was taking pictures, I asked
her about William Eggleston, for whose book *The Democratic Forest*
she wrote an introduction. She admires him greatly. "He does drink
an awful lot," she says.

I use the delayed-release switch to make a picture of myself in the
presence of greatness. For this I have to stack some books on a small
table and set the camera atop them, then move a chair next to hers.
The thing fires prematurely a couple of times. She takes a photographer's interest in all these proceedings and is graciously forgiving.

She adores Jim Lehrer and Robert MacNeil. She has already read
MacNeil's novel and thinks it wonderful. She tells me she is even
closer to Roger Mudd, who lives in McLean, Virginia, and with whose
family she always stays when she is in that vicinity. She tells me that
Roger Mudd was finally successful in getting rehabilitation for his
ancestor, the Dr. Mudd who treated the injured John Wilkes Booth
after the assassination and, as a result, lost his citizenship. She says,
"That must be where we get the saying 'His name is mud,' don't
you think?"

Promptly at six she goes to the ancient television set and turns on
"The MacNeil-Lehrer News Hour." She never misses it. The image
is disgracefully bad.

She offers me a drink, or would have done so, had I not mentioned
in some connection that I did not drink. Then I felt that I should have
a drink, if only to make it possible for her to have one. I wondered
how exactly she was going to get any dinner. It must happen that very
famous people are left utterly alone for no other reason than people's
reluctance to intrude upon them. There is no sound of any other
presence in the house. She seemed genuinely glad of my company
and reminded me more than once of my mother's eagerness to have

someone to talk to. (Back home in Princeton, Jim Seawright assures
me that a large network of friends keep tabs on Miss Eudora.)

The general topic of drink brings up that of bootleg liquor and
moonshine. When she was young, she and her crowd would have to
go across the Pearl River over into Rankin County to buy drink. It
was never actually moonshine, she was careful to emphasize, but the
real stuff—"Old Crow and things like that"—just completely illegal
in Jackson. To evade the law, the bootlegger kept moving his place of
business. Once, going after a supply, she encountered a little black
boy sitting on the bridge reading *Time* magazine. When he saw her
coming, he silently raised his arm, never taking his eyes from the
page, to point her in the new direction. He'd been left there to divert
traffic. She relished the detail of his reading that particular magazine.
The same arm that had enacted Bessie Smith's entrance showed me
the boy's languid gesture.

I find it oddly reassuring that she lives just as much surrounded by
junk as I do, things that a self-respecting second-hand dealer would
keep out of sight, or give away. There is a dim oil over the mantel.
The mantel itself would look better if it were more cluttered with
stuff. As it is, the one or two things there have no way to hide their
painful drabness. Large porcelain statuettes of a fairytale king and
queen. The sofa looks as though it might be comfortable, but the sofa
is unavailable, being under an avalanche of books. Her chair is a
prosthesis, and is now frozen in some midway position, but she seems
unable to relax into it. She spends the whole time bent slightly
forward, her arms folded in her lap.

We speak of other friends that we have in common, and especially
of the artists who hail from Jackson, Mississippi. My colleague James
Seawright, the noted sculptor and head of the Visual Arts program at
Princeton, comes from a Jackson family that has long been close to
her. She calls Jim, not surprisingly, "Jimmy." I don't recall mentioning the Princeton composer Milton Babbitt, from Jackson, but she is
fond of the writer Richard Ford and his wife Krystina, who have now,
she informs me, actually moved back to Mississippi (Oxford) after
having lived restlessly all over the United States, including Princeton.
Richard's incessant displacement contrasts with her stubborn lifelong fixity in the place where she was born.

Her eyes dip back into the columns and she remarks again on my drawing of the owl. Talk of cartooning brings up the comic strip "Peanuts" and its creator Charles Schulz, whom she has met at various times. He donated money to a local black college. She was with him at some other meeting of writers and artists and recalls that students asked what the *inside* of Snoopy's doghouse looked like. Schulz said, "It is vast, with great chandeliers and staircases. But only I know that. You will never see it except in two dimensions." About this answer she said, "That's so good. That's just like a writer. A writer has to know all about the inside of a thing even if he is just going to show a little bit of it."

I tell her that *Punch* is for sale and will cease to exist if no buyer can be found. "No! Don't tell me that. A world without *Punch!*" This reminds her of P. G. Wodehouse. She has bought a complete set of his works and keeps it by her bed. "I've read most of them one by one, but now I have the set." When she wakes in the wee hours and can't get back to sleep, she reads Wodehouse. I say that I read Wallace Stevens in the same way, especially the "Adagia." She approves of this. "They're like injections," she says.

The biography of the novelist Henry Green by his son Sebastian Yorke lay near her chair. She'd met Green, she said, during her brief period of living in England, and loved him, both as man and writer. Green once told her, just after they'd met, that his best book was his autobiography *Pack My Bag*. "It's the best thing I ever wrote, but you'll not find it anywhere," he said. But she said she did find it and liked it tremendously. I said I'd found it unreadable, full of sentences that made no sense at all, and that I must now, on her assurance that it was good, have another try.

Byron De La Beckwith had been rearrested some months ago to be tried again for the murder, in Jackson in 1963, of the Mississippi civil rights leader Medgar Evers. I bring up this name with some misgiving. One of the most powerful things she ever wrote is "Where is the Voice Coming From?" She produced it in one rush of inspiration and outrage immediately after hearing of the murder on the radio. She'd entered with uncanny prescience into the soul of a bigot and murderer and produced an overwhelming monologue of envious, spitting hatred. So accurate had been some of her imaginings that the *New Yorker* had anxiously besought her to alter certain details, which turned out to jibe all too closely with the facts that came out when Byron De La

Beckwith was arrested for the first time, before the story could
be printed.

A look of dismay comes over her face at this name. She does not
think he will ever be convicted. She savors the bizarre name of the
suspect and says, "Someone told me I'd thought the killer was a
Snopes when all the time it was a Compson."

I asked her what she made of David Duke, and a look of deeper
dismay came over her face. "All the De La Beckwiths were for him,"
she said.

Leaving, I said I'd send her copies of the pictures if they came out.
"But please don't bother writing," I said, thinking of how difficult
she'd said it was for her to correspond. "Oh, I'll write," she said.

An Interview with Eudora Welty

Clyde S. White / 1992

The interview, videotaped in Eudora Welty's home in Jackson in May 1992, is part of a projected documentary film on Eudora Welty planned for high school and college students. Transcribed by Clyde S. White; edited by Sarah Griffin and Peggy Whitman Prenshaw. Reprinted by permission of Clyde S. White, Cabisco Teleproductions, Carolina Biological Supply Company, Burlington, NC.

Clyde White: Would you describe the childhood world of Eudora Welty?

Eudora Welty: It was a wonderful childhood, owing to my parents, who were very much aware of a child with imagination. I think I must have awakened in my mother a latent sympathy with a child with a lot of imagination. They spent so much time and effort to get books for me, which they were not easily able to afford, but beautiful illustrated books. Read to me all the time and talked to me. So they admired my wishes and stimulated them. That was the best gift you could ever give to a child.

White: What were your father and mother like?

Welty: They were different from all the others in Jackson because everyone in Jackson had lived here forever. My parents came here as newlyweds. They came here from Ohio and West Virginia, and they had both been country schoolteachers when they married. My father had lined up a job and rented a house, and then he'd brought his bride to Jackson. So they started out completely new to everything here. They always liked new experiences, and they always liked being in Jackson. So I grew up in a household of discovery. My father liked driving around the countryside and finding things and going to see things. That's something most of my friends never did. I was so lucky from that start. It was an open world. I felt adventurous.

White: How about your mother? What impact did your mother have on your life?

Welty: She had a big impact on my life because she was a marvelously sympathetic mother. She read to me every night and told me

231

stories. She was one of six children, the only girl and the oldest, and she never complained about anything. She grew up in the mountains in West Virginia and was a country schoolteacher.

Everything was different in Mississippi. She had been warned by her family against catching malaria and dying immediately. They couldn't imagine anybody coming down into the swamps—that's what they thought of the place. So my parents were quite brave to come down and very adventurous—romantic, really—to start out that way. My mother had lots of imagination. And they were both very much sticklers for truth-telling and really learning things. I'm glad of that! I have so many friends whose parents pampered them. I knew one whole family where they said, "They don't have to be smart, they're so sweet!" That wasn't me.

White: You took a lot of summer trips with your parents. What were those trips like, and how did they affect you as a fiction writer later on?

Welty: Well, they just fed my love of a story. Stimulated it. I think my parents were the same way. They wanted to visit both families in the summer time in Ohio and West Virginia. We had a car. In those days there were hardly even any maps to be had down here. They used the AAA automobile Blue Book, which told you how to get somewhere. You could set your speedometer to zero, and the book would tell you "six tenths of a mile past white church on right." There weren't too many signposts. It told you the times that the ferries crossed the river—there weren't too many bridges on the way up. On the big rivers like the Kentucky and the Tennessee, you used a ferry boat. We were so adventurous. You never knew what was going to be around the corner. One summer we all camped out in a tent, but I don't think that was very good.

White: You traveled quite a bit while you were working for the WPA and took a lot of photographs. Would you talk about those trips and the people you met?

Welty: It was totally unexpected. I didn't realize how little I knew about where I lived. I lived in Mississippi's only city—it was a small one—in Jackson, the capital. I'd never seen any of the rest of the state until I went to Columbus, Mississippi, to school, and then I didn't see but one place, Columbus. Later I traveled all over the state and I could see the great differences created by geography—how the

Delta was different from the piney woods, and both sections, from other parts of the state. The people had grown up so differently and were situated so differently—rich people in the Delta and ragged poor up in the clay counties to the north and in the piney woods to the south. You could see the history of the state almost written on the people. At that time it was quite clear. Now everything is amalgamated.

White: How did the impressions that you gathered from all those trips affect you as a writer?

Welty: Of course, I never thought about using anything in writing at the time. I was just learning, which was a good thing. I saw the countryside purely as a sightseer or as somebody who was writing about it for the paper. The travel opened my eyes. I had no idea of the differences within one state—in background and in everything. I constantly learned a lot. Sometimes I could take the family car—not always too easy on the family—and see more that way. It was an eye-opener. In fact, everything I did when I was growing up was an eye-opener. I must have been half-asleep till I got in my teens. I learned everything at one time.

White: "Death of a Traveling Salesman" was published in 1936. How did you come up with the idea for that story and those characters?

Welty: A couple who were friends of my parents who lost their house (as so many in the Depression did) moved in and lived with us for a while. He was a traveling salesman. I had no idea about writing about anything he described, but one sentence he said sparked that story. He had been somewhere and the woman of the house had said, "Go and borry some fire." That just opened a whole world to me. To get a light at night—of course, there would have been no way to do it except with a fire. Things were down to a minimum in those days. "Go and borry some fire" just started me off, and I wrote this story. It had nothing else to do with this friend of the family. Nothing to do with him. I made up everything around it that would lead to this. I didn't know I was going to do that exactly, but doing it taught me something.

I asked Hubert Creekmore, another writer who was a friend of mine who lived up the street, to read it. He said, "Why don't you try this little magazine *Manuscript*," which took unknown young writers, "published in Ohio." I sent it to them and they did take it. That

probably spoiled me to think that life was very easy. You send
something off and it gets taken. To see it in print is what turned the
trick, I think. It made it real—that you could write something and
make it appear, not just in your head.

White: What happened after you got that story published? You must
have known then, perhaps, that you would be a writer.

Welty: But I had always wanted to be one—had always wanted to
write. It was an odd feeling to have something read, to have it
accessible to other people. It made you feel naked at first and kind of
scared. But I got letters after that from other magazines and publications who were in those days on the lookout for young unknown
writers. Then I could respond to that. I didn't sell in any other place
for a long time, but it made me feel that I was connected with the
world. I could not only read, but I could write something someone
else could read. It sounds very simple, but it's like a revolution in
your brain. Well, you can imagine.

White: Would you talk about some of the people who influenced
you during your first years as a writer?

Welty: I was always a reader, but I was never conscious of being
specifically influenced by any writer or reader. I'm sure there were
lots of unconscious influences, but when I was writing a story it was
all of a piece in my head. Of course, seeing how experience was
translated into words was familiar to me from fairy tales on. But then,
I loved to read. I'm sure there were unconscious influences such as
Chekhov and people I loved to read—Katherine Mansfield—oh, all
kinds of influences. I read everything.

White: What about Faulkner? Did his writings have an effect on
you as a writer?

Welty: Not any that I could put my finger on. Of course, he was this
huge presence in one's life. But I can't imagine going to a writer for a
direct influence—for a specific piece of advice like "What do I do
here, sir?" It's too bad you can't do that. The awareness of him was
sort of magical. To think there was a great narrative artist like that
just there to be read, like a sight—Niagara Falls or something—that
you could just go stand in front of and be awe-stricken by. I wasn't
advanced enough or trusting in myself at all enough to profit by him.
There's no direct influence, but the learning of what could be done by
such a genius as that was enough. It meant a great deal to me.

White: You've written about the importance of revision in your writing. Would you talk about that?

Welty: It took me a little while to learn that I ought to revise, and that I could revise. I was too prone just to dash things off spontaneously—I suppose it was very arrogant. The more I understood what I was trying to do, the more I saw what there was to be done. It's too bad there isn't something one can read that will tell you what to do on page two of your manuscript. But I think revising opened the door to the world of fiction and to the world of trial and effect and the approach to the imagination—that's everything. I don't think I trusted myself to be too self-conscious about things. I was afraid I couldn't have followed through. That came later.

White: You've written that many of the heroines in your stories are schoolteachers, but that you yourself did not want to be a schoolteacher. Why not?

Welty: Well, those are two different things altogether. I mean, I loved schoolteachers and revered them. But that doesn't mean that I thought *I* could be one. At that time when I was growing up in the South, there was not much a woman could do to earn a living. You either got married or you taught school. That was it. I think there was a kind of horror to assigning yourself to one kind of oblivion or another if you wanted see the world and do things. I didn't think that I *could* teach. I was smart to realize it, smarter than I knew. I couldn't teach. I wanted to do almost anything else and be independent and my own boss. It worked out I could do almost the next thing to it anyway.

White: Would you discuss your use of families in your fiction? How do you view the family?

Welty: What interests me most is human relationships, and the natural element for those to happen in is the family. The family relationship is the first one a person learns. From that, you learn what your relationships are going to be with other people. As a fiction writer, what fascinates me are human relationships. The easiest place to observe these or to remember them is within a family. That sounds like something simple, but of course it's not simple.

White: Would you tell me about the origins of *The Golden Apples?* Did your reading of myths and fairy tales have an impact on your writing *The Golden Apples?*

Welty: I'm sure it did, as did several things besides fairy tales—the Yeats poem, for example: "Though I am old with wandering/ Through hollow lands and hilly lands,/ I will find out where she has gone,/ And something, something . . . and touch your hands;/ And pluck till time and times are done/ The silver apples of the moon,/ The golden apples of the sun." That's not remembered exactly now. I left out a line. But that poem, when my mind was clearer, stayed with me in a very articulate way most of my life. It was the feeling of quest and searching for the rewards of love and beauty, which is a fairy tale idea.

As time went on, I realized that the stories I was writing were related, which I didn't realize at first. People were there in other names, but they were the same characters at other times. It's just like your imagination to play tricks like that on you! But you catch on eventually if you just keep at it.

I thought it was particularly applicable in the Mississippi Delta, where people sort of live a dream world, or so it seemed to me. In those days, when it was just plain cotton country, it was as distinct as anything in this world from any other part of the state. I got so I recognized people from the Delta when I was at college. I still feel I can recognize them. ("That girl is from the Delta. I can tell it by her walk.") There's just something about them.

I wanted to call up the idea that people were living in kinds of self delusions about things, and I thought that the Delta was just the kind of miasma of light and reflections from white cotton fields—and the sun on the huge rivers or even the small rivers, like the Sunflower. It's set off, like living in a mirage. To me that went with the idea of *The Golden Apples*. It's all a search and a wish for something romantic. So it seemed to me that that joined the stories which at first I had not realized belonged together. But some of the characters were the same as the characters in other stories at a different stage in life. I was pleased at the idea of a connectedness of *The Golden Apples* and of that overlying poetic yearning that ran through everything, which I thought was enough of a joining together.

White: Would you talk about the character Virgie Rainey?

Welty: Of course, she's necessary because she was the answer to all the others. She was the only one who was a realist and questioned things. She was also the only one who was really talented, owing to her teacher. It's strange the way your mind gradually invents something and makes a whole narrative of it in a suggestive way, not specific so that you can follow it. I loved writing that book because it all came to me so slowly and orderly until it all fitted together. It was just a wonderful, fortunate experience to write it.

White: Would you talk about Virgie Rainey and Miss Eckhart? Can you compare them?

Welty: Miss Eckhart was a teacher, one of many teachers that I seemed to have written about. Virgie was like the subject of what she was teaching, only in a very loose way. Miss Eckhart was the only one who could have taught Virgie anything about the art she could practice. It had just happened that by great good fortune they'd been thrown together. Miss Eckhart knew that, but Virgie was too self-centered and too young and too unbelieving probably to understand it. So it was rather tragic. But I think that often happens in a small town.

White: How have the South and Jackson, Mississippi, changed over the years?

Welty: Jackson has always been the only city in Mississippi. It's the capital and where all the state offices are. When I grew up, it was twenty-five thousand people, which is a big town. Everything else was small, little villages, as in Faulkner. He makes all that so plain. Every town is sort of a little microcosm of a society. Thank God things did change a lot in the South. At the time I was writing *The Golden Apples,* I don't think much had changed. Jackson itself has changed incredibly, just accelerated itself into trying to become more civilized. Well, it's always been civilized, but I mean in a different way, more aware of humanity.

White: People have referred to you, of course, as a southern writer, a regionalist. How do you respond to that title?

Welty: I don't respond to it. I don't think I'm speaking for only the people in Jackson or even on my street. I'm just speaking for human beings. But you have to have a point by which you observe them and through which you understand them. You can't just sit in a chair in Coney Island and watch people parade by. That wouldn't teach you anything. But a life lived in a community does. A sense of time and development is with you from earliest childhood. That's important in a narrative, in a story. Consistency and the arrow of change are all integral parts of drama.

White: You have said that your novels have come upon you accidentally. Do you consider yourself a novelist?

Welty: As I write each novel, I'm the novelist of that book. But I think I'm more naturally a short story writer. I don't plan well enough to be a novelist. They have happened sort of accidentally. I start a short story, and I realize that I have the foundation there for something of a different scope in time or bigger cast of people or more development. So then I work it out that way. But I don't start it thinking that I'm going to do a novel of a certain shape and size. I just don't have that kind of mind. So I have to learn each one anew. Nearly all of them have started out as a story, including the longest one, *Losing Battles*.

White: What is the origin of *Losing Battles*? How did you develop or come up with the idea for it?

Welty: I read the county papers in Mississippi as a result of working for the WPA. I worked for these little papers, reporting on WPA projects, and I got carried away by the reports sent in by their reporters from such-and-such a cross roads or community. You know, "Miss So-and-So after the freeze last week had all her preserves to blow up in the basement." About that particular story, I wrote to the correspondent, "Could you tell me, when the preserves blew up, if they all blew up at once or one by one?" He just wrote back, "As a result of the freeze all of our preserves blew up. Yours truly." Just what was in the paper—I never got my question answered. But everything was there if you'd only interpret it, things that would never happen in Jackson, and very touching stories. They would deal with people like those in *Losing Battles*. The smallest item is news: "Someone came through town last week from Memphis to buy some bottled water" was in the paper. Family reunions were in there. All the things that go on in the country.

Then my mother was ill for a good while and we had live-in people to help me with her. They're nearly all what is called in the paper "settled white Christian ladies with no home ties." Doesn't that make you want to cry? They were the ones looking for work like that. I had a number of them work with me. I learned about their families and how they lived, which you would not know in a town like Jackson about the poor, poor conditions in north Mississippi. And I just started writing. They had such a sense of fun and a sense of family. It just grew, that story did.

White: Would you tell us about the importance of place in your fiction?

Welty: I think it's very important, particularly in the South where places have remained the same for so long. Of course, now everything is changing, as it should. But for a long time nothing seemed to move. Place is very important. It has a kind of poetic truth to me. In Mississippi, which is an old, long-ago-settled state, everything has a past. We sort of know what it was like when the Indians were here, then when the Spanish were here, then when the English were here, then when the French were here, then when the British were here, and then when we were here. There are records and memories of places. You would be aware of the history of places when you went to visit them, even when there was no physical reminder visible any longer.

White: Would you talk about *The Optimist's Daughter?* What was the origin of the character Laurel?

Welty: That story really sprang from my own life in an indirect way. It was so much about vision and eyes. My mother had had lots of trouble with her eyes, and she'd had an operation such as I gave the judge in *The Optimist's Daughter.* In those days you had to nurse a cataract operation case for weeks. Not move on the bed. I learned a lot and thought a lot about vision and the tricks it could play on you. It was really about vision, inner and outer. My mother had died—in fact, the death of the judge sprang from my own experience with the death of my mother. It was not like that at all, but it was the same sort of experience. Certainly there was nobody in my life that was like Fay. It's a good thing there wasn't anybody like Fay.

White: Would you talk about the inner journey that Laurel experiences?

Welty: Of course, that *is* the story. It's what it is about. She had to get accustomed to thinking of her parents as people with emotional and dramatic lives of their own that she might not have known about—to accommodate all that into her knowledge of them and her love of them, to accept death and other changes, for instance, the intrusion of Fay. All of course are just parts of ordinary life.

A lot depended on her point of view. I made her an artist who lived in Chicago, which would be as far as I could think of from living in Mississippi, so that she could have a refreshing point of view, a learning point of view—somebody who had not been prepared. She realizes she hasn't been prepared for anything, like the death of her fiance. Oh, no, she was married to him, wasn't she? The death of the one she loved. The story of her mother that had been very mysterious to her, she had to come to grips with that—and the realization that there are many things that you might not understand at the time. You might not understand them ever, but they're there, mysterious, and have their right to exist. The story of human relationships is what interested me.

I don't know where I got the plot idea. My brother had fought at Okinawa, and I knew about the experiences of some men. Most of the boys I knew were in the Air Force or the Army and had fought all through World War II. So I knew the feelings that she would have had for men who had gone off to war. That doesn't explain the connections I found in there, but they're there.

White: What were the origins of "The Demonstrators" and "Where Is the Voice Coming From?"

Welty: In a way they were responses to much criticism that we were living through in Jackson at the time of the race riots. They weren't race riots, but I was thinking in modern terms. We made troubles for ourselves in all kinds of ways—stupid actions, incomprehension, and so on. But I do not think that such actions spoke for everybody. There were always people of feeling and sensibilities and integrity who were trying, both black and white, to come together then. It was not an open and shut situation. It never is anywhere.

But I received many a midnight telephone call from strangers saying, "What the hell do you mean down there, sitting on your ass, not getting out working for civil rights? You don't understand anything about black people." Or, "You don't have any sympathy for them." Which wasn't true. I had been writing about injustice all my life. That's what it was all about, injustice. Plenty of people like me were aware of this and doing what they could. But just because of my address, Jackson, Mississippi, I was supposed to be a lout and a bigot and everything. That got to me. I thought I would write some stories to show what it was really like here, how it was so complicated and how motives were so mixed. How nothing is simple.

White: How did you feel about winning the Pulitzer Prize? How does that make you feel?

Welty: Wonderful, of course. It also gives you a feeling of connection with the world, which is not too common with writers. You're pleased when it's read or when it's liked, and also you feel that your peers thought it was all right, people who were doing the same kind of work you were. So it means that much more. I was thrilled.

White: Most of your works are affirmative. Is the tragic spirit alien to your work?

Welty: No, I think there's tragedy deep inside most of them. I don't think you can draw the line between tragedy and not- tragedy because so many things imply something tragic just as they imply something humorous. I don't think anything should be denied any quality. I don't consciously do so because life doesn't. Implications are there.

White: Would you recall for us your first meeting with Reynolds Price and the relationship that has grown over the years?

Welty: Have you already asked Reynolds? Have you got his side of it?

We had a wonderful meeting. It really is a story. He was still at Duke, a senior, I think. Of course, I didn't know him. I was going from one college to another giving readings to help my income out, and I was invited to come to Duke by his composition class. It turned out that I was doing it all by train, by day coach. I was coming from somewhere in South Carolina, maybe Converse College, and not getting into Durham until two o'clock in the morning. So I wrote and said, "Please tell me what hotel I can stay at, and do not meet me because I do not want to be met at that hour. I just want to know where to go."

So the train came in and I looked out. I couldn't see a light anywhere. The town was totally dark. I began to wonder about getting to the hotel. As I stepped off the car, I saw this slim, young man in a white suit standing all alone on the platform. He came up and asked me if I were I. And he said, "I won't speak to you." I had said I didn't want anyone to be nice to me or speak to me at that hour or anything. "I won't speak to you, I won't do anything. I'm just going to carry your suitcase for you and see that you get inside the hotel."

Of course, that was Reynolds. Neither one of us said a word. He took me over to the hotel and bid me goodnight and went away in the sweetest, most feeling way. It was just so kind because honestly I don't know what I would have done. The town was pitch black dark, no street lights even, no porter. It was a fool idea I'd had that I could arrive at that hour. The next day I found out who he was, and, of course, it was Reynolds. The idea was entirely his own. He sympathized with my wish not to be talked to at that hour, not to make trouble, not to be a burden to anybody. But he was not going to let me get there unprotected, unguarded. That was typical of him.

It was the beginning of a fine friendship that has never ceased. We have been the dearest of friends all these years. We see each other whenever we can. Later he became the editor of the Duke magazine and went right on writing. I read some of his stories at that time. Any fool could have seen that they were holding star-quality writing in their hands. I knew that besides being a very fine gentleman he was also a first-rate writer, all right there for me to see.

White: How do you spend your spare time? Do you read a lot?

Welty: I read all the time. I do, I read all the time. Now, of course, I'm the only one in my family left, and I live alone in this house. I can just take it easy if I want to, or else I can work like a demon if I want to. I don't work like a demon as often as I used to, though I would like to. I do love to read, as always. I used to do a good bit of reviewing. I don't do that anymore because the deadline thing defeats me. I just hate it. I've quit doing it. But I still write things because I want to.

White: Will you have more books coming out?

Welty: You never know—I don't know. I love to write. I'll never stop that, never stop loving to write. So we shall see.

Eudora Welty, in Her Own Words

David Streitfeld / 1992

From the *Washington Post,* 4 December 1992, Sec. D, 1, 3.
Reprinted by permission of the *Washington Post.*

The details are lost in the mists of memory, but it seems that the members of an amateur literary group once sent an invitation to Eudora Welty. "Bring us one of your stories," they urged. "Don't bother to read it. Just tell it in your own words."

Welty recounts this anecdote slowly, the way she must do most things these days, but as she does, unfettered delight spreads across her face. "Don't you like that?" she asks, and repeats: " 'Just tell it in your own words.' It's one of my favorite, favorite remarks."

The much-honored grande dame of American letters has come to Washington this week to receive another in a long row of prizes. This time it's the PEN/Malamud Award, given for excellence in the short story. At the ceremony tonight, she'll read one of her works—in her own words, even. She's not positive, but thinks it'll probably be the "The Wide Net," maybe abbreviated for public consumption.

"Oh, you've heard of it? I don't think I've ever met anyone who was familiar with it."

Welty is as low-key as they come, but this is going a bit too far. "The Wide Net," the title story of her 1943 collection, is one of her most celebrated—the tale of the October day when William Wallace Jamieson's wife, Hazel, left him a note saying she had had enough and was going to the river to drown herself.

This takes place in southern Mississippi, on the Old Natchez Trace, the landscape Welty made her own and has rarely strayed from. It's the same in life: She still lives in the state capital, Jackson, in the home her parents built. It's become a local landmark of sorts, with strangers arriving at the door all the time.

These days, the physical frailties to which one is prey at 83 means she's often at home when they show up. Too often. " 'I just thought I would like to come by and speak to you'—you know, kind of neighborly. Although they aren't my neighbors, they're from out of town."

Eudora Welty is a forgiving sort. In this she is special. Famous writers tend to be both troubled and troublesome—you'd have been downright frightened to knock on the door of Mississippi's other great contribution to literature, William Faulkner—but it takes a huge amount to get Welty riled. So she generally ends up indulging her visitors.

Often, they want to be writers themselves, and are searching for the secret. As if there is one. "Everybody wants to express something. But they don't attach it to any idea of work. I mean, it's a serious business to write about your life."

Or talk about it. Interviews are bad enough—"An hour?" she asks about this one, conducted yesterday morning in the dark, unopened bar of the Mayflower Hotel. "Is it really going to take that long?" But sometimes her callers belong to an even worse species: They're hopeful biographers, delighted to delve into her personal life (Why did she never marry? Why has she stopped writing?).

She thanks them and says she'd rather not. She dealt with all she cared to, which was her childhood, in a set of lectures a decade ago called *One Writer's Beginnings*. She wrote the book more for herself than anyone, almost as a form of therapy. "Thomas Mann said the past is like a well," she said. "Once you start into it, it shows all the things it's been holding all this time, and you can look at them."

The past has always haunted Southern fiction, but Welty's work often had a double helping: Much was set a generation or two back—in the 1920s or the '30s, and sometimes much further. When she talks about historical events, you kind of feel she was there.

Jackson, she notes, "was burned by Sherman three times. How do you burn a town three times? He was on his way to the siege at Vicksburg and every time he passed through it he would burn it. It was called Chimneyville, that was all that was left. There's not any so-called antebellum Jackson because it was all burned." And then, unexpectedly: "That's kind of nice, I think. It's a fresh start."

When she talks, she looks straight at you, and leans forward as much as she can. She excuses herself for staring. "Somehow," she explains, "by looking closely you can hear better. . . . It's maddening not to have your hearing. A lot of my work comes out of overheard remarks. Now I can't overhear them."

She didn't do this intentionally—merely by going somewhere in downtown Jackson, she was bombarded. People would come from all parts of the state to do their business there, and the accents and intonations and expressions varied wildly.

"You could tell where people were from by words they used or the expressions. It was fun to be a detective. But now everybody speaks in a homogenized way. When have you ever heard anybody say recently, 'I have a gnawing and a craving for it,' which I overheard somebody say. Or, 'Do you like fresh meat?'—that means freshly killed." She smiles, taking pleasure in the shape of the words.

There are other changes wrought by modern life. Welty may be a beloved figure in Jackson, but that didn't stop the band of robbers that broke into her home two years ago.

It was Thanksgiving before last. She had been out to an early dinner, and walked right in on them. "I realized when I opened the door that things were all wrong," she says. "I had just gotten in the night before from a trip. My suitcase was still standing in the hall where I put it down but it had been opened, and things were strewn all over. I felt cold air blowing, and realized they had burst in through the French doors. So I went to the phone and called the police. I said, 'There are people in my house, they're in here right now.' They said, 'Lady, get out!' "

She dismisses the incident now. "It was just teenage boys. I think they were looking for Christmas presents. The funny thing was, they took all my gloves, including my pair of white kid evening gloves. You don't have very many of those in a lifetime."

She'd like to dismiss something else, too: the idea she has written herself out. Actually, she still has things she wants to say in fiction, and maintains that "the next time I have an idea to work out, I'll do it." Ideas, then, aren't the problem; arthritis is. Dictation isn't the answer. It doesn't work for her. There is no answer.

In one sense, this doesn't matter. It was said of E.M. Forster that his reputation increased with each book he didn't write, and something of the same has occurred with Welty.

Her fame chiefly rests on her four books of short stories, the last of which appeared in 1955, along with three short novels that appeared around that time. In the last 20 years, there's been the usual tidying up—a *Collected Stories*, a book of essays and, unexpectedly, the bestselling *One Writer's Beginnings*—but no new fiction, nothing to obstruct the view of that luminous and long-ago work.

Sometimes an award sheds luster on the winner, and sometimes it's the other way around. During its five years of existence, the PEN/ Malamud Award has been in the latter category, but will presently be making an effort to reorient itself slightly toward the former.

"To make the award known, you do have to have winners who are known," explains Ann Malamud, the widow of Bernard. "And there is a legitimate place for awarding a prize for a body of work." This explains the selection so far of John Updike, Saul Bellow, George Garrett and, last year, Andre Dubus and Frederick Busch, none of whom has been exactly unheralded in his time.

"I think," says Malamud, "what we are going to try to do is to have lesser-known people in between the better-known. I think my husband would have wanted that. He was a schoolteacher all his life. He was interested in young people and encouraged them."

He was also, at the other end of the scale, interested in Eudora Welty. Ann Malamud mentions finding a paperback collection of her work, "13 Stories," in her house and discovering the margins were laced with her husband's commentary.

There are more mundane connections, such as the fact that they were clients of the same literary agent, Diarmuid Russell. That operation, now called Russell and Volkening, is in the hands of Tim Seldes—husband of Washington writer Susan Shreve, who will introduce Welty tonight. The literary world often moves in such neat circles.

Welty has previously won the Pulitzer Prize, the American Book Award, the American Academy and Institute of Arts and Letters' Gold Medal for the Novel, the Hollins Medal, the Brandeis Medal of Achievement, the Howells Medal, the M. Carey Thomas Award, the National Medal for Literature and the Presidential Medal of Freedom. Aside from the Nobel, nothing much seems to be lacking.

"I don't know how many I've gotten," she confesses, but adds that they still matter. "I think it goes back to a childhood pleasure—that something has come, not necessarily deserved. Just manna from heaven."

The ceremony will be at the Church of the Reformation, across the street from the Folger Shakespeare Library. There's space for 600 literary-minded folk, but don't bother: The event sold out quicker than any done under the auspices of the PEN/Faulkner Foundation within memory.

After the reading, everyone will walk across to the Folger for a reception. Traditionally, the honored author gets mobbed at this point, but Welty is fragile enough to need protection from too enthusiastic a crowd. A mass book-signing, for instance, is out.

She's had enough strange experiences with that phenomenon anyway. "Sometimes," she says, "people ask you to do the damndest things—to write 'to so-and-so, the prettiest, smartest girl I ever saw.' And I say, 'I've never ever seen this girl. I can't write that. *You* have to write it.' "

And the young man will respond: "Oh, I couldn't say anything like *that*. It takes a writer."

In her own words, if possible.

Seeing Real Things: An Interview with Eudora Welty

Jan Nordby Gretlund / 1993

From Jan Nordby Gretlund, *Eudora Welty's Aesthetics of Place* (Newark: Univ. of Delaware Press, 1994), pp. 401-24. Reprinted by permission of Associated University Presses.

Gretlund: On the basis of your early story "Acrobats in a Park" I assume that you have read the poetry of Rainer Maria Rilke.

Welty: Of course, I have, but I do not remember when, or where.

Gretlund: There was a translation in 1939 by J. B. Leishman and Stephen Spender of the *Duino Elegies* . . .

Welty: Yes, I love those. I remember reading those long ago.

Gretlund: And in that edition there is a print of Picasso's painting "La famille des saltimbanques," and one of the elegies is on that painting.

Welty: It could be that I saw it,—not with the poem, but I saw the Picasso. I saw his paintings pretty early. I have always been fascinated by painting, and especially by that school. I used to see most things in Chicago at the Art Institute, which is a marvelous museum, and they were the earliest people I saw.—When I went to the University of Wisconsin in Madison, I had no idea what I saw, but I used to go down to Chicago to see the Impressionists, whenever I could. I went frequently.

Gretlund: I know that you are a painter yourself.

Welty: You couldn't take anything I did in painting seriously. I loved it, and I studied it, but I had no serious ambition about it. I wouldn't dream that I had any ability for that; I just loved painting. I studied art when I was growing up here. There was a good painter named Marie Hull who gave lessons to young people right here in Jackson. I knew a number of Jackson painters. There was quite a number as I was growing up. And when I got to the University of Wisconsin [when] I was a junior, they had a wonderful art history course, and I minored in that. I majored in English, and minored in art, because they had such marvelous professors and marvelous chances to see the real thing. I could go into Chicago and see the real things; that was just wonderful.

It's very different from studying writing because that was something you had to do almost in solitude. You can go to many good classes in literature, which I did, but the act of writing I didn't think I could learn that way. Any practice in it is of course valuable, that's the way you learn.—I had some marvelous professors in English literature, which meant everything, I would have chosen them any day over a professor in writing. The one I liked and got most from was at Wisconsin—Ricardo Quintana. He was a Swift and Donne man.

Gretlund: Did you read Swift and Donne?

Welty: I did read Swift and Donne, but I read everything contemporary, too. I just read whatever came to hand; I just read all the time. I was coming along when you could read Proust and Thomas Mann, all those people were publishing. And Chekhov—I sort of dictated my own, what I would read, by my own taste. It wasn't that I spurned anything else, but it was just that I was so eager to read them. By Thomas Mann I read *The Magic Mountain,* of course. My mother was reading *Joseph and His Brothers,* but I never did read that, although I meant to. I read *Buddenbrooks,* and later probably in the early 40s or maybe late 30s I read some of the tragic shorter things that he wrote. I don't think they were translated in the early 1930s, or maybe they were and I didn't know it.

What happened in those days was that the Modern Library was invented, and Proust and Mann began to appear in print. I think Proust was one of the first things that came out; and *Swann's Way* was the first. I remember going down to Macy's, I was in New York, and there used to be fights in the aisle over getting hold of them, everybody was so eager. And Macy's and Gimbel's, the store across the street, had price wars on who was going to make it cheaper. There was a day you could get it for seven cents! That's when I was going to Columbia, 1930-31, I think. Although it could have been other times I was in New York, because I went every time I could. Anyway, that was a marvelous gift to everybody, to start the Modern Library.

Gretlund: I see you as more of an Agrarian than most people do.

Welty: I just don't know about it. I didn't write with a philosophical basis to what I was doing. I had no philosophy I was pursuing, and no aesthetics, I'm just writing as a tale-teller. But they were very good

to me at the *Southern Review;* they were just like godparents to me.
They accepted my work and printed it. It was a godsend. But there
was no philosophical or any other [theoretical connection].

Gretlund: But wasn't there a spiritual kinship? After all, my count
shows that you were the darling of the *Southern Review,* as you had
more stories published in the first series than anybody else.

Welty: Really. I didn't know that. It was just that Peter Taylor was
a little younger than me, or he would have been ahead of me.

Gretlund: Did you ever read *I'll Take My Stand?*

Welty: Eventually I did. I think I must have just read it out of
curiosity, probably because it was written by these people whose
other work I liked, and who had been good to me. But I didn't read
much like that. I was a big fiction reader. I didn't take any part or
even much interest in the Agrarian pursuits. I didn't know enough to
begin with. I didn't have a good background. And I had no philosophical convictions that I would apply to writing. I remember when I met
Robert Penn Warren, much, much later. I didn't meet people in those
days, and Jackson is quite a distance from Baton Rouge, but I went to
Baton Rouge one time to drive a friend, the journalist Herschel
Brickell, down there. And we met Katherine Anne Porter. She had
invited me to come and see her, and she was then married to Albert
Erskine, and we all three went to lunch at their house.

It was a good while before I ever met Cleanth and Red. But when
we all did meet, they were so likable and wonderful and so good to
me that I didn't feel out of place. I was pretty shy about the whole
thing. I felt that I would never be of interest to them, because they
had such a philosophical investment in all this, and I didn't have any.
This was in the late 1930s. Katherine Anne wasn't married to Albert
for very long. The whole thing was a big mistake. He died recently.
When I moved from Harcourt, Brace, my agent Diarmuid Russell
wanted me to go to an editor I liked, and he had asked different
people that might be interested. One was Albert Erskine. He had then
gone on to be president of Random House. I hadn't seen him since
these days at Baton Rouge, when he was a bridegroom really, and he
was so good to me. He published *Losing Battles.*

Gretlund: In *Losing Battles* you have two academics, Julia Mortimer and Judge Moody, with names that seem to mock them. And
there is a critical debate about the novel's opposing the values of

academics and farmers. Do you blame the farmers for their willful
ignorance, or do you mock the academics and praise the family?

Welty: The family above all. And also the love of the tale, the
talking. The way you keep the family going is through the
stories.—The names are good old Mississippi names, I wasn't trying
to be cute or anything. I always liked the name Moody. Don't you
like that?—I laid it in the part of Mississippi that is the most rural and
uninvaded. I chose a place on purpose that had not been infiltrated by
anything else. Far from being the Old South, and all that stuff, these
people—all they had was each other. And there are so many people
in Mississippi like that.

Gretlund: And the setting is definitely Mississippi? Several critics
have argued lately that the novel is really West Virginia transplanted.

Welty: My mother is from West Virginia, you know. It is the same
strain of people, but those people did not come here from West
Virginia. [The heat, the drought, and the dust] is Mississippi; it's not
West Virginia. But there is a simplicity and a directness and a relish
of tales and things like that which they have in common.

Gretlund: Isn't it surprising for the author of "Place in Fiction" to
hear the argument: Welty wrote about the northeastern corner of
Mississippi, but it is really West Virginia!

Welty: That's absurd! I tried to get a part of Mississippi where they
had nothing, Tishomingo, because I wanted to show what they did
have was each other and the family tales and the family solidarity.
That's all they had. And I thought that was a good basis for a novel.

Gretlund: Baton Rouge is not a presence in your fiction, but New
Orleans certainly always was, from "The Purple Hat" to *The Optimist's Daughter*. Mississippians seem always to have been fascinated
by New Orleans. It appears that it was only rivaled by Memphis.

Welty: That was literally true, I think, when I was brought up.
People had one city or the other to which they went to consult
specialists of any kind, or to make an important purchase, like a
bridal gown, or something like that. And also it was a place of
pleasure, where you went for your flings. Of course, in North Mississippi, Memphis is the only place. And *here* people were divided
between Memphis and New Orleans. Always it was just one or the
other. You didn't go to both! New Orleans is such a wonderful stage,
a wonderful theater, for anything to be acted out. It is native to it to

be like that. It is much more of a change from ordinary life than
Memphis is. Memphis could be almost like Jackson, but New Orleans
is like a French place. It still is. It is very deep, I mean it is layers of
life, and not easy to know. It is mysterious, a good city. When I wrote
"The Purple Hat," I was trying to show off having been to a gambling
hall. We used to go down there on dates, to meet with friends. In
those days we would go and dance to wonderful jazz music that we'd
just walk in to, right off Royal Street. It was very easy to go down
there and get into this completely different world. I didn't know
Memphis very well, but it was, I think, much more countrified; New
Orleans was an old, old city, and fascinating. It cost very little to go
there, but you had to have enough money to afford what was little,
which not many of us did.

But I remember being able to catch the streamliner train that began
to come out of Jackson, Tennessee, to New Orleans; it would go
through Jackson [Mississippi] some time between five and six in the
morning and arrived at New Orleans about 10 o'clock or 10:30. You
could get off the train, and walk around all the day—you couldn't
afford a hotel, you had nowhere to sit down. We had no money, but
we were young and did not need a place to sit down. You could walk
all through the Quarter and eat one good meal there, at Galatoire's or
something, and have one drink in Pat O'Brian's Courtyard, and then
walk back to the train at six o'clock in the evening, get on, and ride
home. You could do the whole thing for about ten or fifteen dollars! It
was the only way we could have done it; it was during the Depression.
We always went from the station to the French Quarter and just stayed
there and went up and down. If we had enough money, we could go
into the Monteleone Hotel, which is on Royal Street, and if we ever
spent the night it would be there, because you'd just walk out into the
French Quarter in the morning. All those little streets down there,
you had certain places you went to, to revisit.

I never did go for shopping. I didn't care about going to the shops.
But I went to get to hear the wonderful jazz by the old people in the
Preservation Hall, since it started. I remember Sweet Emma played
the piano. She would come in wearing a house dress and her hat, and
she'd put her purse and a bag of groceries to take home afterwards on
top of the piano, an old upright, and sit down and start in. I have

some of her records. She was just like a good housewife coming to give it a good cleaning down where she played.

Gretlund: But most of the traveling performers you saw right here in Jackson.

Welty: Yes. They really were nationally known, and the only reason we ever got them here was that they had to lay over one night between Memphis and New Orleans. This was when I was nine or ten years old.

Gretlund: When did you hear Fats Waller play in Jackson?

Welty: That came a good deal later. I didn't go to hear Fats until . . . he didn't come here until in the 20s. I had all his records already, he didn't burst upon my horizon, he'd already done that. I never would have set out to do "Powerhouse," because I wouldn't have thought I could. I was just so keyed up that I just did it. I did have the good sense to know that I had no basis to rewrite anything, I just didn't know anything except what I wrote down.

Gretlund: Sometimes fiction becomes fact. Your Mike Fink story in *The Robber Bridegroom,* in which he rides into an alligator, is now registered as an official Mike Fink story in Blair and Meine's *Half Horse Half Alligator.*

Welty: Oh, I just made that up. But it is in the spirit. I mean, the whole thing was in the spirit of that extravagant time. I tried to make it like [a tall story]. Mark Twain, you know, referred to all those things, too, when he wrote *Life on the Mississippi,* and when he wrote *Huckleberry Finn.*

Gretlund: But you add an element. Your Mike Fink is a depressed mailrider of modern times. It is sad to see him in his reduced state.

Welty: I know it. It's as in the fairy tale tradition. Well, those were people who frequented the Trace, really. Mailriders had to go there. I had to have somebody like that for another character. I read a lot of histories of the time . . . .

Gretlund: *The Devil's Backbone,* perhaps?

Welty: I have read that one, and another one by [Jonathan Daniels], but there are plenty of histories of the time, which you can read. It was really true, really a fact that . . . . Did you read a story I wrote called "A Still Moment"? The three men that meet there on the Natchez Trace, that could have been physically possible, because the three people were around there at the same time. I just imagined what it would have been like, but it would have been possible. I read a lot of things that made me write it, like the letters of Lorenzo Dow, the mad, they say he was mad, evangelist. He made dates a year ahead that he would be back at this clearing in the wilderness, and he would be there. He and his wife exchanged letters while he had this life. I read those letters, they are just wonderful. It was a time of extravagance and romantic ideas. It was the times that made me write those stories.

Gretlund: Did you know that "A Still Moment" is probably the story by you most often referred to and commented on?

Welty: Really. It is just as well. I don't know what to say. That really is strange! I'm very proud of the fact that Robert Penn Warren told me he liked that story the best. That part about Audubon, I guess, is based on the truth. Not Audubon in my story. He was all down in there, painted his way down. I've seen some of his paintings in old houses down there. And in his diaries he would write about his horror as he walked the streets of New Orleans and saw great tables in the market of slaughtered song-birds for sale, just to eat! It's fascinating to read. It is the only time I ever wrote out of things I've read instead of out of living. Those were such romantic "facts."

Gretlund: Your fascination with the early history of the Natchez Trace is expressed with much humor. And the humor has stayed with you right up to *The Optimist's Daughter,* in which it comes out as satire on the social classes, especially in Fay's mourning scene.

Welty: I got one review in French that said the only person worth saving in that was Fay and that all these other people were trash!

Gretlund: And that is not exactly what you had in mind?

Welty: Not exactly.

Gretlund: Was the French critic right in so far as your criticism was leveled at all social groups in Mount Salus?

Welty: It is against the humans. What it is against are the people who do not know the meaning of their own experiences, as I came out and baldly said about Fay: people who don't know the meaning of what's happened to them. They are not sensitive to what's going on around them. They don't see. And it has nothing to do with the classes or anything like that. It is just the human ability to know what your own experience means. Some people never learn what happens to them.

Gretlund: Do the Fairchilds of *Delta Wedding* ever realize their shortcomings? They don't always treat their black laborers as human beings.

Welty: Which was probably exactly what was going on at the time. They didn't even realize what they were doing.

Gretlund: I have the impression that Troy Flavin, the overseer, is having a relationship with one of the black girls on the plantation, i.e. with Pinchy.

Welty: I get more letters about Pinchy. "What does it mean," they say, "Pinchy is coming through." Well, I should have explained that. It is just a term that meant that you would get religion. She was going through that, which I had heard from time to time. But a lot of things I didn't have the wits to realize would need to be explained. I just took it for granted that everybody would know what that was.

Gretlund: Wasn't it unusual for Ellen Fairchild, the plantation mistress, to go down and witness the "coming through"?

Welty: Not if she liked Pinchy. I guess it was a family feeling toward the people she was looking after. No, I think that would be taken for granted. You'd help them whatever they were going through. It was what they call maternal. I'm sure it wouldn't be accepted now. I mean, it would be very strange now, I guess. I know whenever it was cold weather here, we used to take blankets and go over to where our maid lived and take her more covers. . . . They relied on us; when a sudden freeze came down, they wouldn't be prepared. Jackson was smaller then. All of us were closer together than now. Our maids lived on the other side of Greenwood Cemetery. Of course, that's terribly looked down on. You're not supposed to be paternal, or that kind of thing, but that was the need of the moment: they were cold. Nobody would do that now, for everybody's sake. They would think we were looking down on them.

Gretlund: Talking of racial relations in Mississippi, what do you think of the efforts to bring Byron De La Beckwith to trial again?

Welty: He is a monster! Of course, he should have been convicted in the first place. He is a horror! I don't know what is up right now. You know my story ["Where Is the Voice Coming from?"] is about the murder he is charged with, the one I wrote the night it happened. The reason I wrote the story is that I thought: "I should know exactly the kind of person this is." And I did know, except as somebody told me: "You thought it was a Snopes, and it was a Compson." But I wouldn't exactly agree, I don't think De La Beckwith is a Compson.

Gretlund: What do you think of the black-white situation in Jackson today?

Welty: Well, I may not have an ear close enough to it. At least it seems to me to be open always—so far as I can tell. You can always talk. And there are a good many black leaders who are prominent now, and people in office. I mean it is doing all right, it is slow, too slow, too late, but . . . not too late, can't be too late.

Gretlund: Is there any part of Jackson where it is dangerous for white people to go?

Welty: I wouldn't know it, if there was. And it might be just as dangerous for bad white people being there as for any black people. Things seem to be awfully slow. When I fractured my back and went to the hospital, the fracture mended, and I did exercises and came home. They sent me with this nurse, Daryl Howard, and said: "Keep her!" And that's what I've done. I can't really afford to, but I do. I really am fortunate. Daryl comes at seven o'clock in the morning, brings me some coffee in bed, and then she stays through breakfast and lunch, half a day every day, just to get me going, and she tells me most of what I know about the black situation. She's black and she's highly intelligent, you know, well-educated children and so on.

The other night her daughter, who has a night job (her daughter is married, both of them have night jobs), was standing outside the place where she works, just one of these all-night places, a decent place, but the hour was bad, and a man drove by where she was standing at the curb and said: "Throw your purse in the car or I'm blowing your brains out!" They mean it, too, when they say that. She was really terrified, and who wouldn't be? She did what he said, she threw her purse into the car. And she was terribly upset, of course.

Gretlund: Was it a white man driving the car?

Welty: I don't know. I don't even know if she knew. It could be either. I mean, it happens with either. Anyway, the poor girl was hysterical after it happened, as she well would be. She's married, but her mother went over and spent the rest of the night with her. It was such a terrible thing. She went down to look at a line-up to see if the man was—the one,—but she didn't find him. But that kind of thing goes on—too much—and among decent, educated, self-sufficient, self-respecting people that are going about their business. And this kind of thing happens, and it is just entirely too much, and I don't know what's being done about that. It's gotten more rampant, and more taken for granted, I believe, than it ever was before.

Gretlund: The identification with your place that you just demonstrated is characteristic of your fictional characters. But recently, it has been argued that the male MacLains in *The Golden Apples* are not really of their town, because mostly they are not in Morgana.

Welty: That's their part of being of Morgana. They are of it; that's why it matters. That's just a fact. I can remember things like that happening here. It just enters into the legend of a town: "Remember about Mr. So-and-so, he left his hat on the banks of the Mississippi River and disappeared."

Gretlund: Are the male MacLains essential for an attempt to define the identity of Morgana?

Welty: I think so. And also, their stories never die. Everybody's crazy about them, for the reason that's the way they act. They are just . . . romantic figures. I can remember some in my childhood.

Gretlund: There is another critical idea that I would like to hear your reaction to. Its origin is the scene in *Losing Battles* where Granny Vaughn after the celebration of her ninetieth birthday invites Vaughn, the youngest boy, to come to her in bed. It has been argued that this scene shows the dark side of humanity in your work. I disagree.—I believe the old woman sees the outline of Grandpa Vaughn's hat on the boy and in her exhaustion believes she is addressing her late husband.

Welty: You are probably right. It was just natural for her to say that. You know she was the mother of them all. And would just welcome them . . . . I am sure that was it: she was thinking of Grandpa, or . . . . She was able to take care of anybody's problem, no matter what.

Gretlund: If readers are looking for the dark side of life in the novel, they could take a look at Miss Lexie's nursing of Julia Mortimer. Why does she starve her patient?

Welty: Oh yes. That's a horror. There are people like that, and there are some nurses like that.—I don't know. There's some kind of cruelty in some forms of nursing. I don't mind to say this, we had a whole lot of nurses in our family. I had to have a whole lot of them for my mother, and I had that same thing, called "good country ladies with no home ties." They would advertise: "Settled white Christian lady with no home ties will come and stay with you and help you nurse your . . . ." And that's just what she needed, but it depended on the person. There were some that were just horrors, but some of them were just as kind as could be. They were old ladies without anything to do, and they would say: "I am glad to get this job because it's getting to be cold weather," you know, time to come in. Just country people that were alone.

I had to get somebody to help. Just the need to be two people to lift her. She was very particular who she had. She fired one nurse because . . . well, I had her read to her, because I was busy somewhere else. This nurse mispronounced "gesture"—as in "he made a gesture"—my mother said: "You're fired!" She was hard to please. You would be too, if you loved to read and couldn't. We read all day long to her. I read, and we had recordings for the blind. I read whatever she liked to hear. She liked the Bible. She liked the Book of Esther, she loved the King James' version of the Bible, she loved the sound, she loved the poetry of it. She was an intelligent person. And she relished the sound of it. She wasn't too crazy about the recordings I got her. She liked *me* to read.

Gretlund: I read your fiction as a contribution to the tradition of realism, specifically to a Chekhovian brand of realism. What is the relation between "a sense of place," with its emotional connotations, and your idea of realism?

Welty: The physical surrounding has to be exact and has to be right. That's how you make it right: use place to identify . . . an emotional content. I'm just thinking of it also as a tactic in the writing of fiction that you can use place "to place" things, in the verb, and it identifies. Well, it is like that long piece I wrote on place.

Gretlund: It is the emotive contents of your aesthetics of place that make it impossible for critics to distill it into a few words. How can you hope to define the principles of something which is based on emotions?

Welty: I don't know. I wouldn't be able to.—And is it really necessary?

Gretlund: I believe that the best way to study the Weltian concept of "a sense of place" is to read your fiction, book by book.

Welty: Yes, that's where it exists!

Gretlund: I like your phrase from "Some Notes on River Country" where you wrote: "A place that was ever lived in is like a fire that never goes out."

Welty: It's very poetic, I'm afraid, but I believe it, though.

Gretlund: What was the origin of your famous essay on "Place in Fiction"?

Welty: We were to give a series of lectures at Cambridge University, and this was the opening one. And I was panic-stricken to think I would be addressing Cambridge students. Also more than that, they were from all over England and taught American subjects at English schools. I had tried to think of something that I could legitimately bring up . . . . I'm not a scholar or anything like that, that's why I thought that place in fiction was the bridge.

I was sitting there panic-stricken before I read my first speech, and one of the teachers that came in, while I was sitting there, just seemed in passing me to get a telegraphic message from me. Probably because he was a Scot. Anyway he stopped and said to me: "You will do grand!" Which was so kind of him. I was petrified.

Gretlund: Who invited you to Cambridge?

Welty: It was something they have every year, English teachers of American subjects in sixth form schools and colleges and universities, the teachers of all these come to sometimes Oxford, sometimes Cambridge. And it was funded by two groups. I think Britain paid for the passage over on a boat, and the U. S. paid for your maintenance. We had to go on an American boat one way and an English the other. It was a terrible American ship, "The America" or something. The English ship was a Cunard, but not one of the big boats. It was fine. In fact, I loved and enjoyed it both ways.

They want some on all subjects, I mean not just English. There was another on English literature, I can't remember his name now. He's from Cornell. This was a perfectly nice man, but we weren't especially congenial. The ones I liked were the English teachers of American subjects, and we had a long enough time to become really acquainted. It was a wonderful experience. John Hope Franklin was there, and many good people. So it was like a faculty just like in a college. It lasted six weeks. It was three lectures to do twice. The sixth form teachers had a second assembly, and we also had to address them.

Gretlund: Did you simply repeat "Place in Fiction"?

Welty: No, it was in three parts. It was longer than what I used for printing. I had quite a lot of examples which I thought they needed, and which I wouldn't have left in, especially in America. I worked on it, months and months I think, trying to get something. They were going to invite one writer. The others were all teachers. I was invited as the only practitioner.

So I wrote a paper as a practitioner about using place. I tried to get something that would join us together for my speech. I was so scared. I'd never made a speech anywhere before, and I just started out at Cambridge University! I could not turn it down, it was such a chance to go over there. We stayed at Peterhouse, and I made lots of friends that I kept for years, in fact some until they died.

Gretlund: It must make you sad that many of your friends are now dead.

Welty: It's just terrible. It is. I feel terrible about it.—I'm very glad to still be alive, and I really don't think about old age too much. The only thing, the worst thing about it, is that on account of arthritis I'm not very well able to travel. So all the things that I love to do . . . for instance, I wasn't able to go to the the funeral of my editor Albert Erskine. The funeral was in Connecticut, his home. I had planned to go, but the doctor told me not to try it. I felt so bad about it, he'd been so good to me.

I haven't been to New York now for several years. Some of the people I always went to see are still there. I always stay at the Algonquin, still do.—It's just that I don't want to be on anybody's hands. What I would do, would be to get a car and a driver that could be mine while I was there. I tried with taxis, which was very hard; getting into the taxi and getting out is hard for me. But if you get a car and a driver—I still do that, I have them meet me at the airport and be waiting when I get off the plane, and they take me straight to the hotel. And that's very helpful. You can do things to make it easy for yourself.

Gretlund: Do you have manuscripts that you are still working on?

Welty: No, I just wish that I could get some things written that I want to write. It is just too physical, writing.

Gretlund: Couldn't you dictate, maybe to a tape recorder?

Welty: No, I can't do that. I can't dictate or any other thing. I need to do it myself. I just don't think in the terms of sound, the page is where I work.

Gretlund: And yet some of your stories are at their best when you read them aloud.

Welty: Well, that's good. I mean, I make some of my living doing that. I'm glad I got some that fill that bill. I'm often asked to read "Why I Live at the P.O.''—It has to be short, and that means it has to be early. I got more long-winded as time went on. I really enjoy reading. It is the only thing I will do—I don't lecture.

Gretlund: Was the last piece you wrote for *The Norton Book of Friendship?*

Welty: Yes. Of course that wasn't writing, but editing, except for the introduction. I'm not sorry I did that. We [Ronald Sharp] had a good time doing it.

Gretlund: It gave you a chance to pick some of your favorite people and place them in an anthology.

Welty: Right!

The Domestic Thread of Revelation: An Interview with Eudora Welty

Sally Wolff / 1993

From *The Southern Literary Journal* 27 (Fall 1994), 18-24. The interview combines conversations conducted in Welty's home on 26 July 1989 and 15 June 1993. (See also above, "Some Talk About Autobiography.") Reprinted by permission of Sally Wolff and *The Southern Literary Journal*.

"Yes, I have heard that this happened. . . ." Eudora Welty replied, as we talked about events that took place in Mississippi during the Civil War. I was inquiring about an incident at the beginning of her story "The Burning" in which a mounted Union soldier rides his horse into the foyer of a plantation house. Her spoken response, similar to her literary one, draws on a deep sense of Southern heritage, folklore, and history. In her story, Welty initially focuses on hearth and furnishings, stressing thereby the intrusion, disruption, and calamity, as well as the lasting scars of soldierly conflict, on domestic order and setting.

Welty: . . . In Natchez [Mississippi], in one of the old homes, they say you can see a long mark on the cabinet in the hall where the spurs from the soldier's boot scratched the wood as he rode into the house.

It was common for the soldiers to go through the house and take things, and burn down the houses, even the schoolhouse. Sherman put everything to the torch. I've seen photographs that were made of Jackson. It looked like Vietnam. Jackson was burned three times. We were on the way between east and west, and Sherman burned every time he came through. Jackson was called Chimneyville because all that was left standing were the chimneys. He was thorough.

Wolff: A good number of your characters drown, or you describe their deaths in drowning terms. Judge McKelva's face, for instance, in *The Optimist's Daughter,* appears "quenched," as if "he had laid it under the surface of dark pouring water and held it there." Has anyone in your family drowned?

Welty: No, no one close to me has drowned. There's a lot of water in Mississippi, though. Mark Twain said, laughing at himself, that he didn't know how to dispose of characters, so he drowned all of them. They would go out in the yard to hang out the clothes and fall in a bucket of water or drown in the well.

Wolff: That is how Clytie drowns.

Welty: I hadn't realized the similarity; yes, she falls into the rain barrel. I didn't know what to do with her, either.

My mother was scared of drowning. Mother was terrified of drowning. She was afraid of her children drowning. She was scared for us to go swimming, and though she was a fearless woman in other circumstances, she didn't want me on a boat to go to Europe.

In West Virginia, people had no way to get anywhere except by water. The mountains went down to the rivers. Folks had to go by boat on water. My mother went that way when she took her father to Baltimore. She took him first on a raft, which was even scarier. She was pretty fearless.

People's lives did end in the water there. Those are treacherous rivers. They are icy and rapid, and if you tried to walk on stones, the water would just sweep you down. It had a power to it, but it was exciting. The roads were almost non-existent then. West Virginia was a pretty young state when she was there.

My father had us all have swimming lessons, and we swam here in Livingston Lake. It was just like warm milk.

Wolff: Where did your mother go to school?

Welty: My parents had to work hard to get the money for school. My mother taught school every year to get enough money to go to summer school. She eventually graduated from a teaching college in West Virginia down the river from Charleston [West Virginia]—one of the state colleges.

She showed me the careful notes she had taken in school. She showed me the maps she kept of Dante's *Inferno*. Her father had brought books back from Virginia in a barrel, "up river."

The course of the interview shifts. What is the significance, for her, of a rural setting in stories such as "A Piece of News," "The Wide

Net," and "Death of a Traveling Salesman," which are essentially
about love?

Welty: I learned a great deal about Mississippi when I worked for the
W.P.A. and traveled around the state. For the first time I saw that
Mississippi was a rural world—I found it much easier to write about
than a town. It's a simpler society to describe. It was a different world
if you went outside the city. I got to know it pretty well with my
journalistic jobs and the W.P.A.

Wolff: What did you see?

Welty: What I discovered was the people in the rural setting. Their
lives didn't change with the times. They were poor. Their conditions
didn't change and were really terrible. It was all so much worse than
I could have imagined. They had no radios, no TV's. They were living
in small shacks and cabins and were cut off from things.

These people were the opposite of what they easily might be—
pinched and bitter. A friend of mine also had to go into rural areas to
buy land for the roads, and, oh! the tales he told me of poverty he saw.

I discovered still more by visiting all the county seats. It was an
education that I had again when I attended the M.S.C.W. It was the
first state college for women in the country. At the time, everybody
could go to school there, and it was cheap to go there. Some students
were ill-educated. The teachers were the best educated people around.
The school had a cross-section of girls from the rest of the state and
many from poor homes. But their families were happy. Their mothers
sent them baskets of fried chicken from home. They were good
country people. It was a poor, poor time in history, when I look back.

Wolff: How did this understanding affect your writing?

Welty: These stories are all part of the same rural setting. You have
to set the stage for a story. You have to have something to identify it.
I used to take all the county newspapers and read them all. That's
what got me interested in what went on in the state of Mississippi.
Just the naked news.

The newspapers back then would have letters from little towns in
the paper, by the family of the reporter or the correspondent. What
Ruby Fisher reads in the newspaper was the kind of thing that would
be in these newspapers: "So and So became shot," or "The Sunday
visitors in town were. . . ." That gave me a picture of what life was

like, much as I think it did for Faulkner. I did know people like that. They are the material of southern gothic. Jackson was not typical of Mississippi at the time because of its size. It's the only place of its size in Mississippi.

Wolff: You have written a great deal about love.

Welty: I suppose I have. What other kind of story is there? It's the basis for any kind of structure of the story—narrative and plot—the drive, the spirit, what makes the human. It's the center of all the stories. Human relationships are all that matter. What other human relationship would be as complex, as true, as dramatic an emotion?

Wolff: The marriage of Becky and the Judge seems to possess qualities which make it one of the best.

Welty: Well, it lasted the longest.

Wolff: In the earlier versions of your novel *The Optimist's Daughter,* up through its publication in the *New Yorker,* Philip Hand, the husband of the protagonist, Laurel Hand, does not appear. Why did you decide to omit the scenes you had first written about their courtship?

Welty: There wasn't time for any of it. I played Laurel down from the beginning—she's the eyes. But when I started developing the novel more, I decided to concentrate on Phil's death rather than on the earlier material. I wanted to imply more than I said about Phil.

It wasn't that more material didn't exist. World War II was still fresh in my mind. So many details come to mind that fit. My use of him changed. He remained the same. That was his function in the novel. I wanted to convey his reality. Everything had to be in its proportions, since he was in a short novel.

Writing makes its own contribution. I see things when I go back and re-read that I'd forgotten were in the novel. But they do exist in it.

Wolff: Is it correct that you decided to add Philip Hand during the year after the publication of the *New Yorker* story, since the next set of revisions contain the first references to him?

Welty: The reason I did not publish it in novel form for one year was to give it time. Lots of things came to me during that year. I was able to make right use of what I had. I didn't want anything to cloud over the last section. I really love that part when Laurel thinks of him going around the house. I just sat down at the typewriter—that's the way I revise—just sit down with the manuscripts.

Wolff: Did you base your characterization of Phil on your friend John Robinson [Jackson friend and fellow writer]?

Welty: Everybody is asking about John Robinson these days. No, I did not. He did not have Phil's character. My brother [Walter] made a breadboard and had double-jointed thumbs and goes with the character. My brother saw action in the war. Walter went through the battle at Okinawa. But I felt I had too much about Chicago, so I kept things out that were not contributing to what I was trying to do. Also, I didn't know where a young married couple would live in Chicago. I knew a number of painters who went to the Art Institute and the first art gallery I went to, and that has meant the most to me.

Some of the language was Walter's as I think I've said. I use names, too. I keep a list of Mississippi towns. There was a Banner. I remember the exact ways things were said. Some of the remarks for *Losing Battles* came right out of the mouths of people helping me when my mother was ill.

Wolff: Phil was killed six weeks after Laurel married him, his body was never found, and he was eaten by birds he would have known and loved. What is the source in your imagination for the violence of this death?

Welty: I knew so much of that. My brother died of rheumatoid arthritis before he was forty. It was his life—he wanted it.

Wolff: When Phil cries for the life he wanted, isn't that also Laurel's wanting it, and yours?

Welty: It is a communication between them—that's what she felt, too. She's the one who could hear it. It was a reality to her. That was the meaning it had for her: she got the meaning. It was not lost on her.

Wolff: The image of Phil with his mouth open like a funnel is similar to a description you wrote of George Fairchild in an early version of *Delta Wedding*. You describe him as "a figure strangely dark, alone as the boogie man, back of them all, and seemed waiting with his mouth set open like a drunkard's or as if he were hungry."

Welty: It's almost like a trance or a dream. I've seen people like that before. Nothing physical can be invented. If you think about French and Italian art of the thirteenth-century period, it had people with grimaces like that.

Wolff: Is his open-mouthed image more suggestive of horror, fear, or longing?

Welty: Longing. That would be more like it, I think.

Wolff: Your other portrayals of marriage have happier endings.

Welty: Yes. I like Jack and Gloria. She has this idea that "We're gonna get off to ourselves." She thinks it'll work. She is naive in thinking she can do it—get away from the family.

Wolff: Your metaphorical writing often involves sewing, threading, or referring to cloth or parts of dresses: in *The Optimist's Daughter,* for example "It seems to Laurel that the voice could have torn cloth." Why do you often think in sewing terms?

Welty: People had to sew back in my mother's day. Babies had regular trousseaux of hand-made and embroidered clothes, all done in the home. They sewed tea napkins—you know, small linen napkins with scalloped edges. People embroidered all day long—underclothes even. There was not much money to buy clothes, so people did sew a lot and provide for their own. We had a sewing woman who came and spent the day at our house. People knew sewing women.

Once my mother had just embroidered a beautiful dress for me, with pretty wreaths and hoops in the pattern. I was at a friend's house for a party. We were playing outside, and I was hiding near the woodpile. Another girl spotted me hiding and brought a whole pile of kindling down all over me. My dress was dirty and torn. When I got home, I saw Mother outside, and I prayed and prayed to Jesus to mend my dress before Mother came in from milking the cow. She had worked so hard on the dress.

Wolff: You have said that when you are revising your work, you cut pages apart and pin them together in some other configuration. Is revising a story or a novel like pinning a dress pattern?

Welty: Yes, in a sense. I had never thought of it in that way, but laying a pattern allows you to experiment. Does it work better here, or here? I probably did get that from sewing. It gives you more maneuverability. I did so much revision as it was.

I got some of that from working in newspapers, where you worked with long rolls of paper on your typewriter and where you were really able to patch something together.

Wolff: Do you plan stories by certain patterns? For instance, the weather often figures in your stories about love. In "A Piece of News" the storm accompanies the marital crisis, as it does in *The Optimist's Daughter* during Laurel's crisis.

Welty: I plan a story by its dramatic sense, not by a particular pattern. That's the dramatic end of writing. But the weather is an important part of a story. The weather depends on the crisis; the crisis is coming out of the weather. The crisis is the cause of the weather.

Wolff: Do you sew?

Welty: No. But my mother did. She tried to teach me to embroider. My mother had to leave the room when I threaded the needle—she couldn't stand to watch. I wasn't good at all.

Eudora Welty

Leslie R. Myers / 1984-1994

A series of unpublished interviews conducted by *Clarion-Ledger* columnist and arts critic Leslie R. Myers. Most of the interviews were conducted at Welty's home on Pinehurst Street. Related stories subsequently appeared in the Jackson newspaper. Grateful acknowledgment is expressed to Myers and *The Clarion-Ledger*.

9 January 1984

[On the publication of *One Writer's Beginnings*.]

Myers: What did you learn about yourself in reviewing your life?

Welty: Well, I guess the things that surfaced in the book are the things that are most important to me—the things that made it, that I did not eliminate.

Myers: How did writing fiction help prepare you for your autobiography?

Welty: It was through writing [fiction] that I learned a lot about my feelings about people, not that I write about [particular] people. In fiction, I've learned so much about myself. Not in a literary sense, but in a deep sense—how my imagination works.

Myers: To you, what's the essence of the book?

Welty: I think I'm quite lucky to have all the strands in my background—none of them quite usual . . . the type of family I grew up with, the feelings. The kind of household we had was so amicable, but we were all individuals. We all got along with one another. And there was the fact I was born a first-generation Mississippian from families that went way back in different parts of the country [Ohio and West Virginia]. This book belongs not only to myself, but to my family.

Myers: Your memory is remarkable. You recall everyone so clearly.

Welty: It not only applies to members of the family, but friends. Their lives seem to be of a whole.

You learn so much from the organ of memory. It's the things you realize are indelible to you. I think it must have been Thomas Mann, a German writer, who said that memory is a well—almost bottomless.

The more you remember, the more comes into your memory. It fills up. It's *there*. It's like a vein in the earth you can tap.

I've gotten letters from people who read excerpts [of the book] in *The New York Times* and *Vanity Fair* who said they'd remembered things from it. I was touched.

Myers: Socrates said learning is actually remembering. Plato, who is even better, wrote about our shared sense of memory.

Welty: We all do have a common memory. And that [Socrates] could be true—even if I did learn.

Myers: Was this book something you always wanted to do, or did Harvard talk you into it?

Welty: Oh, *certainly*. They argued me into it! I'm not a lecturer. They invited me to come and I said, "Of course not! I'm not a scholar or anything." But they said what I could do that nobody else could do was write about myself and my work.

I'm glad now that I did it. But I would have never, never, never, never thought of it myself. I wouldn't have done a straight autobiography. But I would dissect what in my life had affected me as a writer.

Myers: How did you decide on the book's three chapters— "Listening," "Learning to See" and "Finding a Voice"? They're unusual.

Welty: I started with them. I'm glad I did. This [autobiography] was so different from anything I'd done. It was three lectures to begin with at Harvard. They invited me to Harvard to give these lectures, later to be published in a book. They called me up and wanted me to give the names of the lectures—so I had to think of them!

I'm glad I did, because that's how it happened. Those three subjects really have to do with my work. The chapters are expanded from the lectures. They're really the same, but I did write them again. I tried to expand and be more specific.

Myers: What was the autobiographical lecture experience like?

Welty: I dreaded doing it. I didn't know I could.

Myers: You are much more humorous than your reputation—not so shy. As a child, in your book, you were almost boisterous.

Welty: I enjoy life. I don't run up and down the stairs hollering to people anymore—but I might, if they were here.

Myers: Your childhood is so interesting to read about; why do you think that is?

Welty: That's something you can never judge yourself. I don't think I was so different as a child. Our day was different. We were readers. We didn't have television. Traveling was different from today; you were conscious of the countryside. Now you're not conscious of the countryside. Now, you just get on a plane and get off. It [traveling] is the type of thing that interests a child with a buzzing imagination looking for anything that will *buzz* it. You respond to that.

Myers: How do you really catch a doodlebug?

Welty: You put a straw down a hole and, naturally, the doodlebug will come up. But a child thinks you call them up!

Myers: Whatever happened to bottle trees? I heard there might still be one around Mize [Mississippi].

Welty: All the ones I used to know about are gone.

Myers: Are you anxious for the book to come out?

Welty: Well, it's definitely non-fiction. When I'm writing a book, I don't think about anything else—what people will say. But, when it comes out to the public, I've never cured myself of a panic about what will people say and whether they'll understand it.

But . . . I think I've worried more about my novels and short stories than about this autobiography. Your imagination is very protected. A work of the imagination is really closer to a writer. Whereas, your life just happens.

Myers: Why did you decide to end your autobiography in your early adulthood?

Welty: I don't say, this [book] is it . . . this is everything. I've only suggested. But I had to end it somewhere. [At book's end] I refer to stories that I wrote later on, after college. After that, I was an adult and a lot of other things entered into my life.

I didn't try to give any revelations. I didn't think they pertained.

Myers: I don't recognize any of your fictional characters in this book—as people. And I didn't expect to.

Welty: Oh, yeah. You couldn't do that. You couldn't put a whole, real human being into a story. You make up a character to fit. You pick up rags and tags and pieces of things and gestures.

Myers: You wrote that Miss Eckhart (in "June Recital"), more than other characters, "came from me," yet she seems so unlike you.

Welty: Miss Eckhart, she was wholly an invention of mine. But we shared our art. There're probably no two people less alike. Virgie [in the same story] was very talented, very alive, very much of the world herself. I think most of my characters could touch base with her. She embodied the spirit I wrote about.

Myers: Always seeking. I laughed out loud about you and [three-years-younger brother] Edward. You two were like that together—spirited, seeking. Were you usually the comedian or his good audience?

Welty: We probably vied to be the comic. Of course, we had to have an audience. We had a similar sense of humor—and of the absurd.

Myers: Why is travel often a thread that runs through the book?

Welty: I've always loved to travel. That's why I put so much about trains in the book. And trains seemed so much my true nature—always moving.

I'm glad I came along not too late to take my trips to Europe by boat—to take a long time going there, to see how big the ocean is and to see land, coming upon it. I remember the first land I saw was Spain and they had red earth, like red clay in Mississippi. You could hear the bells of goats up on a hill. Now it would be a matter of coming down in Madrid airport. I got the experience of leaving and arriving. It's so great.

Myers: Although you never wanted to teach, you write that school-teachers "are to a great extent my heroines." You recall your mother taught school and you credit teachers who influenced your life. Why do teachers work so well in your fiction?

Welty: It is a good kind of character. It's usually someone who thinks for herself—often a heroic, lone character. They often fill a role in the community, like Miss Duling (her first grade teacher at Davis School in Jackson). I often use small communities because everything has boundaries and everyone has roles that fit right in. They usually have a pivotal role in the community, but I don't want to write about mayors!

I loved learning and I loved going to school, and admired my teachers. Miss Duling—she was marvelous.

Myers: I've noticed that you handle groups so well, in nonfiction and fiction.

Welty: I love stories with a bunch of people interacting together—a bunch of kids camping, a bunch at a wedding, a bunch at a family reunion, a bunch at a recital—*any* excuse to get them together.

Myers: Being able to name the book's chapters before you started tells me that you already knew where you were going.

Welty: It doesn't exist as a story for me unless I see it as a whole. The end should be implicit in the beginning.

Myers: What is your favorite short story?

Welty: Usually, the only story in a writer's life that he thinks about is the one he's working on. But I think it's the stories in *The Golden Apples*—"June Recital" and I love "Moon Lake."

Myers: Will there be a second autobiography?

Welty: Another? I haven't thought about it. . . . No. I don't think so. I think I've done my stint. I love to work in fiction.

Myers: What is the life of a fiction writer?

Welty: Your time is your own. It's the most wonderful time because it's your time. You were for it and it was for you.

Myers: What advice would you give to young writers?

Welty: You're going to have to find a way to support yourself while you write. What I would do, if I had it to do over, would be to take a job that has nothing to do with words. I'd save them for myself. I would like to do work with my hands, like be a gardener—to make something you can look at, complete and finished.

Myers: What's next for you?

Welty: Well, I want to get back to my fiction. That's the main thing I want to do. I want some uninterrupted time. There hasn't been any in the past two years [while writing the book]. I'm *not* going to make any speaking dates in the next year. Of course, we're right in it [1984]. I'm not going to do it! I want to write some short stories.

Myers: What have been your greatest rewards?

Welty: Ah! Work and friends—just to put it in two words. I don't know if I put it in my book or not, in so many words. But . . . I *love* to write.

11 September 1987

[On the French award to Welty of the Chevalier de L'ordre d'Arts et Lettres medal to become a Knight of the Order of Arts and Letters.]

Myers: Congratulations. I didn't even know they still had knights.

Welty: I was certainly amazed. It's not like anything I could have

ever imagined—to be a knight, or a knightess. Isn't it wonderful? It
all sounds so alluring.

Myers: I know your books are translated into several languages.
They're obviously reading them in Paris.

Welty: Well, it certainly will please my French publishers. I think
they would be delighted to know it. They might feel justified.

22 November 1989

[On the publication of *Photographs*.]

Myers: You've talked about the "mind's eye picture" you use in
fiction writing. Do you use the same mind's eye to take photographs?

Welty: No, I don't. In fiction, you're seeing *into* people and their
minds and their thoughts. You're trying to feel them, to see relationships.

A photograph is just what is evident to the eyes. Both are valuable
to the eye, but they're not the same thing to me. But I guess you
could say that both of them are part of my interest, my curiosity—my
wishing to know—about the world around me. It's the people in
photographs that interest me.

Myers: What do you look for in a photograph?

Welty: Usually, they announce themselves. I'd be walking down
the street with a camera—and there it was, all out in front of me. I
didn't set out to photograph anything because I didn't know what I
would see. I took pictures without preparing at all.

Myers: I never see you taking pictures anymore. Do you?

Welty: My eyes are not right for the new cameras. I can't use the
viewfinder very well—those little tiny things. I long ago stopped
taking cameras on trips because I find that they distract me. I find I'm
thinking about the picture instead of what I'm looking at. I'm not a
photographer any more.

14 December 1990

[Concerning Welty's birthplace and childhood home until age thirteen, located at
741 N. Congress Street, Jackson.]

Myers: What was childhood like there?

Welty: It was just a congenial place to grow up. We were a very close family and a very happy family—and very busy. We felt our house was at the center of things. We were close to the library and to the State Capitol. We were close to Davis School, which was the center of our lives, outside of home.

Myers: How did you pass the days?

Welty: We had our own rooms and we would charge up and down the stairs all day, play out back in the sycamore tree, play jacks on the sidewalk. We played outdoors at night—everybody in the neighborhood did. We'd catch lightning bugs, and we'd cut choo-choo boats out of pasteboard shoe boxes and pull them up the sidewalk. We played in Davis School yard like it was our own yard.

16 April 1991

[At Davis School, where Welty was to be honored at the Davis School Homecoming Festival on 20 April.]

Myers: It sounds like they've made you the all-time star student.

Welty: It's an honor to be asked. Of course, I'd come. I love Davis School and I'm proud to do anything for it.

Myers: Did you know the bell that your stern teacher, Miss Duling, always rang is lost? So the school children are writing stories for you, all titled "The Mystery of Miss Duling's School Bell."

Welty: I'm afraid of that bell! I'm scared of it. (Laughs.) She was like the sound system in the school. She stalked the halls. We were all scared of her. But she was the reason it was such a good school.

Myers: Does being here feel like it used to?

Welty: It's the same site. But it's not the same building. It's entirely different. Mine burned down. Well, the location seems right and I can see my old house. So it still feels like home.

13 November 1991

[On the awarding of the National Book Foundation's "Medal for Distinguished Contribution to American Letters," the publication of *The Norton Book of Friendship*, edited by Welty and Ronald A. Sharp, and the reissues by Harcourt Brace Jovanovich of a fiftieth-anniversary hard-cover issue of *A Curtain of Green and Other Stories* and eight other works of fiction in paperback.]

Myers: Is all of this happening at once a bit overwhelming?

Welty: Well, we'll see. It seems like a lot to me because of the National Book Foundation.

Myers: Did you know you're only the fourth person to receive the medal?

Welty: No, I didn't. I'm in mighty good company.

Myers: Have you planned your speech?

Welty: They just want me to say something briefly. They suggest I reminisce. I'm going to be at a table with my publishers. That's awfully nice. My editor, John Ferrone, will be there. I think one of my old editors, Robert Giroux, will be there.

Myers: *Curtain of Green* also is coming out in a special series for its 50th anniversary. Do you feel like it's been fifty years?

Welty: Yeah, I sure do. Well, it seems like both, both at the same time. I think both are true. They still are with you, your books. But time did fly by.

It's a nice-looking book. It really is pretty. I'm proud that they brought it out. I don't know if it's on bookshelves yet. I've got a copy.

That book, the first one, it's so unbelievable it came out to begin with. As a first book of short stories by an unknown person, certainly the odds were against it—more against it than I ever knew. I didn't know anything about publishing. It was really Diarmuid Russell who got it done.

Myers: Does the anniversary make you look back?

Welty: It sure does. The sad part is that so many of the people connected with it are no longer with us—my editor, [my agent] Diarmuid Russell, and the friends I had who came to the first party for the book. Not many are still living. I wish they were so they could be a part of this.

Myers: Did you have any clue fifty years ago that you'd become one of the most respected writers in the world?

Welty: Oh, no! I'd have been *insane* if I had had such an idea! (Laughs.) Maybe some people feel that way about their first book. But no, I really would have been insane. I don't suppose I'd say that. I didn't say, "Fifty years from now you'll be sorry you didn't publish my book," to all the people who rejected my book!

Be careful or maybe they won't give me this book award. (Laughs.) They'll say, "She does not deserve it, after all. We'll take it back!"

Myers: The medal also carries $10,000. Do you have special plans for the prize money?

Welty: I could just use it, that's all. I wish I did have a wonderful project that I could just turn it into, like going to Europe. I'll probably use it for needs. It [writing] is not a way to make money. Writing is the last way!

Myers: Of course, the National Book Foundation presents the annual National Book Awards. Looking back, I see you won for fiction in 1983 and were nominated in 1973, 1971, and 1956.

Welty: Really? I also was once on the jury to help choose the National Book Award winner. When they spoke of reminiscing, I thought about what it was like to read all of those books. Every publisher sends you their books. There were three judges and you had to get together. I remember when Walker [Percy] won for *The Movie-goer* [in 1962]. That was so wonderful.

Myers: There also are eight paperbacks being reissued?

Welty: Yes. They're pretty, too. They have covers by [artist] Barry Moser.

Myers: How did it come about that all nine books would be re-printed?

Welty: It's all a publishing event. I'm just pleased to see it. It's nice to be kept in print.

Myers: Is your *Norton Book of Friendship* out yet?

Welty: I don't know. It's very new. I'm just a co-editor. Ronald Sharp is the other editor.

Myers: You've never done any book like it before.

Welty: No. It's brand new. We worked on it about two years. I loved doing it. It's a very handsome book. We were proud of the way we organized it, too. We tried to make it an interesting book. I don't know if we did, or not.

Myers: How did you come up with the idea?

Welty: I didn't. Norton has a whole series of readers on various subjects and I was asked to do it by the publishers. I jumped at it because I liked the subject and I like the idea of a chance to go back and look up a lot of things and reread them. They said we could use any [literature] we wanted—from any country, any century.

I would have done it any time. I just waited awhile to be asked, it looks like. It really was a pleasure to do it. But it was hard work, too, to choose—in the face of everything you could have chosen. Friend-ship certainly means a great deal to me and always has.

Myers: You've written wonderful things about friendship, but you left your own writing out.

Welty: Well sure I did.

Myers: How did you come to work with Ronald Sharp on this?

Welty: As far as I know, they [the publishers] picked us both together. I met him a long time ago at Kenyon College. One of his teachers there was a friend of mind. We did all the work in Jackson. He came here. It was very generous of him to do all the traveling. We wrote back and forth for about two years. It was an undertaking!

The book sort of grew as it went. We were a good combination because we're so different. He's an academic person [a former *Kenyon Review* editor], and I'm a fiction writer. He's a man and younger. He's from the Middle West. We brought two different kinds of experience to it—and we both love reading literature.

Myers: What entry about friendship is most special to you?

Welty: There are so many favorite things in there. When we were doing this book, there was no end to a favorite this and a favorite that. It's like trying to pick out a star in the sky!

There's a wonderful group in there, when the Russian writer [Ivan] Turgenev became a friend of [Gustave] Flaubert, who wrote *Madame Bovary*. When they started to correspond, it was so funny. They said, we are like two moles burrowing toward one another. They wrote before they ever met.

Myers: What's next?

Welty: I don't know. I'm just trying to get through it! (Laughs.) Sooner or later, I'd like to get back to writing a short story that I started writing long ago. It's a group of stories. It might be bad luck to talk about it. I don't ever talk about something that's unfinished. It's just superstition.

8 October 1992

[New Stage Theatre, a Jackson professional theater, staged *Edna Earle*, with an 14 October opening gala honoring Welty. The one-woman show was written and performed by New Stage founder Jane Reid-Petty. The play is based on the character Edna Earle Ponder from Welty's 1953 novel, *The Ponder Heart*. Welty has been a board member for the theater nearly since its 1965 founding. Several of her works have been adapted there in such productions as *The Ponder Heart*, *The Robber Bridegroom* and *A Season of Dreams*. The ongoing Eudora Welty New Plays Series also was founded at New Stage in 1984.]

Myers: I know you've seen Jane's *Edna Earle*. What are your impressions?

Welty: I think it's just a splendid thing. She [Reid-Petty] was such a sensitive reader and translator. It [the play] is a beautiful thing on its own. I think it just throbs with life.

Myers: Why have you never written a play? So much of your writing has been translated to the stage, even Broadway.

Welty: I always wanted to. I don't know. It's just a different world entirely from the one I deal in. In a novel, you're free to tell the reader what's in the mind of the character. But in a play, you have to bring it out in action. A play—it's a different talent altogether.

Myers: But I still think you have it. Your characters are known for their dialogue.

Welty: I do a lot of listening to speech, overheard remarks. It's my specialty. I had to learn it [dialogue], too. But it's fascinating to learn.

12 November 1993

[Welty was chosen as the "cover girl" for a 1994 Mississippi Writers calendar published by the Mississippi Department of Archives and History. The twelve writers pictured in the calendar included Tennessee Williams, William Faulkner, Margaret Walker Alexander and Richard Wright. The cover picture was a 1924 photograph of Welty—wearing a stylish 1920s dress, with a "flapper" hip sash and a string of beads—as she boarded a train.]

Myers: Well, you're the cover girl. Tell me about that great picture.

Welty: It was taken in New Orleans as we were about to catch the Sunset Limited to Los Angeles. I was going with my father on a trip to California for the occasion. That's why I'm wearing such a strange dress. (Laughs.) That's what I thought was right for California.

My father said. "Pick out a dress and that will be your present for the trip." So I picked that black, sheer dress. It was my choice at the age of 15.

It was a wonderful train, through the Grand Canyon and everything!

11 February 1994

[After the 1963 assassination of civil rights leader Medgar Evers in Jackson, Welty wrote "Where Is the Voice Coming From?" In this third Jackson trial on the murder charge, Byron De La Beckwith was found guilty on 5 February 1994.]

Myers: We're doing a story on Mississippians' reactions to the Beckwith verdict last Saturday. I thought you'd want to say something about it.

Welty: I'm glad something is finally done. I'm glad of the trial and I'm glad of the verdict.

I'm on record for what I think of this, of that event [the assassination]—which is, I think it's deplorable.

Myers: I remember that "Where Is the Voice Coming From?" was about it.

Welty: I wrote it that night it happened, when no one knew who did it. But I knew what kind of mind did it. The story is told by the murderer himself. I knew what *kind* of person did it. We all knew it.

Myers: I guess Beckwith [formerly of Greenwood] reminds everybody again of Mississippi's grim past.

Welty: Just be glad it [Mississippi] also does produce a Medgar Evers.

An Afternoon with Miss Welty
Joseph Dumas / 1994

From *Mississippi Magazine*, May/June 1994, 30-34. Reprinted by permission of Joseph Dumas.

See that box on the end of the table? Someone sent me a plume from one of the wild swans of Coole. The giver knew she idolizes W.B. Yeats. His "The Wild Swans at Coole" (1917) memorializes Lady Gregory, her son Robert, and their famed estate, Coole Park, in verse. It is a favorite of hers.

She, herself, has been called the greatest living short story writer in the English language. Every major writing award is hers save the Nobel Prize, for which she has been frequently mentioned.

Four collections of short stories, five novels, a collection of essays and reviews, and a best-selling autobiography were written principally in an upstairs bedroom overlooking her tree-lined street near Belhaven College in provincial Jackson. The house is part of her legend. She has lived and labored there for more than 60 years. Pasted to the brown door is a sticker in patriotic colors pledging her political allegiance to "Clinton/Gore." For years, passersby have slowed their cars in front of her house and strained to see her typing at the upstairs window of her bedroom.

But Eudora Welty, who turned 85 in April, has not climbed the stairs in well over a year. "I'm afraid I won't come down," she said, adjusting her tall frame that now leans permanently forward. Last year she fractured her back.

Eudora Welty's father, president of the Lamar Life Insurance Company, built the sturdy burgher's cottage on Pinehurst Street. "This was built when I was a senior in high school. When I was younger we lived on North Congress Street. Not long ago, someone asked me to show it to them and I did and the people who are there invited me to come in, but I didn't want to.

"They bought the house and refinished wood and everything. I was so pleased to hear that it was just like my father had it."

281

I had unintentionally arrived a half-hour early for our appointment.
She had nonetheless appeared promptly in the semi-dark, formal
living room, her silent footsteps carrying her in the unassuming
manner by which she is known. Like Phoenix Jackson, her aging
character in the much-anthologized "A Worn Path" from her first
collection of stories, *A Curtain of Green and Other Stories,* Miss
Welty is moving slowly and learning to live with the realities of aging,
including cataracts and arthritis, which have halted her professional
writing and robbed her of the discipline the craft once imposed. "I
think what I miss when I am not working is that I haven't got this
thing to grip me; this piece of work that I want to lose myself in,"
she said.

Humor, nonetheless, abides. "I can barely remember what I had
for dinner," she said, then proceeded to rhapsodize on the importance
of food in the South.

"One of the things about Mississippi society—and no telling what
society and other place—there is so much talk about food, and I just
love putting things like that in stories. That shows so much. I love
some of the fancy party dishes, you know, like sweet potatoes *s-t-u-
f-f-ed* into an orange rind," she purred.

"Say, what did you *have?*" she drawled in a voice like honey-
butter poured slowly over velvet. She does it again and you begin to
smell her vivid description.

"In the South people eat all the time. That's the way they mark
any occasion."

Asked about trying a voice-activated computer to ease her writing,
Miss Welty looked puzzled. "You mean it types when you speak?
That's kind of scary isn't it?" She laughed. "How do you know what
it's saying is what you said?" She laughed again.

"I don't think in terms of speaking. I have to see it on paper. I
don't think I could ever dictate, especially a story. . . . You can't do
that by voice. I couldn't. Maybe you can learn anything. But I'm so
inept. I can type. I'm used to the typewriter, but [now] that's what is
hard to do.

"I think in quiet. I don't know if I could think with something
whirring and talking back to you. I'm too old and set in my ways. I'd
probably talk back to it!"

In spite of the trials it has given her, age does convey privilege. I asked her about the *The New Yorker*'s new incarnation. For many years, the magazine serialized her stories. She was blunt in her opinion. "I don't like it. It has none of the ease and casualness of the old *New Yorker,* the way it used to be. People didn't take themselves so seriously, like E.B. White and all those good people who wrote for it."

The New Yorker published one of her most passionate stories more than 30 years ago when, in June 1963, Medgar Evers was assassinated across town. It is, in fact, the only one of her stories she attributes to an actual circumstance.

"I was just so fired up that I couldn't take it!" she said. "I thought, 'Put yourself inside that man.' I thought I knew so well what that kind of mind was like, I could write it in the first person."

Indeed, the fictional killer in "Where is the Voice Coming From?" published the following month, bears an uncanny parallel to Byron De La Beckwith, who withstood a third trial for Evers's murder in January of this year and was found guilty.

"We had to check every detail to be sure that it wouldn't possibly conflict with something that really happened. See, there hadn't been anybody arrested, of course. You see, I wrote it instantly. No one had been even spoken of.

"I had to move it out of Mississippi for one thing. I had to be sure I didn't have the same kind of automobile. . . . I had to change everything. I couldn't mention the governor although I mentioned Ross Barnett as if he came from another state.

"They did want to publish it immediately. They didn't wait (for me) to mail it. So we did it all over the telephone. In the meanwhile, since they'd got it, some things had happened and they didn't want coincidence anywhere. Reality was what I had just written, you know . . . but they could take no chances on any coincidence with reality.

"I wrote it in the first person because I felt I knew what that kind of person was thinking—I've lived here all my life. Of course, somebody said to me afterwards, 'You were wrong because you thought it was a Snopes and it was really a Compson.' " The Snopes and Compson families, are, of course, characters created by fellow Mississippian William Faulkner in his fabled Yoknapatawpha County.

Now that writing has become difficult for her physically, how does Eudora Welty while away the hours? Reading. "I have a book I read at bedtime and one I read when I get up in the morning." When I told her I did the same thing, she nodded and dismissed those who think reading more than one book at a time is peculiar.

"I would die if I couldn't read!" she exclaimed, then contemplating that, added, "I'd better not say that." Beside her on an end table was the book *Jazz Piano: A Jazz History* by her good friend, Dr. Billy Taylor, the music consultant for the CBS network show, "Sunday Morning." Otherwise, new books in shiny dust jackets were piled on tables and spilling over onto the Chinese rug. An ornate poinsettia, blood-red, stood in front of the faux fireplace, "looking like a fire," she said.

Visiting with friends, literary and otherwise, is another pastime. Novelist Nadine Gordimer popped in not long ago. "I liked her so much. She writes marvelous novels. We sat where we're sitting now and talked a long time."

Private traveling now replaces the grueling lecture schedule she once maintained. With relish, she recounted one of her last college engagements. "Within the last couple of years I was invited to read a story. When I got to the podium and started to read, I found I did not have my glasses. So I decided I just wouldn't say anything about it all," she said, her voice raising in laughter.

"I thought, I've read this story so many times that I don't need it. So, I had the book, I had it open. And I just went through it all from memory. I didn't know I could do it, but, it just all came to me. If I had known I had to do it, I would have been panic-stricken. But I didn't want the person who had brought me there and who introduced me to know anything about it. I decided I wouldn't even tell him, but I did, afterwards," she said. "I was proud that I had read it all! They thought I was reading out of the book and I didn't know I knew it. It had to be done—what else could I have done?"

Now her forays out are confined to intimate settings, mostly with friends who join her for dinner at favorite spots about town. "I'm a little hard of hearing," she says, so I move and, finally, we sit facing one another, knees nearly touching. "I have an old friend who wrote me not long ago and something sticks in my mind. She said, 'I'm 90 years old now, and I feel like there's somebody else living inside my skin and not a friend.' I loved that!

"Isn't that wonderful? I know what she means. I understand. I guess she feels her body is not obeying her. She didn't mean an enemy but not a friend."

Friends are another thing Miss Welty misses, sorely—more than writing. "It's a strange feeling. It's something that old people like myself feel often because you think back to the days when your familiar friends were around you and with whom you could talk and whom you counted and could discuss the nature of things; then you realize it isn't anymore." It's not difficult to make new friends, she explained, but it is hard not to miss special people.

Diarmuid Russell was one of those special people. Russell and Volkening, Inc., is the New York literary agency which has placed her work since 1940 and was founded by Diarmuid Russell and Henry Volkening. For 33 years, Mr. Russell, who died in 1973, was her agent. He was the son of A.E., the Irish poet and mystic who was a boyhood friend of W. B. Yeats.

Miss Welty was one of the firm's first clients as Michael Kreyling records in *Author and Agent: Eudora Welty & Diarmuid Russell*. In a letter dated June 24, 1940, Kreyling reports, Miss Welty wrote to Diarmuid Russell, "No, I shall never be bitter if you do not sell (the stories), but only struck with the weight of your influence if you do. I feel that I am fortunate to have you to criticize them. When I was going to school at the University of Wisconsin, in the winter afternoons when the snow kept falling, I used to sit in the stacks in the library in the Celtic division reading all the books they had of your father's and Mr. Yeats' and copying things into a notebook, not for use, but just to have. . . ."

In December 1992, Miss Welty made a rare trip to Washington to receive the Pen/Malamud Award for excellence in the short story. It became, unexpectedly, a reunion.

"Tim Seldes gave a party for me," she said, her eyes suddenly full of sparkle. "He invited some of my old friends that were writers who came from Russell and Volkening like Anne Tyler and Peter Taylor.

"You know, it was so much fun and I was remembering how Anne and I met in Baltimore. I forget which one of us said it and the other agreed, 'Whenever I don't know what to do about something, I think, "What would Diarmuid do? What would he say?" ' That's true. When people write you in the mail, 'What would Diarmuid say?' " she repeated, voice low, sharp as a razor.

"The point is, you do know what he would say. The answer comes with the question.

"He was marvelous. He did everything for me. And for all the people who worked with him."

She shifted position. "Of course, nobody is there now that was when I began. Nobody is like Diarmuid or Henry, but you don't compare people or anything else. It's not what the agency does for me, that's perfectly fine. It's just that I miss Diarmuid. . . . Tim bought the agency from Diarmuid. He just 'took me over' at that time. He's a nice man."

She returned to her memories of Russell. "He edited *The Viking Portable Irish Reader* (1946). I remember his saying, 'I've got to have Lady Gregory in there.' She was very important. She did perhaps more for other people than for herself. She was so wonderful—vital! They couldn't have done it without her.

"The first time I went to Europe at all I went to London and that was shortly after World War II. They were still suffering from the effects of the war and the deprivations. People were planting victory gardens in the bomb sites. It was a great difference between then and when I came back later.

"A year or two ago I went over to see my old friend V.S. Pritchett. He and his wife are old friends of mine. We have *rendez-vous* in this country; sometimes over there. I do love London. I love Regent's Park. I remember seeing a black swan in Regent's Park following a spray of white swans, just as though the ballet would start in a minute. . . .

"I was a friend of Elizabeth Bowen who lived in Regent's Park. I used to love to go to her house. I forget which number it was. It had been bombed. All those beautiful houses had been bombed. She lost the house she was staying in. I remember she was one of those people who went out at night and made people put their lights out.

"She escaped back to Ireland. She was so troubled because Ireland took no part in the war.

"You know they wouldn't declare themselves. She felt very bitterly about that. She was another Anglo-Irish person like Lady Gregory and Yeats. That whole strand of people was so extraordinary.

"I loved her. And I was glad I got to meet someone [of that strand]. Of course, she was too young to be in that group, but Diarmuid

Russell could distinctly remember being patted on the head by Yeats when he was a little boy."

Miss Welty thought so much of Elizabeth Bowen that *The Bride of the Innisfallen and Other Stories* is dedicated to her. Her first work, *A Curtain of Green,* was dedicated to Russell.

"I have one of A.E.'s paintings Diarmuid gave me. Let me get it for you," she said, pushing a button on the recliner in which she was seated. A motor whirred; then, suddenly, she was standing.

"I have this wonderful chair," she explained. "Someone left it to me. You can go all the way back and the footrest will come up. It could be the works! I just use it to sit in."

She left and returned as quietly as she entered the room the first time. This time she carried the oil painting she speculates was done more than a century ago.

"Wait. Let me wipe the dust off it; I don't want to get it on your clothes." She dusted the gilt frame. "He painted all his life. He'd go up to Donegal to paint. I have a whole set of his books upstairs."

Before I left, she indulged me by signing her book, *Photographs*, taken during the Depression when she was a publicity agent for President Franklin Roosevelt's Works Progress Administration. While making the inscription, she revealed, "I was a southpaw when I was born and they broke me. . . . It was when I went to school. I started in the middle of the year. I would go to the blackboard and write with chalk in the left hand.

"My father said—he was a Yankee—he said, 'The world was made for right-handed people.' Well, he's right in that. He said, 'Everything is done for their convenience.' They just didn't let me use my left hand. My mother came from a left-handed family; she, herself, was right-handed, but she had five left-handed brothers and an ambidextrous father.

"Since my right hand is so arthritic, I've been doing things with my left hand like eating. I can do everything but write and brush my teeth."

Our conversation wound down and back to the folkways of Mississippi and the South. Told of a bus depot with signs printed "North" and "South" with no other designation than departure times, her china blue eyes blazed. "Like that's all you need to know," she said. "That's perfect. I love it!"

Then she leaned over and asked, "Could I use that in a story sometime?"

Eudora Welty

Danny Heitman / 1994

From *Sunday Advocate Magazine* [Baton Rouge, LA], 17 July 1994, 16, 18. Reprinted by permission of the Baton Rouge *Advocate*.

JACKSON, MISS.—At age 85, the writer Eudora Welty is a fine old tree, bent and knotted but sagely alive. A fractured spine gives her posture a parenthetical curve. She walks with a pronounced stoop, very slowly, navigating even the broadest floor like a tightrope. Touched by a Delta drawl, her voice is faint but deliberate—a voice the novelist Reynolds Price called "shy but reliable as any iron beam."

Welty can no longer climb the stairs to her upstairs study, can no longer hammer at her cherished Smith-Corona electric typewriter. After years of arthritis, her hands are as stiff as wire.

But age, that capricious craftsman, has sharpened Welty's best features into high relief. Her wide blue eyes display the calculating clarity of stained glass, and their color shifts slightly in fresh slants of light. They stand out all the more in Welty's lengthening face, her jaw slackened by gathering years.

"I've been so blessed that my vision is still working," said Welty, sitting in the parlor of her home in downtown Jackson. Though writing is hard for her, Welty remains an avid reader. In the otherwise neat brick house where Welty has lived most of her life, one sees numerous stacks of books. Like most rooms of convalescents, the parlor is gathering upon itself a bit, so that treasures can rest at easy arm's length.

Clearly, Welty's treasures are her books. A copy of Jim Lehrer's memoir, *A Bus of My Own,* sits on the sofa with a small pile of others. "Isn't this terrible, this mess?" Welty asked, surveying the room from a blue cushioned chair. She tries to keep a good detective mystery on hand—"you can read one a night"—and Welty's also been rereading Elizabeth Bowen and Chekhov.

And, of course, her library includes a fresh copy of *A Writer's Eye,*

Welty's latest book and her second collection of criticism. Just published by the University Press of Mississippi, *Eye* assembles every book review Welty ever wrote—67 pieces penned over 42 years. Most of the reviews originally appeared in *The New York Times*, where Welty spent the summer of 1944 as an intern.

The internship established Welty as a frequent *Times* reviewer, heightening her profile and helping fund her real vocation as a writer of fiction. Welty can't thank Robert Van Gelder enough for giving her that chance.

Van Gelder was the unconventional *Times Book Review* editor who befriended Welty and hired her for the summer. He had followed her early fiction and thought Welty would be just the fresh face he needed. "I was a complete innocent," Welty recalled. "That's what Van Gelder liked. He liked trying somebody out who had never done this before. The summer before me, he had put a psychiatrist in the job. I liked that. It was refreshing. Robert Van Gelder often invited people to come in for a summer with new life and breath. He did lots of things that were unusual."

As a young journalist, Welty reveled in New York's bustling newspaper industry. "At that time, the *New York Herald-Tribune* was still going, a rival newspaper," Welty said. "You know, every newspaper needs a rival. So it was really hot competition and really more fun that way. I'm glad I had that experience."

Even after leaving her internship, Welty continued to file reviews from Jackson. "It was interesting, you know, you get a book today, and your review is due in two days. I kind of enjoyed that. It was part of the excitement of being assigned to do a book, that you did it immediately."

But soon, deadlines lost their charm. "I often wished that I could pull something back through the slot of the post office after I had mailed it and change it," Welty said. "You had to use snap judgment a lot, of course, but I'm not very good at that. I don't think I'm the ideal reviewer for a daily newspaper. It upsets me now, just to hear the word *deadline*. And since I was trying to write fiction at the same time, I always had this fellow feeling for the author. I couldn't stand to say something too damning."

Back in Mississippi after her brief stint at the *Times,* Welty was starting to realize that Jackson would be home for life. She had tried

New York once before, as a graduate student in advertising at Columbia University.

In the dead of winter, her mother would send her boxes of camellias to remind her of home. "It was wonderful to be up there with the ice and snow, and these lovely tropical flowers would come," Welty recalled. Later, Welty revived the tradition herself, carefully shipping blossoms to her friends up North.

"I sewed the stems to the inside edges of the boxes so they wouldn't move about or jostle and hit each other. It was my own invention," Welty said. "I only tried to send four or five blooms in a box on overnight express. I'd wrap the stems in wet cotton. In those days, you could go down to the train station and put things on the express and they'd get to New York the next day."

In 1931, during her first year at Columbia, Welty received a more ominous message from Jackson. Her father, a prominent insurance executive, was dying. Welty left school and returned south to help the family.

"My father had leukemia, the first case I'd ever heard of," Welty said. "The doctor told us about it, and he said, 'Hide the encyclopedia so your father won't look it up.' Of course, he already had."

Though removed from New York, a time-honored mecca for aspiring writers, Welty's career thrived. She quickly found a universe in her own backyard. As a publicity agent for the Works Progress Administration. Welty traveled the backroads of Mississippi taking pictures.

"I learned about my native state for the first time," said Welty. "Jackson is just about the only large town here. If you want to learn about Mississippi, there's more to learn here than you can learn in any one city. So the WPA gave me a chance to go everywhere in the state."

Welty's photography deepened her powers of observation and her skill for illustration, two strengths that mark her fiction. One of her early short stories, "The Whistle," demonstrates her power to paint a large scene in a small space:

Night fell. The darkness was thin, like some sleazy dress that has been worn and worn for many winters and always lets the cold through to the bones. Then the moon rose. A farm lay quite visible, like a white stone

in water, among the stretches of deep woods in the colorless dead
leaf. . . .

Welty's short stories are worlds unveiled in delicate economy. They
are like paperweight villages in the palm of the hand, small but
endlessly arresting.

Crisscrossing Mississippi also honed Welty's ear for regional ver-
nacular. She gained a reputation for flawless dialect with stories like
the widely anthologized "Why I Live at the P.O." The story popular-
ized another Welty technique: Put the reader within earshot of a
character, then let him eavesdrop as conversation tells the story. In
the comic monologue of "P.O.," a small-town postmistress reveals
the family feud that exiled her to live in her mail room:

> Of course, there's not much mail. My family are naturally the main
> people in China Grove, and if they prefer to vanish from the face of the
> earth, for all the mail they get or the mail they write, why, I'm not going
> to open my mouth. Some of the folks here in town are taking up for me
> and some have turned against me. I know which is which. There are
> always some people who will quit buying stamps just to get on the right
> side of Papa-Daddy.

After the WPA job, Welty's rise as a writer came quickly. John
Rood, editor of the little magazine *Manuscript,* published her first
short story, "Death of a Traveling Salesman," in 1936. "That was the
first time I sent him a story, and immediately, he took it," Welty said.
"And I thought, 'Is that the way it happens? You just put something
in the mail and they say okay?' Well, I was just lucky."

Following that initial acceptance, Welty's critical acclaim and her
resume grew. Her short story collections and novels established her
as one of the South's most celebrated writers and gave her international exposure. In the 1950s, an invitation to lecture came from
Cambridge. "I'd never talked in public before," Welty said. "I
thought, 'Why not start at Cambridge?' "

Though wide traveling and honors like the Pulitzer Prize gave her
the freedom to thrive elsewhere, Welty always returned to her ances-
tral home in one of Jackson's oldest and finest neighborhoods. "One
good thing about my kind of writing is that you can do it anywhere,"

Welty said. "But I write best in the part I know, as far as fiction goes—things I can have an opinion on and understand and try to identify, motives and trends and things, and have some basis of objectivity and judgment."

Welty wrote book reviews less frequently as her fiction career prospered, which meant that she was more often the subject of reviews herself. She can only remember one review that deeply hurt her—one written by the influential critic Diana Trilling. "She said that my writing was so self-conscious, that I was aware of my style and what I was trying to do, like I was showing off," Welty recalled. "I was very hurt by that, and I was surprised. I don't think that was true. I hope not. But I remember how sharply that cut."

It isn't surprising that Eudora Welty would bristle at the label "show-off." She is studiously modest about her work, habitually crediting her success to the generosity of others. "I think of myself as so lucky. Always, I've been treated so well," Welty said. "I sent my work to editors without knowing anything or anybody, and the quarterlies were at very first encouraging to me and gave me publication. Things you never dream of. I feel very fortunate with my editors, my agents and everybody."

Welty's success has made her an unwitting tourist attraction. Fans often arrive on the porch seeking an audience or an autograph—so many that the typically gracious Welty has had to put a "Do Not Disturb" sign on her front door. But when asked about the burdens of fame, Welty denies that she has any.

"I don't have all that much (celebrity). I don't write that kind of book. I have no sense of being trapped. I'm not under demand to be a fixture or anything. I do what I please. People are generally very considerate and nice to me," Welty said.

Almost to disprove the point, an admirer from Birmingham, Ala., knocked on Welty's door during her interview. He was a lifelong fan who wanted to meet his idol. Too occupied to see him, Welty had a guest gently turn him away.

Welty eats out at neighborhood restaurants, runs errands around town, entertains friends and makes infrequent appearances at local bookshops. Despite declining health, she also tries to accommodate occasional interviews. But Welty cherishes her privacy and maintains a few rules for guarding it. She doesn't want her personal letters published, doesn't want a Welty biography, and has no plans to extend her own slim memoirs.

"I'm a professional writer, but I write what I think is of professional interest, of objective interest in the world," said Welty. "I don't think of it as being a confessional kind of profession. Some people do, and that's all right. But this is what I think."

Welty broke her rule against autobiography in 1984, when she published *One Writer's Beginnings,* an account of her childhood. *Beginnings* grew from lectures Welty delivered at Harvard, and she thought it was worth doing for its window into the genesis of her craft. "I was glad I did it because I never thought of my work in those terms of how things came about, but I don't intend to go any further with it," Welty said.

One Writer's Beginnings is also notable as the last new writing that Welty has published. In 1991, she co-edited *The Norton Book of Friendship* with Ronald Sharp, an omnibus of pieces by other writers.

Welty also published a collection of her photography in 1989. *A Writer's Eye,* like the picture book, was gathered from her archives.

Welty said she's still trying to write more things, though her health has slowed her. Her hands aren't swift enough for her typewriter, she has trouble writing in longhand, and she finds the prospect of dictation troublesome.

"I don't have direct access to the page as I once did," said Welty. "I couldn't ever dictate anything. So I don't feel as objective or as free as I normally did. I'm not complaining because I'm getting along so well."

A year and a half ago, Welty injured her back, and age and arthritis have complicated her recovery. "When I came home from the hospital, they told me I had to move downstairs for awhile and had to change my way of life somewhat," Welty said.

A nurse comes every morning to cook breakfast and handle household chores. The nurse also drives Welty on errands and to the beauty parlor. Welty's prized camellias have to take care of themselves. "The garden is gone. It makes me ill to look at it," Welty said. "But I'm not complaining. It's just the state of things."

Welty has an electric lift chair so she doesn't strain herself standing up. "It works like an ejection seat," said Welty. "Sometimes, I wish I had one over there on the sofa to get rid of the company."

Since her back problem developed, Welty hasn't driven her 1979 Cutlass Supreme, a maroon, canvas-topped stick-shift that was the focal point of some comic political theater. When Welty, a lifelong Democrat, put a Michael Dukakis bumper sticker on her fender in 1988, it was removed three times.

"I think I live in a Republican neighborhood," said Welty, grinning broadly. "I don't know who did it, but I thought that was kind of funny. I feel like a lone Democrat in Jackson sometimes, including voting for Clinton."

The Cutlass is still in her garage.

"Everybody wants to buy it, but I don't want to sell it," Welty said. "I still have the feeling that if it's in the garage, then someday I might just jump in and take off."

Index